CHURCHILL'S
BESTIARY

CHURCHILL'S BESTIARY

His Life
Through Animals

—

PIERS BRENDON

MICHAEL O'MARA BOOKS LIMITED

First published in Great Britain in 2018 by
Michael O'Mara Books Limited
9 Lion Yard
Tremadoc Road
London SW4 7NQ

A CIP catalogue record for this book is available from the British Library.

ISBN: 978-1-78929-050-9 hardback print format
ISBN: 978-1-78929-051-6 in ebook format
ISBN: 978-1-78929-086-8 in audiobook

Every effort has been made to trace the copyright holders of images in this book.
Any errors or omissions that may have occurred are inadvertent, and anyone with any
copyright queries is invited to write to the publishers, so that a full acknowledgement
may be included in subsequent editions of the work.

Designed and typeset by K.DESIGN, Winscombe, Somerset

Printed and bound by CPI Group (UK) Ltd, Croydon, CR0 4YY
Follow us on Twitter @OMaraBooks

www.mombooks.com

*The endpapers show a photograph of Churchill's study at Chartwell, with aquarium
on the left. By kind premission of Professor Stefan Buczacki (see page 312).*

To Helen and John

with love

CONTENTS

ACKNOWLEDGEMENTS

My first thanks are due to friends and colleagues at the Churchill Archives Centre. Allen Packwood, Natalie Adams and Katharine Thomson have been more than generous with their help and I have benefited hugely from their unrivalled knowledge not only of the Churchill Papers but of other relevant collections in their keeping. Without their guidance I would certainly have missed gems hidden in files seldom consulted by historians. Thanks are due, too, to Tom Davies for additional assistance. And I must express appreciation to the Master, Fellows and Scholars of Churchill College, Cambridge, for permission to quote material for which they hold the copyright. Several Fellows of the College also made pertinent suggestions when I gave an illustrated 'post-prandial' talk about the role of animals in Winston Churchill's life.

Other copyright holders to whom I am under obligation are Artemis Cooper, Anthony Bonner, Alice Nemon and Curtis Brown on behalf of the Beneficiaries of the Estate of Winston S. Churchill. I am especially indebted to Emma Soames, who kindly allowed me to consult the papers of both her mother and her Aunt Sarah before the cataloguing process was complete. Some copyrights I have been unable to trace and if their owners care to get in touch with me I will make proper acknowledgement in any future edition of this book.

Two eminent Churchill scholars in the United States made valuable contributions to the book. Richard Langworth sent me advance copies of his own essays about Churchill's animals and gave me access to a digitized version of Churchill's speeches. Jim Muller, who is chairman of the board of academic advisers to the International Churchill Society, gave me prolonged and expert counsel of a kind that he is uniquely qualified to provide. He also allowed me to consult his definitive edition of Churchill's *The River War* prior to its appearance in print.

Peter Pagnamenta read an early draft of my text and made instructive and constructive comments. Kedrun Laurie furnished me with a number of significant pointers on the subject of hunting. Donald Rayfield has been a mine of information about everything to do with the animal kingdom, and much else besides. I also benefited from help in particular instances from Paul Cartledge, Minnie Churchill, Ian Craig, Pam Gatrell, Ronald Hyam, Cita Stelzer and Jane Williams. For further aid and encouragement I am grateful to Rex and Goody Bloomstein, to Henley and Penny Smith, to my brother Dominic, who has always believed in this bestiary, and to my wife Vyvyen, who acted as midwife to the animals that appear below as they emerged from their womb in the word-processor.

My literary agent Laura Morris not only arranged for the publication of the book but made crucial suggestions for revising the penultimate draft. Louise Dixon, my editor at Michael O'Mara Books, has seen it through the press with heart-warming enthusiasm and meticulous efficiency. Her picture editor, Judith Palmer, has been resourceful and indefatigable. And her copy-editor, Helen Cumberbatch, has done a brilliant job, saving me from an embarrassing number of solecisms and downright errors. Any that remain, needless to say, are my responsibility.

No friends have been more supportive than John Burningham, who cheered me with his inimitable wit, and Helen Oxenbury, who created the marvellous illustration on the dust-jacket. To them I dedicate the book.

Piers Brendon
Cambridge
August 2018

TIMELINE OF WINSTON CHURCHILL'S LIFE

1874 30 November Born at Blenheim Palace, the son of Lord Randolph Churchill (third son of 7th Duke of Marlborough) and Jennie née Jerome

1886 August-December Lord Randolph Churchill Chancellor of the Exchequer

1888 April Winston to Harrow

1893 September Became cavalry cadet at Sandhurst

1895 24 January Death of Lord Randolph Churchill

1895 February Commissioned Second Lieutenant in Fourth Hussars

1897 Campaigned with the Malakand Field Force on North West Frontier of India

1898 2 September Took part in charge of 21st Lancers at the battle of Omdurman

1899 October To South Africa as war correspondent for the *Morning Post*

1899 November Captured by the Boers and imprisoned in Pretoria

1899 December Escaped

1900 Fought in various engagements as Lieutenant South African Light Horse, while continuing to report as war correspondent

1900 October Elected Conservative MP for Oldham

1904 31 May Crossed the floor to join the Liberal Party on the issue of free trade

1905 December Under-Secretary of State for the Colonies

1906 January Liberal MP for Manchester North West

1907 East African journey

1908 April President of the Board of Trade and MP for Dundee

1908 12 September Married Clementine Hozier in St Margaret's, Westminster

1910 February Home Secretary

1911 October First Lord of the Admiralty

1914 October Took part in defence of Antwerp

1915 February Naval attack on the Dardanelles, which discredited him

1915 May Removed from Admiralty to become Chancellor of the Duchy of Lancaster in Liberal–Conservative coalition government

1915 November Resigned and took up painting as a pastime to keep the 'black dog' of depression at bay

1916 January–May Served on Western Front first with Grenadier Guards and then as Colonel 6th Battalion Royal Scots Fusiliers

1917 July Minister of Munitions

1919 January Secretary of State for War (and Air)

1921 February Secretary of State for the Colonies

1922 Bought Chartwell, a country house near Westerham in Kent

1922 November Lost his seat at Dundee after the fall of Lloyd George's coalition

1924 October Having moved to the right, elected MP for Epping and appointed Chancellor of the Exchequer in Stanley Baldwin's Conservative government

1925 April Returned Britain to the gold standard

1929 May Lost office when Baldwin's government defeated in the general election

1931 January Quit the Tory shadow cabinet over the Indian question

1936 December Shouted down in the Commons for supporting Edward VIII during the abdication crisis

1938 September Denounced Neville Chamberlain's Munich settlement with Hitler as 'a total and unmitigated defeat'

1939 September First Lord of the Admiralty, once again, at the outbreak of war

1940 10 May Succeeded Chamberlain as Prime Minister

1940 June Rallied the nation with 'fight on the beaches' and 'finest hour' speeches

1940 20 August Acclaimed Battle of Britain pilots: 'Never in the field of human conflict was so much owed by so many to so few'

1941 June Welcomed Stalin as an ally after Hitler's invasion of the Soviet Union

1941 August Met President Roosevelt at Placentia Bay and agreed Atlantic Charter

1941 December Declared war on Japan after the bombing of Pearl Harbor

1942 February Japanese took Singapore, which Churchill called 'the greatest military disaster in British history'

1942 June Roosevelt sustained Churchill, who was in America when Tobruk fell

1942 August Visits to Cairo and Moscow

1942 November Ordered church bells to be rung after Montgomery's victory at El Alamein

1943 January Casablanca Conference

1943 August First Quebec Conference

1943 November Teheran Conference

1943 December Churchill seriously ill in North Africa

1944 June Visit to Normandy shortly after the D-Day landings

1944 September Second Quebec Conference

1944 December To Athens to prevent Communist takeover of Greece

1945 February Yalta Conference

1945 8 May Victory in Europe Day

1945 23 May Formed 'Caretaker government' before general election

1945 July Potsdam Conference

1945 26 July Heavily defeated by Labour at the polls. Churchill himself elected MP for Woodford

1946 5 March 'Iron Curtain' speech at Fulton, Missouri – first major salvo in the Cold War

1946 19 September Speech in Zurich calling for a United Europe

1950 23 February Narrowly defeated by Labour in the general election

1951 26 October Victory at the polls and again Prime Minister

1953 23 June Incapacitated by a major stroke but made a slow recovery

1953 October Won Nobel Prize for Literature

1955 5 April Resigned as Prime Minister

1964 July Left the House of Commons

1965 24 January Died in London, exactly 70 years after his father

1965 30 January State funeral and burial in Bladon churchyard, near Blenheim

1977 12 December Death of Clementine Churchill

INTRODUCTION

One of Winston Churchill's key characteristics was his fascination with the animal kingdom. This aspect of his life has never been thoroughly examined, yet animals of all sorts were a crucial element in his existence from the very start. Winston was born prematurely on 30 November 1874 in his grandfather's magnificent residence, Blenheim Palace, a baroque masterpiece designed by Sir John Vanbrugh, decorated by the likes of Grinling Gibbons and set in grounds shaped by Capability Brown. Ever impatient, Winston arrived at a gallop. A bold rider, whether in the realm of sport, politics or war, he sustained the pace almost to the end of his long life. But he always preferred horsepower measured in sinews rather than cylinders, deprecating the replacement of man's trusty steed by 'the infernal – I mean internal – combustion engine'.[1]

Blenheim Palace was the gift of a grateful nation to Winston's famous ancestor, the first Duke of Marlborough, and it took its name from his great victory over the forces of Louis XIV's France in 1704. Like other English country houses, Blenheim was an integral part of the natural world. Its honey-coloured stone was quarried from the Cotswolds. Set amid garden, park, lake, grove and cascade, it seemed to be the ultimate efflorescence of a landscape refined by art. It was the nucleus of an estate teeming with animals, domestic and wild; the former to be cherished and the latter killed. These distinctive roles reflected the convention well established by the Victorian age, and unhesitatingly adopted by young Winston, that a gentleman spent much of his time hunting, shooting and fishing, while doting on the horses, hounds and other furred or feathered friends with which he surrounded himself at home.

At Blenheim twenty gamekeepers, dressed in brown breeches, green velvet coats with brass buttons and black billycock hats, ensured superlative field sports. During shooting parties, often attended by royalty, guests let fly at clouds of pheasants and on one record-breaking day Winston's cousin Sunny, ninth Duke of Marlborough, assisted by four others, slaughtered some 7,500 rabbits. Foxes were pursued with equal abandon and Blenheim's huge, Doric-columned stable court housed a score of thoroughbred hunters, which Winston bestrode with joy, as well as the same number of carriage horses. Harrying hares was the particular passion of Winston's father, Lord Randolph Churchill. According to Sunny's statuesque second wife Gladys, whom Winston disliked, Blenheim Palace was 'murderous with heavy people & talk of guns, game etc.'.[2]

Yet Blenheim was celebrated for the pedigree cocker spaniels which the dukes bred, and Gladys herself was so besotted by dogs that, after becoming estranged from her husband, she virtually turned the house into an immense, stinking kennel. Animals had always been valued at Blenheim which, like Lord Derby's Knowsley Hall and other stately homes, had once boasted a menagerie of exotic beasts. Farm animals were also prized, particularly cattle, whose status was denoted by the extravagant opulence of the Palace's dairy, where a fountain, which in any other place would have adorned the entrance to the mansion itself, was provided simply to cool the milk and butter. Whatever function they fulfilled, animals were part of the tenure of Winston's existence. He was brought up in symbiosis with the so-called 'brute creation'.

As a small boy Winston was a keen 'bug-hunter', adept at netting butterflies, dragonflies and moths. Encouraged by his father (who was the seventh Duke's younger son) he later pursued game with hound, gun and rod. He revelled in the excitement of the chase, telling his mother (Jennie, née Jerome) that fox-hunting was the greatest pleasure in the world. In India Churchill became an ardent pig-sticker. In Africa he dispatched, among many other large quadrupeds, three rare white rhinoceroses. At home he could blaze away at pheasants until it gave him a headache or spend six back-breaking hours vainly casting flies for salmon. Often he was invited to enjoy the 'sporting' amenities of Scotland, typically by his close friend Archie Sinclair, who wrote to him from Thurso Castle in September 1922:

The salmon fishing is sure to be good, the snipe are coming
into the bogs – Edwin [Montagu] and I shot 16 in 1½ hours
yesterday and the light was bad or we could have had many
more – stags are coming onto the ground, and we go after the
grouse with dogs or drive them according to the weather.[3]

All this was well calculated to appeal to Churchill, who rode to hounds,
shot birds and beasts, and fished well into old age.

Yet from his infancy upwards Winston was devoted to domestic
animals. He kept guinea pigs and tame bunnies – while slaying wild
rabbits. He had an affinity with felines and in letters home he signed
himself 'The Pussy Cat'. At St George's Ascot, his prep school, he was
smitten by 'a dear little fox-terrier puppy'.[4] At Harrow he sold his bicycle
to buy a bulldog, the purpose of which escaped his fond nanny, Mrs
Everest, 'unless it is to keep us all in terror of our lives'.[5] Churchill always
found time for animals despite prodigious military and literary exertions
and a political career which saw him rise to glittering heights as President
of the Board of Trade, Home Secretary, First Lord of the Admiralty,
Minister of Munitions, Secretary of State for War (and Air), Colonial
Secretary and Chancellor of the Exchequer. At Chartwell, the pocket
Blenheim in Kent that he acquired in 1922, Churchill accumulated an
extensive menagerie. He lavished care, cash and emotion on the welfare
of its inmates, who became part of his extended family.

Churchill's daughter Sarah rhapsodized over the advantages of
their family life in the country, recalling especially the dogs and the
nags, nice old tame hacks which she called blackberry-picking horses.
Nor did she forget her tortoise Ptolemy, whom she ceremoniously
buried in one of her father's cigar boxes thinking he was dead, only
to discover, when a gardener unearthed him from the rose bed, that
he had been hibernating. After Churchill's defeat at the polls in 1945,
Sarah comforted her 'darling darling darling Papa' with a delectable
picture of his rustication at Chartwell. 'No lovelier plot of land exists,'
she wrote, 'and we could till the land and milk the cows and feed the
chickens and you could have an enormous bell you clanged when you
wanted to see us.'[6]

Dwelling amid fauna and flora, Churchill maintained, was the ideal form of existence. He went further, once remarking that 'The world would be better off if it were inhabited only by animals.'[7] Robert Boothby, his parliamentary private secretary in the late 1920s, exaggerated when he said that Churchill had little regard for human life, least of all his own, but that he 'would cry over the death of a swan or a cat'.[8] But it is true that Churchill's eyes filled with tears during the Second World War as he contemplated the effects of bombing not only on people but on German cats and Japanese dogs. He also wept on discovering that a group of people waiting outside a shop on the route to Chequers was queuing for birdseed. In none of this was Churchill unusual, for mankind has always related to the beasts of the field, the birds of the air and the fishes of the sea in complicated, varied and irrational ways. Like other members of the aristocracy, he was the heir to two conflicting traditions: the Georgian and Victorian development of blood sports as a symbol of national virility; and an increasing sympathy for animals fostered by the Romantic movement.

By the nineteenth century the British ruling class had elevated fox-hunting into a chivalric cult. Formerly a pursuit fit only for 'bumpkins and boobies'[9] such as Squire Western in Fielding's *Tom Jones*, it was now extolled not just for ridding the countryside of vermin but for instilling the cavalryman's virtues of dash and pluck. Churchill himself echoed (but slightly misquoted) Mr Jorrocks's opinion that fox-hunting provided all the glory of war with only 25 per cent of the danger.[10] Similarly, stags were culled not only to improve the species but to hone the stalker's art. Salmon were hooked for eating and for edification, angling being seen as part of a pastoral idyll in sharp contrast to the swarming life of mean city streets and dark satanic mills. Also intrinsic to a wholesome rural existence was the seasonal assault on pheasant, partridge and grouse. Prince Albert was partly responsible for transmuting this from an informal field sport into an organized massacre; and few took larger bags than his grandson, King George V, which did not stop him weeping over a dead garden bird.

Such sentimentality was encouraged by the growth of humane feelings that culminated in the romantic recognition of the innocence, freedom, beauty and vitality of creatures like the skylark, nightingale, albatross, field mouse and even the fly. Empathy for animals was further encouraged by Darwin's theory of evolution, which demonstrated the kinship of all creatures great and small. Genetic propinquity encouraged emotional intimacy. People who talked to their pets, and most owners did, might now bridge the gap between the species. According to a recent study, 'personifying animals and befriending them is a normal and natural human characteristic'.[11] Churchill himself was the complete anthropomorphist. He not only invested animals with human traits but enrolled a huge cast of them in the psychodrama of his existence, directing the action and devising the dialogue.

Thus he offered his thoroughbred colt Colonist II an enticing reward for victory, which apparently explained why he came fourth: 'I told him this is a very big race and if he won he would never have to run again but spend the rest of his life in agreeable female company. Colonist II did not keep his mind on the race!'[12] Churchill wrote letters as if from his poodle Rufus. He claimed to have established telepathic communication with his sheep Friendly. During the Second World War he accused his cat Smoky of semaphoring state secrets with his tail to the pelicans in St James's Park. He encouraged his budgerigar Toby to drink whisky and brandy from his glass, but when purchasing a similar bird to give to Field Marshal Montgomery he stipulated that, like Monty himself, it should be a total abstainer from alcohol. Late in life he was overheard addressing one of his guppies (tropical minnows) in these terms: 'Darling, I do love you. I would make love to you if only I knew how.'[13]

Such was Churchill's tenderness towards the livestock farmed at Chartwell that he opposed the slaying of any creature to whom he had said 'Good Morning'.[14] And on one memorable occasion he asked his wife Clementine to carve the goose because it 'was a friend of mine'.[15] Nevertheless his *sine qua non* was meat. Churchill demanded that the masses – humble folk in cottage homes, to use his own terms – should be fed on the roast beef of old England and he himself liked steak or lamb cutlets for breakfast, washed down with white wine. He once rejected a delicious salmon on the grounds that the war would be won by carnivores. As for vegetarians, they were (with the exception of his friend and scientific adviser Professor Frederick Lindemann, later Lord Cherwell) beyond the pale. Churchill even joked with Stalin about the diet of Sir Stafford Cripps, his sometime ambassador to the Soviet Union, saying that Cripps 'lived on pea and lentil, with an occasional orgy on a carrot and a pumpkin as a New Year dinner'.[16] Nut-eaters, fruit-juice-drinkers and other food faddists died young, he asserted, after a long period of senile decay. Churchill's own diet, though, did not alter his conviction that kindness to animals was the mark and the duty of civilization. And rapport with them was a unique source of pleasure.

To an uncommon degree Churchill was amused, intrigued, enchanted and besotted by animals. He adored zoos, carnivals, fairs, gymkhanas and circuses, enjoying especially the frolics of wrestling bears and acrobatic sea lions. He was thrilled by the burlesque performance of a parrot at the Monte Carlo casino. He treasured big beasts presented to him, which were housed in Regent's Park: among them his lion Rota, his leopard Sheba and his white kangaroos Digger and Matilda. These last two he proposed to receive at an official ceremony in 1947, saying that the photographers could snap him as much as they wished – 'in the kangaroo's pouch if they like, with my legs all sprawling about'.[17] Imitating the practice of the ancients, he engaged in what would become known as 'panda diplomacy'. Churchill relished animal stories, especially those of Rudyard Kipling, and confessed to roaming the jungles with Mowgli and fighting for dear life in the skin of the mongoose Rikki-Tikki-Tavi against the cobra Nag. He liked to recite Kipling's verse in his bath, twiddling the taps with his toes, and it has even been suggested that the cadences of his 'we shall fight on the beaches' speech owed something to the seals in *The Jungle Book* who 'fought in the breakers, they fought on the sand, and they fought on the smooth-worn basalt rocks of the nurseries'.[18]

Certainly animals occupied a prime place in Churchill's imagination. He identified with them and *was* identified with them: R. A. Butler (while deploring Churchill's lack of a spiritual side) called him a 'magnificent animal'.[19] Animals supplied Churchill's family with terms of endearment. Winston was Pug (or Pig) to Clementine's Kat. Returning home he would utter a sharp woof-woof, answered by her enthusiastic miaow; and they often ended letters to each other with sketches of their four-footed avatars. Their offspring, collectively known as the 'kittens', had individual animal nicknames: 'the Puppy Kitten' (Diana), 'the Rabbit' (Randolph), 'the Bumblebee' (Sarah, later called 'the Mule'[20] because she was stubborn and wouldn't breed), 'the Duckadilly' (Marigold) and 'the Chimp' (Mary). Unlike many patricians, who notoriously preferred their horses and dogs to their children,[21] Churchill was an affectionate parent. He played animal games with his brood, chasing them in the guise of a bear or a gorilla. The latter he imitated with uncanny accuracy, crouching behind bushes and jumping out with his arms swinging limply, baring his teeth, beating his chest and emitting 'a blood-tingling roar of "Grr! Grr!"'.[22]

Perhaps his impersonation was enhanced by the fact that, in the opinion of David Lloyd George at least, Churchill physically resembled a gorilla. During the course of his career he was compared to a remarkable variety of other creatures, among them lion, tiger, buffalo, bull, bulldog, bullfrog, chicken, duck, rat, caterpillar, spider, maggot, mongrel, puppy, donkey, warhorse, orangutan, dinosaur, dragon, hippopotamus, wild boar and rogue elephant. Not all such characterizations were hostile and some were expressions of affection. Churchill's daughter Mary likened him to a charming porpoise and his daughter Sarah to a 'divine tortoise'.[23]

Time and again Churchill himself employed animal imagery, which loomed almost as large in his rhetoric as the military metaphors for which, as a soldier, he instinctively reached. The two modes were often complementary. Thus Churchill greatly admired 'the conception of a well-armed infantry battalion working with the élan and combined individualism of a pack of hounds'.[24] And in the midst of the Blitz, in February 1941, he proposed to give a lecture on strategy at the Imperial Defence College after the war:

> It will be all animal stories – nothing else. You remember how Foch said, 'I am like a parrot – *un perroquet*. First I grasp with my beak, then with one claw' – and so on. Then there is the tiger sprawled and the tiger crouched. I once had a horse that got badly rubbed in a ship coming over from Ireland. The inside of one hind leg was quite raw. It would have kicked a man's brains

out if he had tried to doctor it. The vet put a twitch on its nose, and then he could rub the leg with disinfectant and do anything he liked, while the horse stood trembling. That illustrates the initiative. I told them that story at the time of Gallipoli. Once you grab the enemy by the nose, he will be able to think of nothing else.[25]

Other familiar animals, cows, sheep, chickens, pigs, were grist to Churchill's mill, often exploited as a source of oratorical entertainment, which disarmed opposition in the Commons. He described writing a speech as laying an egg and he told Labour MPs, 'I do not wish to cast my pearls before … those who do not want them.'[26]

To characterize both friends and enemies he also conjured up exotic creatures with names to match. He dubbed the battle-scarred Antipodean General Bernard Freyberg 'the Salamander … of the British Empire'.[27] He mocked Bernard Shaw, saying that the world was amused by 'the nimble antics of this unique and double-headed chameleon, while all the time he was eager to be taken seriously'.[28] Lenin, though, was 'as mildly amused to stalk a capercailzie [wood grouse] as to butcher an Emperor'.[29] Churchill described the Irish Republican Army as 'a miserable gang of cowardly assassins like the human leopards of West Africa'.[30] He rejected a rapprochement with Nazi Germany by recalling the 'fable of the jackal who went hunting with the tiger and what happened after the hunt was over'.[31] He also branded Mussolini as a jackal and, still more obnoxious, a hyena. The Soviet Union tested, though it by no means exhausted, his feral lexicon. He represented the Bolsheviks as snakes, vultures, crocodiles, wolves, bears, hyenas, vampires, typhus-bearing vermin, the tapeworm killing the Russian dog, 'the nameless beast'[32] foretold in Muscovite legend and, above all, as baboons, hopping and capering amidst the corpses of their victims and the ruins of civilization. When a Russian trade delegation led by Leonid Krasin visited London in 1920, Churchill asked the Foreign Secretary Lord Curzon, 'Did you shake hands with the hairy baboon?'[33]

In using animals as emblems of virtue and vice, Churchill was drawing on a tradition that stretched from Aesop to Orwell – who of course depicted the Communist leaders as pigs. Such symbolism had a universal appeal (though Churchill did say that *Animal Farm* should not be given to the Russians because they would not understand it). Allegorical creatures were especially effective as agents of satire, none more so than Jonathan Swift's Houyhnhnms, whose equine perfection afforded a terrible contrast to the repulsive depravity of the Yahoos. But whereas *Gulliver's Travels* veered into misanthropy, that older form of animal literature, the bestiary, concentrated on morality.

Originating early in the Christian era, bestiaries reached a peak of popularity during the Middle Ages, when animals were still regarded as being more of symbolic than scientific interest. Medieval bestiaries disseminated improving lessons and pleasing parables derived from the book of nature. Sumptuously illustrated, adorned with maxims, myths, marginalia and folklore, they exhibited the brute creation in all its glory, menace and multiplicity. Indeed, they showed rather more than the works of God, since bestiaries also contained imaginary creatures: dragons, centaurs, mermaids, gryphons, basilisks, phoenixes, unicorns. All these vivid compilations, however, might have taken their epigraph from the Bible: 'But ask now the beasts, and they shall teach thee; and the fowls of the air, and they shall tell thee.'[34]

This book is a Churchill bestiary. It aims to shed light on his life by reference to the animals which played such a significant part in it. The book also explores the way in which Churchill made use of animals in his work with pen and tongue. This was epitomized by the image he minted on his eightieth birthday, when responding to parliamentarians assembled in Westminster Hall to pay tribute to his service to the state and especially to his eloquent wartime leadership: 'It was a nation and race dwelling all round the globe that had the lion's heart. I had the luck to be called upon to give the roar. I also hope that I sometimes suggested to the lion the right place to use his claws.'[35] The king of beasts, like every other animal relating to Churchill, takes its alphabetical place in the following pages. Arbitrary divisions are made for the sake of convenience. Thus there are separate entries for Dogs, Bulldogs and Poodles; for Horses, Polo Ponies and Racehorses; for Fish, Eels, Goldfish and Golden Orfe, Tropical Fish and Whales; for Snakes and Boa Constrictors; and so on. The entries vary in length, depending on the role each beast played in the story. These roles often overlap and conflict. Faithful dogs vie with miserable curs. The lion does not always feature as the king of beasts but sometimes as royal vermin. Churchill is likened to Pooh Bear but warns that Red Bruin is padding across the steppes on bloody paws.

Repeatedly we encounter the paradox of the animal-loving hunter, a telling analogue of the soft-hearted warrior whose humane values were at odds with his aggressive instincts. Churchill's attitude towards animals reflected his nurture as a grandee and his nature as a sybarite – he was not one to rationalize, let alone to ration, his pleasures and he deplored the consequences of intemperate self-restraint as much as he despised the hobgoblin of consistency. Here he spears hogs but scratches the backs of pigs. He hunts foxes but keeps them as pets. He likes fishing but loves fish. Churchill declares that making concessions to Gandhi is like feeding cat's meat to a tiger (hardly the most apt comparison in view of the Mahatma's well-known pacifism and vegetarianism), and later admits that the one thing he wants to do before he dies is to 'shoot a Manchurian tiger'.[36] Yet in old age he himself hopes to be reincarnated as a 'lovely tiger'.[37]

Still, the inconsistencies add depth and texture to the overall picture. This picture aspires both to entertain the general reader and to interest the scholar, drawing as it does on much original material, notably from files largely neglected in the recently digitized Churchill papers. On display here is a heraldic tableau blazoned with anecdote, vignette and commentary. It is a multi-coloured tapestry embroidered with contemporary observations, a rich pageant embellished by Churchill's wit, wisdom and wayward genius. It is a talking picture, abounding in quotations that transmit his voice across the gulf of years. It is also a moving picture which, like bestiaries of old, not only adorns a tale but points a moral – especially in the realm of ecology. Advancing through these pages is a cavalcade of beasts who have shared the Earth with mankind throughout history. Their fate, as numbers decline with terrifying speed and the natural world faces unprecedented prospects of environmental catastrophe, is now bound up with our own more tightly than ever before. In the shadow of extinction, creatures of flesh and blood are all one.

THE BESTIARY

ALBATROSS

Churchill invoked this majestic wanderer of the southern skies at the climax of an important parliamentary speech in 1935. By then his own high-flying political career had stalled and he seemed to have lost his way. Not only was he at odds with the National Government but he had also fallen out with most of his own party over the question of giving India limited self-rule. Having led a diehard Tory campaign to prevent what he saw as a cowardly imperial surrender, Churchill now had to concede defeat. More galling still, the chief proponent of the Government of India Bill, the Secretary of State Sir Samuel Hoare, was an old enemy. Churchill publicly compared Hoare to a cow that gave good milk but then kicked over the pail, and privately he wished to 'break this bloody rat Hoare's neck'.[1] In Churchill's dramatic Commons peroration he acknowledged that Hoare would win the vote for his measure but he suggested that the victory would be to him what killing the albatross had been to Coleridge's Ancient Mariner.

Misguided though Churchill was in attempting to hold back Indian independence, he correctly forecast that it would both lead to bloodshed in the subcontinent and herald the fall of the British Empire. Hoare would have to accept the blame for the part he played in bringing down this soaring creation. Churchill quoted the Wedding-Guest's poignant question and the Ancient Mariner's anguished response:

> 'God save thee, ancient Mariner!
> From the fiends, that plague thee thus!
> Why look'st thou so?' 'With my crossbow
> I shot the Albatross.'[2]

Churchill hung the guilt round Hoare's neck like the dead bird. It was a curse that he not only pronounced but fulfilled.

Hoare cravenly supported Neville Chamberlain's policy of appeasing Hitler, and when Churchill became Prime Minister in 1940 he exiled Hoare to Madrid where, as ambassador, he had to deal with another fascist dictator, General Franco. His fate was at once ignominious and appropriate. Hoare was 'very clever' but, in the words of King George VI's private secretary Sir Alan Lascelles, 'a bit *kibdelos* (spurious, base, deceitful)'.[3] There was a good chance that he would be murdered in Spain, the head of the Foreign Office Sir Alexander Cadogan said hopefully, whereas if he had stayed at home he might have become the 'Quisling of England'.[4] So what began as a rhetorical flight of fancy finished, Churchill would doubtless have concluded, as a form of poetic justice.

ALLIGATORS

C hurchill regarded these reptiles as among the greatest villains of the animal kingdom. This was partly, no doubt, because they were armoured and dangerous, lurking in rivers and swamps to ambush their prey. But it was also because they were relics of a prehistoric age, irretrievably primitive and brutish. Saurians were the antithesis of *Homo sapiens* and the enemies of the human race.

Churchill was not alone in his hostility towards them: alligators in China, where they were known as Muddy Dragons, had been nearly exterminated. But it was with conciliation rather than conservation in mind that Churchill approved London Zoo's plan to swap two Père David's deer for a pair of Chinese alligators. These deer came from a herd established exclusively by the Duke of Bedford at Woburn and, although indigenous to China, they were now extinct in the wild. Mao Tse-tung's government was delighted by the exchange, wishing that 'scientific and cultural interflow between our two countries be strengthened and our two peoples' friendship be developed from day to day'.[1] Thus in March 1955, at the very end of his final ministry, Churchill supported an animal transaction that would have been familiar to Assyrian kings, Egyptian pharaohs and Roman emperors. Furthermore, at the height of the Cold War and despite his visceral anti-Communism, he proved willing to treat with China red in tooth and claw and politics. He thus anticipated the era of modern panda diplomacy.

The alligator nevertheless remained prominent in Churchill's pantheon of *bêtes noires*. On occasion he equated it with Mussolini, who was also base, sinister and malign. In an elaborate attack on Britain's appeasement policy in 1938, Churchill amused the diarist Harold Nicolson by speaking of 'this great country nosing from door to door like a cow that has lost its calf, mooing dolefully now in Berlin, and now in Rome – when all the time the tiger and the alligator wait for its undoing'.[2]

ANTELOPE

When Lord Randolph Churchill set off for South Africa in 1891 on a quest for health, gold and game, Winston, then aged sixteen, asked him to bring back an antelope. In his first letter Winston supposed that his father had already 'slain multitudes of lions and natives' and urged him not to 'forget my youthful antelope'. Lord Randolph, fatally ill with what was evidently syphilis, assumed that his son wanted a tame antelope. He doubted if he could obtain one, though he killed many in the wild, regarding the whole experience as 'a concentration of human joy which Paradise might with difficulty rival'.[1] But Winston assured him that he had no wish for a live animal, only 'a head for my room'.[2] He reinforced the point by adorning subsequent letters with sketches of antelope heads. Such trophies were the standard means of advertising the virility of British empire-builders and quite soon, his father having failed him, Winston was able to acquire many of his own.

While taking part in the Boer War in 1900 he witnessed soldiers, eager for sport and venison, pouring fire into a stampeding herd at least 700 strong, 'a regular cascade of antelope'.[3] In 1907, when he was parliamentary under-secretary for the colonies, Churchill went to East Africa on a private sporting expedition, which he characteristically transformed into a semi-official progress. Travelling along the so-called Lunatic Line, the recently opened railway linking Mombasa to Lake Victoria, Churchill sat on the cow-catcher of the locomotive and let fly at any suitable creature that came within range of his gun. He returned from Uganda via the Sudan 'game reserve' and in a single three-hour walk, according to his own account, 'I shot a fine waterbuck, two reedbucks, and two of a beautiful herd of roan antelope, who walked down to the water past our ambuscade.'[4]

In England he got a taxidermist to mount the best heads in his bag: a rhinoceros, a zebra, a warthog, a Grant's gazelle, a Thomson's gazelle and two kinds of antelope – a wildebeest and a Coke's hartebeest. He also gave orders for the dressing of three zebra skins and the construction of a 'rhinoceros table',[5] presumably made from the pachyderm's foot. An antelope might indeed have made an exotic pet but Churchill preferred it as a costly wall decoration.

ANTS

Ever since Solomon hailed the ant as a paragon of industry and Herodotus described India's giant gold-digging ants, human beings have been intrigued by these insects – and Churchill was no exception. Aged ten he asked his father whether there were 'many *ants* in India'.[1] He ascertained the fact for himself when serving as a young lieutenant on the North West Frontier, noting that the scaly anteater, though destitute of beauty, was not without use. During the Boer War he enjoyed watching fights between different species of ants. And he was enthralled by the marching columns of soldier ants that he encountered during his East African safari in 1907.

He observed that they advanced in regular array, fierce, remorseless and inscrutable. Their army guarded its flanks and sent out tireless reconnoitring patrols. Churchill admired the self-sacrificing courage of these creatures, saying that they would rather have their heads pulled off than relinquish their grip on their prey. But he could not resist breaking up their columns with his walking stick, jumping nimbly aside when they attacked him. In 1925 he also witnessed a great battle between rival ant colonies in the Insect House at London Zoo, where he was especially impressed by the gallantry of the vanquished, who carried their underground workers to safety in their mouths.

Like many others, especially military men, Churchill was tempted to seek solutions to the social problems of humanity in the discipline of the swarm and the hive – though he would hardly have gone as far as General Baden-Powell, who informed Boy Scouts that bees were a 'model community, for they respect their Queen and kill their unemployed'.[2] Still, Churchill did write that men and women possessed such self-defeating characteristics that they were only fit for a hugger-mugger world: 'Ants or Bees would be worthy of better things – tho' even they have some bad habits.'[3] Bearing such habits in mind, however, he was particularly struck by the story of ants eating the Emperor Tiberius's pet snake. This was a warning, according to Roman astrologers, about the dangers of the multitude, of which Churchill was acutely conscious. Although respecting the sovereign people, he feared the revolutionary mob. And the advent of Lenin convinced him that the anthill and the beehive were paradigms of Communism, the antithesis of a free society and a liberal world order.

It is not clear how much Churchill knew of the Victorian debate about the degree to which insects such as ants were models of competition or co-operation; but after 1917 he would have endorsed the view, best expressed by the scientist T. H. Huxley, that 'The Societies of Bees and Ants exhibit socialism *in excelsis*.'[4] Retaining a soft spot for delectable honey bees, Churchill maintained that the new kind of slave state being established in Russia was peopled by predatory pismires. The Soviet Union was a standardized, mechanized collective without a soul. It was an ant heap in which the individual was sacrificed to the mass. To his chagrin its creed was extolled by one of his favourite contemporary writers, H. G. Wells. Controverting Wells in 1931, Churchill solemnly declared: 'There is not one single social or economic principle or concept in the philosophy of the Russian Bolshevik which has not been realized, carried into action, and enshrined in immutable laws a million years ago by the White Ant.'[5]

APES

In 1891 Lord Randolph Churchill outraged the British public by stating that the female lust for diamonds was so barbaric that he could only conclude that 'whatever may be the origin of man, woman is descended from an ape'.[1] Even in jest Winston would not have been guilty of such a *bêtise*. He did think, though, that human beings were risen apes, not fallen angels. Influenced by Darwinism, he also believed in the survival of the fittest, as best expressed by T. H. Huxley:

> For his successful progress, throughout the savage state, man has
> been largely indebted to those qualities which he shares with
> the ape and the tiger; his exceptional physical organization; his
> cunning, his sociability, his curiosity, and his imitativeness; his
> ruthless and ferocious destructiveness when his anger is roused
> by opposition.[2]

At the same time Churchill affirmed in his only novel, *Savrola* (published in 1900), that political morality would triumph over physical force in the end and that the nation with the highest ideals would succeed. This message he reiterated in 1940, declaring that the decisive factor in the war against Hitler was 'a cause which rouses the spontaneous surgings of the human spirit'. If it were otherwise, he said, 'how would men have risen above the apes; how otherwise would they have conquered and extirpated dragons and monsters?'[3]

Even so Churchill feared that fascist or Communist dictators could put the evolutionary clock back in the short term. He went so far as to claim that Leon Trotsky, having exhausted the aid of criminals after the Russian Revolution, turned to wild beasts, vainly attempting to

Reflecting Churchill's concern, the Gibraltar apes were treated as part of the garrison, given a food allowance and medical attention.

mobilize the wolves and the apes. Of course the anthropoid tribe was easily depicted as a comic or demonic caricature of the human race and Churchill was not alone in exploiting it for the purpose of satire or vituperation. Shakespeare had likened proud man to an angry ape who played 'such fantastic tricks before high heaven/As make the angels weep'.[4] In *The Hind and the Panther* Dryden reviled the atheist as a buffoon ape. Evelyn Waugh not only lampooned Edward Gibbon as a chattering gibbon but also ridiculed Mrs Ape, the evangelist in *Vile Bodies* responsible for the hymn 'There ain't no flies on the Lamb of God'. However, Churchill had a genuine regard for the Barbary apes of Gibraltar.

These primates were actually macaques, tailless monkeys, but they were popularly known as apes and legend had it that British occupation of the Rock depended on their survival. No one knew better than Churchill that fiction influenced fact, that myth could shape reality. So in 1944, hearing that ape numbers had dwindled despite the addition of new recruits from North Africa, he issued this directive: 'The establishment of the apes on Gibraltar should be twenty-four, and every effort should be made to reach this number as soon as possible and maintain it thereafter.'[5] One of the apes, an affable character with a grey coat, was called Winston.

Churchill's concern for the Gibraltar apes continued after the war. In 1952 he received news about them from the Governor, along with snapshots showing them in fine fettle – one was wearing a sailor hat. The Prime Minister responded that he was 'much interested to read what you say and in seeing the photographs. I am glad they are doing so well and I hope they continue to flourish.'[6]

BABOONS

During the Boer War Churchill was given a small baboon, which was very fierce at first but later 'tamed wonderfully'.[1] Nevertheless he almost invariably regarded these creatures as outlandish and malignant. It was a common perception. With their pointed snouts, serrated teeth and red bottoms, baboons seemed a grotesque parody of humanity. Their very name was probably derived from the old French term for gargoyle and may also have been connected with the medieval Latin word *babinuire*, which meant 'to paint marginal figures in manuscripts'.[2] Here baboons were depicted in various symbolic roles, often as images of sinful and degenerate man.

In Churchill's bestiary it was the Bolsheviks who featured as baboons – an unusual designation since Africans were more often so called, among them one of the 'boys' on Lord Randolph's trek through Mashonaland. Winston saw Bolsheviks as the modern version of Jacobins, who had been represented as simian by cartoonists like James Gillray (though he also conflated Bourbons and baboons). In Churchill's eyes Lenin and his gang were bestial creatures who had not only destroyed tsardom but threatened to consume the Earth. Following the Great War, he struggled to engage Britain against the Reds in the Russian Civil War. 'After conquering the Huns – tigers of the world,' he said, 'I will not submit to being beaten by the baboons!'[3]

When White forces approached Moscow in 1919 Churchill talked of intervening personally and leading them into the city on a white charger. However, such quixotic belligerence had been largely buried in the mud of Flanders. As the tide of battle turned in Russia he was forced to accept that Britain could not quell 'the foul baboonery of Bolshevism'.[4] Churchill's incendiary attempt to dehumanize and defeat the Soviet revolutionaries helped to confirm his reputation as a warmonger. Yet given the enormity of Stalin's crimes, his hatred of Communism can hardly be regarded as ill-judged.

Furthermore, the baboons in London Zoo, to which Churchill was a frequent visitor, soon gave a demonstration of their murderous proclivities. In 1925 the Monkey Hill was opened with a complement of 100 hamadryas baboons who, competing for a few females in a confined space, engaged in such ferocious combat that their numbers halved within two years. Likening this kind of violence to that of Stalin and his henchmen, one recent authority writes, 'Historians have to learn from zoology.'[5]

BADGERS

Lord Randolph Churchill's oratory was redolent of the countryside. Finding suitably rustic nicknames for his political opponents, he enjoyed goring 'the Goat' (Sir Stafford Northcote), harrying the 'rodent' (Lord Derby) and, above all, drawing 'the badger' (Joseph Chamberlain). Winston larded his own speeches with animal imagery which was rich and earthy but, as the drift from the land accelerated, increasingly old-fashioned. Also somewhat dated was the delight he took in recalling the capture of a badger by his uncle by marriage, Lord William Beresford VC, a 'grand sportsman'[1] who had devoted much of his life to polo, pig-sticking, horse racing and big game hunting. As a young officer, Lord William had won a large bet by catching Brock, the mascot of the 10th Hussars in Hounslow, and carrying him back alive in a bag to the Blues Mess in Knightsbridge. Victorians brightened long winter evenings with similar tales of the shy nocturnal creature that Edward Thomas dubbed the 'most ancient Briton of English beasts'.[2]

As such it was both victim and hero. Slain by the Celts for its medicinal fat, baited by dogs over the centuries, devoured during the Second World War and gassed en masse today, the badger has always been persecuted; yet few animals have greater anthropomorphic appeal, as most obviously demonstrated by Kenneth Grahame's *The Wind in the Willows* (1908). Churchill responded to this appeal. He housed a pet baby badger at Chartwell during the late 1930s. And he hung the skin of another badger on the wall of his bedroom.[3] It belonged to an animal that he had accidentally run over when driving home from a 'rather hilarious' evening at the Other Club, a political dining club that he and F. E. Smith had founded in 1911. Apparently the badger died in Churchill's arms. 'They said it had killed one of my swans,' he told his doctor, 'but there was no proof, and in any case I forgave it.'[4]

BATS

Churchill never encountered vampire bats in the flesh, but this did not prevent him from exploiting them for declamatory or even humorous purposes. As early as 1898, in a letter to his mother, he labelled Joseph Chamberlain a political vampire, saying that he had already broken the Radical and Liberal parties and now perhaps sought 'to fatten on Tory blood'. Churchill added a rider, though, saying that he had 'a great admiration for Joe C. He is a man.'[1] By contrast, of course, the Bolsheviks were beasts. 'They destroy wherever they exist,' Churchill declared in 1919, 'but by rolling forward into fertile areas, like the vampire which sucks the blood from his victim, they gain means of prolonging their own baleful existence.'[2]

Yet when a sample of his own blood was taken in 1944 – by the Army's consulting physician in blood transfusion, Brigadier Lionel Whitby – the Prime Minister treated it lightly. After a genial chat about the standards of integrity expected of health practitioners, he asked the doctor (who had previously treated his pneumonia with the anti-bacterial drug M&B) to send him a copy of the Hippocratic Oath. Having read it, Churchill wrote: 'My confidence in the members of the medical profession, already so high, is enhanced by the knowledge that they are bound by such undertakings.'[3] Nevertheless he nicknamed Whitby the 'Vampire'.[4]

Churchill took common or garden British bats even less seriously, though he was annoyed when one intruded while he was dictating to a secretary at Chequers, the Prime Minister's official country residence. It flew through the window and caused her to duck when it dived, interrupting the spate of words. 'Surely,' Churchill expostulated, 'you are not afraid of a bat, are you?' She confessed that she was. The Prime Minister said, '*I'll* protect you. Get on with your work.'[5]

BEARS

Churchill was not unusual in having mixed feelings about bears. He recognized that they were large, dangerous predators. Yet he sometimes imbued them with the attractive qualities that had made teddy bears children's favourite cuddly toys since the time of Theodore Roosevelt and had induced Lord Byron to keep a tame bear at Trinity College, Cambridge, where he proposed that it should sit for a fellowship.

Thus in *The River War* (1899), Churchill's account of the re-conquest of the Sudan, during which he had taken part in the last great cavalry charge in British history, he described Royal Navy gunboats steaming up and down the Nile 'like caged Polar bears, seeking what they might devour'.[1] When serving on the Western Front during the Great War, he likened the sinister clouds of yellowy black smoke produced by shell blasts to woolly bears. Subsequently he suggested that the warm embrace of nominal allies might turn out to be the lethal hug of the grizzly bear.

Yet in the trenches Churchill snuggled up in a sleeping bag which he had nicknamed the 'Womb of the Red Hot Polar Bear'.[2] At Hartsbourne Manor near Bushey, country house of the wealthy former actress Maxine Elliott, he was permitted to disrupt a game of charades because he gave such a hilarious impersonation of a bear underneath a bear rug. As a father he played bear games with his children: when they advanced through a wood calling out 'Bear! Bear! Bear!' he would drop from a tree and chase them; or indoors he would make a tunnel with pictures he had painted and crawl through it growling and snapping. In Canada Churchill was charmed by the roadside bears he encountered, which turned somersaults, did balancing acts and offered other entertainment in return for food. He gave them biscuits.

Winston and Clementine playing at bears with their only son Randolph, who was much indulged, shortly before the Great War.

Churchill did not favour the gory indulgences of the vulgar such as cockfighting and bear-baiting, which had been outlawed in 1835 – though some aristocrats, such as Lord Derby, still patronized cockfighting in the mid-nineteenth century and as late as 1928 the Marquess of Hartington professed to be 'an enthusiast, even an apologist'[3] for the sport. However, in his *History of the English-Speaking Peoples* Churchill did echo T. B. Macaulay's famous argument that Puritans hated bear-baiting, not because it gave pain to the bear but because it gave pleasure to the spectators. Ever the Epicurean and the Cavalier, Churchill maintained that Puritan measures combined cant and malignity: 'Bear-baiting and cockfighting were effectively ended by shooting the bears and wringing the necks of the cocks.'[4]

Of course at least since Elizabethan times, when bears featured on the coat of arms of the English Muscovy Company, Russia had been Ursa Major. Churchill invariably exploited and augmented the symbolism, grasping the Bear's paw in friendship, exchanging growls with it, warning about its sharp teeth and claws. He referred to

Stalin as the Bear in the Kremlin. Most famously, after the Teheran Conference in 1943, he conjured up an aggrieved vision (which took various forms) of the sensible little British donkey (or lion), being squeezed between the great American buffalo (or elephant) and the huge Russian bear. Soviet expansionism in Europe after the Second World War prompted him to further indignation: 'A bear in the forest is a matter of legitimate speculation; a bear in the zoo is an object of public curiosity; a bear in your wife's bed causes the gravest concern.'[5]

Churchill also exploited the furry beast's fabulous attributes. To illustrate the hazards of what he took to be General Auchinleck's over-elaborate preparations for attacking the enemy in North Africa, he told the old story of the man who gave powder to a bear: he mixed the ingredients with immense care and rolled them into a spill in order to blow them down the bear's throat, but *'the bear blew first'*.[6] Zipped into his siren suit or rubbing his itchy back against a door jamb, the wartime Prime Minister increasingly seemed to resemble a bear. Sometimes he was like a bear with a sore head. More often he was 'rather like a kindly teddy bear'.[7] When humming under his breath he was reminiscent of Winnie-the-Pooh. A. A. Milne's Winnie, more celebrated than Baloo, Rupert, Biffo, Yogi, Paddington or any of their kind, was based on an exceptionally amiable bear of that name in London Zoo. It was so called not after Winston but after its place of origin, Winnipeg.

BEAVER

Churchill evidently saw beaver on his journey through Canada in 1929 and in *My Early Life*, published the following year, he used this industrious rodent to illustrate his belief that all human endeavour is at the mercy of time and chance. Having given an account of the efforts he made in 1898 to reach India's North West Frontier to fight in another campaign, only to find that hostilities had ceased, he summoned up a vivid image to express his frustration: 'Thus the beaver builds his dam, and thus when his fishing is about to begin, comes the flood and sweeps his work and luck and fish away together. So he has to begin again.'[1]

As quite frequently happened, however, Churchill's literary imagination exceeded his knowledge of natural history. In 1931 he received a letter from Thomas Gibson, Deputy Minister of Mines for the province of Ontario, pointing out that the beaver did not build its dam in order to catch fish: 'the beaver is a strict vegetarian in diet, and neither catches fish nor eats fish. He subsists mainly on the tender bark and twigs of trees (chiefly birch) which he fells, and the limbs of which he cuts into suitable sizes and floats to that part of the dam where he stores his winter supply. The dam is built to facilitate these operations and to widen the area from which he obtains his food, as the trees on the fringe of the pool become fewer in number.' Gibson finished by saying that he did not want to criticize Churchill's book, which he admired, 'but I am sure you would like to be accurate even in small particulars.'[2]

He was wrong. Apparently Churchill did not reply to Gibson's letter and he certainly did not change his account of the beaver in subsequent editions of *My Early Life*. His obduracy may seem strange, particularly as he corrected mistakes spotted by other correspondents. Moreover he had a great regard for Canada, a dominion opened up thanks to the beaver, which satisfied Europe's passion for fur hats, crowned the Hudson's Bay Company's coat of arms and became a national emblem. Plainly, though, Churchill was too enamoured of his beaver conceit to discard it. Like the peroration of a speech (which he prized, resenting interruptions, particularly from suffragettes), it provided a dramatic conclusion to an autobiographical chapter. Here was a piquant instance of his penchant, deplored by critics and acknowledged by himself, for 'adapting my facts to my phrases'.[3]

BEES

Political animosities in Dundee, which Churchill represented as MP from 1908 until 1922, were often sharp and sometimes poisonous. With characteristic pugnacity he himself once denounced the hostile local press magnate D. C. Thomson as a narrow, bitter, unreasonable, arrogant, conceited being who was 'pursued from day to day and from year to year by an unrelenting bee in his bonnet'.[1]

Inside Churchill's own eccentric headgear, needless to say, whole swarms whirred and buzzed. Ideas pulsated like myriad wings and words took off like drones in nuptial flight. The journalist A. G. Gardiner compared the young politician, with his Napoleonic longings, to 'a hive of bees working under a glass cover'.[2] General Alan Brooke, driven to exhaustion by Churchill's wartime vagaries, later described him as wandering like a swarm of bees from flower to flower but never pausing long enough to gather pollen.

Churchill would have rejected the charge. He admired and in some ways tried to emulate the busy bee, a miniature marvel tirelessly devoted to the task of distilling sweetness from light. One of his favourite books was *The Life of the Bee* (1901) by Maurice Maeterlinck, a future winner of the Nobel Prize in Literature like Churchill himself. It was a celebration of the 'tuneful bearers of all country perfumes'[3] and a meditation on the lessons humanity might learn from their superlative organization. And it illustrated, as Churchill once told Bernard Shaw, that bees had preserved the monarchical principle. Clementine was unimpressed. She complained that Winston tried to educate her early in their marriage by shutting her up for hours with Maeterlinck's volume, which only confirmed her view that 'bees were bores'.[4] Churchill was nevertheless determined that Chartwell – enlivened early on by the dance of 'the Golden Bumble-Bee', a performance put on by his stage-struck daughter Sarah – should be vibrant with the hum and gleam of hymenoptera. During the 1930s two beehives and several swarms were installed in the grounds. Clementine supervised them, with advice from a trained apiculturist.

When Hitler's war came, precipitating the destruction of millions of domestic animals to save them from bombs, gas or starvation, amateur bee-keeping increased. This was not so much for the sake of honey but to obtain the sugar ration given to support the bees. The system was abused but when ministers proposed to stop the allowance Churchill intervened crushingly, asking the Minister of Agriculture what savings would be made by starving the bees of private owners. After 1945 Churchill employed two German prisoners of war to revive the Chartwell bee colony. The operation may have suggested his celebrated quip about the Labour leader Clement Attlee, who had replaced him in 10 Downing Street: 'if any grub is fed on Royal Jelly it turns into a Queen Bee.'[5]

This was grossly unfair and quite unforgettable. When Margaret Thatcher, newly selected as Tory leader, said that she had been unimpressed by Jimmy Carter but that sometimes the job could make the man, one disaffected member of her Shadow Cabinet, Reginald Maudling, quoted Churchill's remark. Clearly the barb was directed at the future Prime Minister not the then President, and it was meant to sting.

BIRDS

Depending on their species and circumstances, Winston Churchill regarded birds as either fair game or nature's darlings. The sharp distinction, though well established, was more arbitrary than obvious. In the preface to Henry Salt's *Killing for Sport* (1915), Bernard Shaw observed that the sportsman and the humanitarian were often the self-same person, 'drawing altogether unaccountable lines between pheasants and pigeons'.[1] He might have been referring to Lord Randolph Churchill, whose denunciation of shooting tame pigeons Salt, a leading campaigner against blood sports, quoted later in the book. Lord Randolph had spoken during a parliamentary debate in 1883 on a bill to outlaw what *The Times* called this 'saturnalia of cruelty'.[2] He condemned the clipping of wings and the plucking of feathers, not to mention the pricking out of eyes, by which its promoters added excitement to the slaughter and said that such pigeon-shooting afforded the most repulsive sight imaginable. Likening it to the abominable amusement of hunting carted (i.e. captive) stags, he nevertheless insisted that there should be no interference with 'the legitimate sport of hunting wild animals for the purpose of killing them and giving pleasure to everyone engaged in such sport'.[3]

It was a pleasure Lord Randolph wanted Winston to share, agreeing with his wife that, at the age of sixteen, their son must learn to shoot. So in September 1891, having advanced from the boyish pursuit of taking eggs from birds' nests, Winston started to bang away at partridges, deeming it very fine sport. He continued to enjoy it for most of his life, adding to his bag such game birds as pheasant, woodcock, quail and snipe – as late as 1950 he did not take offence at being called a guttersnipe in the House of Commons since, 'after all, the snipe is a decent little bird'.[4] Churchill hunted teal in India. He despatched wild duck in Egypt and grouse in Scotland. In Kenya ostrich and bustard fell to his gun. Staying with his friend the Duke of Westminster at Eaton Hall, Cheshire, in 1936 he downed 112 birds in one day, remarking that a year without brandy, the result of a bet with Lord Rothermere, seemed to have improved his eye.

However, unlike the young Charles Darwin, for example, Churchill never became passionate about shooting birds. It was too tame. Why kill grouse on the Yorkshire moors, he exclaimed, when you can go pig-sticking in the endless zoological gardens of East Africa? Of course he was partial to game birds on the plate and he evidently preferred fresh to ripe grouse, which Alphonse Daudet had memorably likened to 'the flesh of an old whore marinated in a bidet'.[5] Churchill ate grouse for breakfast, selected it (and turtle) as a delicacy with which to entertain President Franklin D. Roosevelt on board the *Prince of Wales* at Placentia Bay, Newfoundland, in August 1941, and enjoyed sharing with Admiral Roger Keyes 'two delicious young lady grouses'.[6]

But he was unimpressed by the mystique of the Glorious Twelfth. He mocked Balfour's government for ending the 1904 parliamentary session early so that Conservative gentlemen could get away to undertake the destruction of 'a certain sacred bird'.[7] In 1913 Churchill drew a poignant contrast between the situation of great shooting estates, with their unrivalled sporting facilities, armies of gamekeepers and record bags, and the plight of a broken and dwindling peasantry. In 1936 he attacked the 'dilettante futility' of the Air Ministry, whose programme of erecting radar stations was hampered by its insistence that sites should be chosen which did not 'gravely interfere with grouse shooting'.[8] And he would hardly have sympathized with George VI's preoccupation in late August 1939, namely the Führer's disruption of the excellent sport at Balmoral. Having shot 1,600 brace of grouse in six days, the King had looked forward to killing more and found it 'utterly damnable that the villain Hitler had upset everything'.[9]

If shooting birds was a sporadic recreation for Churchill, one kill gave a significant stimulus to his imagination. A pilot he met while learning to fly before the Great War shot some wild duck for him from

On large country estates, where Churchill enjoyed shooting, field sports
were conducted like military operations.

his aircraft, a lark which prompted Churchill to dilate on the need to
arm planes (hitherto treated as mobile observation posts) for future
aerial combat. Indeed he always kept a weather eye on the sky. While
fighting on the Western Front he mistook a flock of frightened birds
for shell splinters. At Scapa Flow early in the Second World War he
noticed the tell-tale absence of seagulls around dummy battleships and
ordered that food should be thrown into the water to attract them.
And at home he was alert to herons, the enemies of his fish, and to
carrion crows, blamed for the death of his cygnets.

For the most part, though, Churchill regarded birds as blithe spirits.
He liked to hear them twittering as much as he detested the sound of
human whistling. Indeed, on the first page of his *History of the English-
Speaking Peoples* he declared that our Palaeolithic ancestors had been
cheered by the songs of innumerable birds. Churchill was awed by the

brilliant profusion of winged and feathered life in Africa. Birds, he said, were the only bright specks in the sombre picture of the Sudan scrub. He marvelled at the legions of cranes and the multitudes of water fowl that rose from the Nile at his party's approach. And he observed huge pelicans standing on one leg and contemplating the water, while often in the treetops above, equally vigilant for prey, perched a fish eagle 'glorious in bronze and cream'.[10]

On a more domestic level, Churchill was so delighted that a robin redbreast took food from his hand at Chartwell that he had their encounter filmed, though eventually, as he wrote, the bird absconded. He was also fond of the dove that Clementine brought back from Bali in 1935, which his daughter Mary described as 'a dear little pinky-beige bird with coral beak and feet, who lived in a wicker cage resembling a lobster pot'. After its death, a few years later, it was buried at the centre of the walled kitchen garden under a sundial. Engraved around its base, at the suggestion of the traveller and author Freya Stark, was an epitaph written by the Oxford scholar W. P. Ker:

> HERE LIES THE BALI DOVE
> It does not do to wander
> Too far from sober men,
> But there's an island yonder,
> I think of it again.[11]

One of the few sympathetic characteristics of Neville Chamberlain as Prime Minister, Churchill reckoned, was that he too befriended birds, feeding a flock of sparrows, blackbirds and thrushes every morning at 10 Downing Street.

Most of Churchill's avian invocations were benign. He extolled the first Duke of Marlborough as a downy bird. He sometimes called his wife 'Birdling' and late in life he made an audacious attempt to draw a 'Clem Pussy Bird'.[12] Despite occasionally fighting like cat and dog, they were recognized as such an uxorious couple that *Punch* christened them 'The Birdikins'.[13] On his travels in 1943 Winston was code-named Mr Bullfinch, which prompted this message from Clementine: 'The cage is swept and garnished, fresh water and seed are temptingly displayed, the door is open and it is hoped that soon Mr Bullfinch will fly home.'[14]

Describing another partnership later in the war, Churchill likened himself and Field Marshal Smuts to two old love-birds moulting together on a perch but still able to peck. Arriving in Athens at Christmas 1944 in order to prevent a threatened Communist takeover, and warned that the British might have to open fire, he responded seraphically: 'I come here as a cooing dove of peace, bearing a sprig of mistletoe in my beak – but far be it from me to stand in the way of military necessity.'[15] In 1949 he warned a Glasgow audience that Labour would hand out many favours before going to the polls, 'But vain is the net spread in the sight of the birds – especially old birds like me.'[16]

As the years advanced Churchill found painting such a welcome distraction that he called it a perch for a tired bird. And, wryly epitomizing the impotence of age, he replied to someone who pointed out that his fly buttons were undone, 'A dead bird won't fall out of the nest.'[17] His most uplifting image, by contrast, had occurred in the paean of victory he uttered on 8 May 1945: 'I say that in the long years to come not only will the people of this island but of the world, wherever the bird of freedom chirps in human hearts, look back to what we've done and they will say "do not despair, do not yield to violence and tyranny, march straight forward and die if need be – unconquered."'[18]

BIRDS OF PARADISE

In *The River War* Churchill penned a satirical sketch of British battlefield tourists in the Sudan, who sought entertainment by following the drum. He described these visitors as Birds of Paradise, rare and curious creatures that flocked round armies in the field. 'Like the stormy petrel heralding the tempest, they appear shortly before an engagement ... Their breasts are covered with a beautiful bright-coloured plumage, which grows very rapidly and increases with their age. They are very rarely shot.'[1] Soldiers understandably resented such gaudy migrants, who proliferated during the Boer War when Thomas Cook conducted tours to scenes of recent carnage. Before that conflict ceased Churchill had entered the House of Commons, where he himself was soon identified as an avian exquisite.

He preened himself on the dark-green benches of Westminster and practised his speeches in an aerial summer house that he had built in the branches of a lime tree at his mother's country mansion. Ostentatious and egotistical, he exuded animal magnetism, eclipsed lacklustre colleagues and soared into high office. He seemed, wrote Prime Minister Henry Asquith's daughter Violet, who was in love with him, 'a Bird of Paradise, of brilliant plumage and incalculable habits'.[2] The image was irresistible. According to one historian, Churchill cut such a gorgeous figure as Chancellor of the Exchequer in Stanley Baldwin's government that it was 'as if a bird of paradise had alighted in the rooks' parliament'.[3] The impression grew stronger during the Second World War, when Churchill dominated the Commons with his grandiloquent oratory and flamboyant personality, to say nothing of his prime position. The Prime Minister's fitful friend Lord Beaverbrook, owner of the *Daily Express*, went so far as to declare that the national coalition was a sham, its Labour ministers being little more than a chirping chorus on the front bench: 'There Attlee and Greenwood, a sparrow and a jackdaw, are perched on either side of the glittering bird of Paradise.'[4]

BOA CONSTRICTORS

L ord Randolph Churchill directed one of his sharpest verbal barbs at the Marquess of Hartington, comparing the Whig grandee to a boa constrictor. Like the serpent visibly digesting a duck or a rabbit at the zoo, said Lord Randolph, Hartington squirmed at having to swallow unpalatable measures which radical members of his own party demanded. There was only one difference: 'the boa-constrictor enjoys his food and thrives on it and Lord Hartington loathes his food and it makes him sick.'[1] Winston gleefully recorded the gibe in his biography of his father and enrolled the boa constrictor in his own rhetorical bestiary.

He first invoked the reptile in his defence of the Dervishes, who for courageously defending the Sudan against the might of the British Empire had been represented by his late-Victorian compatriots as utterly and hopelessly vile. The smearing process was similar to that of the boa constrictor, he said, which covers the body of his victim with a foul slime before he devours it. Churchill warned that such abuse was not only unjust but dangerous, because when an army became 'imbued with the idea that the enemy are vermin who cumber the earth, instances of barbarity may very easily be the outcome'.[2] The worst instance occurred in 1898 on the battlefield of Omdurman itself where many wounded Dervishes were killed, an atrocity that Churchill exposed in the first edition of *The River War*, though subsequently omitting it.

The boa constrictor, however, remained a favoured figure in his repertoire of invective. Soon after Hitler seized Austria in March 1938 Churchill employed it again, combining the grotesque and outlandish features of Nazi Germany's engorgement in his own inimitable fashion:

> Two months ago I reminded the House of Commons that after a boa constrictor had devoured a goat or a deer it usually slept the sleep of repletion for several months. It may, however, happen that this agreeable process is disturbed by indigestion. If the prey has not been sufficiently crushed or covered with slime beforehand, especially if it has been swallowed horns and all, very violent spasms accompanied by writhings and contortions, retchings and gaspings, are suffered by the great snake. These purely zoological observations, of which further details can be found in Buffon's *Natural History*, suggest a parallel – no doubt very remote – to what has happened since Austria was incorporated in the German Reich.[3]

Churchill had clearly read Buffon, who describes a snake crushing a buffalo like a malefactor upon a wheel and licking the body so that it would 'slip down the throat more glibly'.[4]

However this account is slightly incorrect – the snake's secretions help its expanding jaws and powerful throat muscles to ingest large victims – and anyway Buffon was referring not to a Latin American boa, which is relatively small, but to the enormous East Asian python. In fact Churchill owed less to Buffon than to Kipling, creator of Kaa and the bi-coloured python rock snake, and he was obviously more interested in reptilian imagery than physiological accuracy. He conjured with another serpentine resemblance when Yugoslavia unexpectedly resisted Hitler's invasion in early April 1941. Compared to the bitter disappointment experienced by the Nazi gang, he said, a 'boa constrictor who had already covered his prey with his foul saliva and then had it suddenly wrested from his coils, would be in an amiable mood'.[5]

BUDGERIGARS

Pet birds had long been popular with all classes of people in England and the Churchill family was no exception. Winston was entranced by their antics, admiring particularly his friend Maxine Elliott's bullfinch, which sat on her shoulder and ate seeds out of her mouth. Chartwell became something of a bird sanctuary during the 1930s and among its feathered population was a large, noisy flock of budgerigars, small Australian parakeets. Bred by his youngest daughter Mary and kept in aviaries at the top of the orchard, they were described by Ivan Maisky, the Russian ambassador, as 'blue birds that can speak in human voices'.[1] However Churchill did not acquire a budgie of his own until he was given one by Dido Cairns, the sister of his son-in-law Christopher Soames, in December 1954. Called Toby, he was an attractive cock with a golden face and colouring of azure blue and emerald green. His supplier, Commander Fogg Elliot, told Churchill that he was very attached to the bird 'and would not have sent him to anyone much less eminent than yourself!'.[2]

Once they had been introduced, Churchill found the little creature marvellously engaging. Toby sat on Churchill's spectacles and lapped ink from his pen, embellishing his letters with blots and scribbles. He pecked at Churchill's matches and cigars, fluttering his wings over the ashtray to create miniature simooms. He strutted across the dining table, knocked over glasses, helped himself to grapefruit, fought with his reflection in the silver pepper pot and chattered 'like a schoolgirl at a picnic'.[3] He unravelled the tags that held Churchill's papers together, scattering them on the floor. He chewed the edges of the secretaries' pads as they took dictation, leaving a signature that expressed his wish, said the Prime Minister, to be remembered. He also nibbled at books, thus indicating, in his master's view, that he had read them, and at

Churchill and his budgerigar Toby on board the luxury yacht *Christina O*, with its owner Aristotle Onassis and Maria Callas.

proofs. 'Oh! Yes, that's all right,' said Churchill, 'give him the next chapter.'[4] In fact Toby was such an obtrusive presence that one man who had come to talk business with the Prime Minister expressed surprise that the bird had not contributed to their discussion.

As it was, Toby literally made his mark on visitors. One morning he spent three-quarters of an hour perched on the bald head of the Chancellor of the Exchequer, R. A. Butler, who was discussing the budget with Churchill in his bedroom; as he left, Churchill's private secretary Jock Colville counted no fewer than 'fourteen messes on Rab's pate'.[5] The Chancellor was amused, though Churchill called him 'old cock'[6] while he called Toby 'Darling'. Wiping his head with a white silk handkerchief, Butler sighed: 'The things I do for England....'[7]

Churchill himself saw nothing odd about Toby's conduct, as another member of the Cabinet, Harold Macmillan, observed. A connoisseur of aristocratic eccentricity, Macmillan found the Prime Minister in bed dictating to his secretary, Jane Portal, with a budgerigar sitting on his head:

> He had a cage on the bed (from which the bird had come out) and a cigar in his hand. A whisky and soda was by his side – of this the little bird took sips.... The bird flew about the room; perched on my shoulder and pecked (or kissed) my cheek; flew to Miss Portal's arm; back to the PM's head, while all the time sonorous 'Gibbonesque' sentences were rolling out of the maestro's mouth on the most terrible and destructive engine of mass warfare yet known to mankind. The bird said a few words in a husky voice like an American actress.[8]

Toby acquired a taste for alcohol and he apparently once fell into his master's brandy glass. This did nothing to diminish Churchill's affection for him and he determined to purchase a similar bird for Field Marshal Montgomery. Fogg Elliot offered a sky-blue cock with a white instead of a yellow face and suggested that it should conform to Montgomery's strict standard of temperance. Churchill replied, 'I certainly think the bird should be teetotal!'[9]

Monty was delighted with the gift and Toby himself was recognized as a member of Churchill's family. He did indeed stir up jealousies at first, especially on the part of the poodle Rufus, who walked out in a huff when Churchill played with Toby. But harmony soon prevailed and Churchill was once observed at Chartwell with Toby on his head, Rufus asleep at his feet and Jock, the marmalade cat, curled up on his lap. Toby cheered Churchill during the gloomy years of his retirement, interpolating his favourite expressions into general conversation: 'Good morning, Winston' and 'Who goes home?'[10] He also provided an object of contemplation. 'Answer me this,' Churchill asked his private secretary, 'how is each feather clever enough to know that it should grow green, yellow or black so precisely according to its position on Toby's anatomy?'[11]

Toby was cosseted. At home Churchill acquired two female companions for him, though no romance ensued. At La Pausa, the palatial Riviera home of Churchill's literary agent Emery Reves, Toby enjoyed taking a bath in a silver bowl filled with warm water and rose petals. Muriel Thomson, who nursed Churchill in his extreme old age, woke the budgie every morning and recorded in her notebook the part he played in the ritual of the day: 'Whisky and soda, specs, cards, bird to be brought into dining room near his chair. Tweeds; hanky in top pocket; boiler suit – slippers ... after dinner ... put bird to bed.'[12] Roy Howells, who also looked after Churchill at the time, said that ordering Toby's supply of seed, grit, sandpaper and cuttlefish for trips abroad was almost as important as ordering his master's cigars.

When the Churchills went cruising on Aristotle Onassis's yacht *Christina O* in 1959, Mary Soames asked her mother if Maria Callas, the shipping tycoon's mistress, minded competition from Toby either as a singer or a star. Clementine, who thought the opera soprano 'a good creature domestically but shallow & common', replied that the competition was not with Toby but 'with Papa!'. When greeted by crowds assembled on jetties, Callas 'remarks what a comfort it is to have *some* of the weight of popularity lifted off her shoulders'.[13] Onassis himself expressed a wish to be reincarnated as Toby.

But the bird came to a sad end. At home and abroad he had always been allowed to fly freely in enclosed spaces. Indeed, Lord Moran, Churchill's doctor, had suggested that in case of loss the budgerigar should be taught his master's telephone number, since he could only identify himself by saying, 'Toby, Toby, my name is Toby'. 'Oom, Oom, Oom,' Churchill had replied, 'I don't know my telephone number.'[14] Anyway, one day in 1961 when Churchill was staying at the Hôtel de Paris in Monte Carlo, something frightened Toby and he flew out of the penthouse window. Although large rewards were offered for his recovery, he disappeared without trace. According to Roy Howells, Churchill was heartbroken.[15]

BUGS

Bugs take many forms and Winston Churchill encountered quite a few of them. The most common species is the bedbug, so familiar to Victorians that Lytton Strachey concluded his famous indictment of their age by declaring that 'the beds were full of bugs and disasters'.[1] As a young officer Churchill encountered these bloodsuckers on charpoys in India. In 1939 they infested Chartwell, gravely upsetting the household which had to be fumigated at a cost of £8. Crossing the Atlantic on the *Queen Mary* in May 1943, the Prime Minister informed Anthony Eden that Lady Beveridge had been terribly bitten by bugs who were advancing resolutely, though 'their spearheads have not yet penetrated our citadel'.[2] But Churchill's worst brush with these pests occurred at Yalta, where it was recorded by another kind of bug, a hidden microphone.

Although better informed about intelligence matters than any Prime Minister before him, Churchill was strangely innocent about the fact that Russian walls had ears. When warned that his conversations in Moscow were being monitored he responded angrily, 'We will soon deal with that. The Russians, I have been told, are not human beings at all. They are lower in the scale of nature than the orang-outang. Now then, let them take that down and translate it into Russian.'[3] The insult was hardly liable to deter Stalin, who had just denuded the Crimea of its native inhabitants. While repairing the Vorontsov Palace, damaged by the Germans, in order to house the British delegation to the Yalta Conference in February 1945, he ensured that it was liberally furnished with listening devices. The Palace was an imposing architectural hybrid – a mixture of English Renaissance, Mughal Islamic, Scottish baronial and Gothic revival – and it was embellished with fine sculptures of Medici lions, which Churchill wanted to take home with him. But it was overrun with bedbugs, which bit his legs and feet at night. His complaints about these parasites much amused the Soviet eavesdroppers. Doubtless the bugs, and perhaps also the buggers, help to explain why he denounced the Black Sea coast as 'the Riviera of Hades'.[4]

In Africa Churchill was especially concerned about the harvest bug, which burrows into the skin and causes intense irritation, warding off its assaults by wearing long, soft leather boots. Hence his demand, met at Anzio in 1944, for an amphibious attack well above the ankle of Italy. 'Why should we crawl up the leg like a harvest bug, from the ankle upwards?' he asked. 'Let us rather strike at the knee.'[5]

Smaller but more insidious bugs – bacteria – also plagued Churchill. He was particularly susceptible to chest infections, colds, coughs, bronchitis and pneumonia. The last nearly killed him at the end of 1943, though Lord Beaverbrook assured his daughter Mary that 'it takes more than some lousy microbes to get the better of your father!'[6] Three years later Churchill got a bug in his eyes which gave him conjunctivitis and responded poorly to antibiotic treatment. He consulted Sir Alexander Fleming who was more interested, Churchill told his own doctor, in an unusual bug in his nose, a staphylococcus, which was very resistant to penicillin. Churchill grinned, 'The bug seems to have caught my truculence. This is its finest hour.'[7]

Churchill was much preoccupied by the potential of germs. In 1937 he suggested that a 'hideous kind of warfare may be waged by scientists commanding armies of innumerable microbes which will fight for and against us in the battlefield of our own unhappy bodies'.[8] But he claimed, or at least hoped, that microbes would neutralize one another and thus leave humanity unharmed. He also believed that science could eradicate bugs, failing to appreciate their adaptability and the incidental harm that conducting chemical hostilities against them might cause. During the war he extolled the achievements of DDT, which wiped out pests bearing diseases such as typhus and malaria. In 1950 he declared that man had gained greater supremacy over the forces of nature than had ever been dreamed of before: 'He has conquered the wild beasts, and he has even conquered the insects and the microbes. There lies before him, as he wishes, a golden age of peace and progress. All is in his hand. He has only to conquer his last and worst enemy – himself."[9]

BULLDOGS

At Eton Lord Randolph Churchill not only lived with his pet bulldog but also, in the view of one of his school contemporaries, possessed a determined bulldog type of face. In boyhood Winston was himself described by his grandmother, Clara Jerome, as 'a naughty, sandy-haired little bulldog'.[1] And while at Harrow he too acquired a bulldog, selling his bicycle to help pay for it. Both his mother and his nanny disapproved of this transaction, asserting that the animal would be a dangerous and expensive nuisance. But Winston overwhelmed them with a barrage of arguments. His bicycle was too small and he now had a pony to ride. He hadn't been given a promised lurcher puppy and the bulldog, named Dodo, would produce whelps worth 30 shillings each. His father had kept a bulldog at school and Dodo was tame, affectionate and extremely well bred.

Luckily for his son Lord Randolph took to Dodo, perhaps because pedigree mattered as much in dogs as in humans. There was furthermore a canine hierarchy, ranging from the prince's greyhound and the baronet's borzoi to the miner's whippet and the tinker's mongrel, in which bulldogs now occupied an honoured position. Propagated to bait bulls, they had long been prized among sporting gentry. For that very reason respectable dog owners had rather shunned them during the early Victorian period.[2] But the year after Winston's birth the Bulldog Club was formed and within a decade its cynosure rivalled the collie (the Queen's favourite dog) in polite esteem. Always famed for their courage and endurance, bulldogs naturally embodied the island race's view of its essential character. As early as 1857 Charles Kingsley referred to the 'British bull-dog breed'.[3] And the animal became an avatar of John Bull, who was often pictured with a bulldog (or a mastiff) by his side.[4]

Empire-minded politicians made much of this four-footed incarnation of the nation, none more so than young Winston Churchill in his first election campaign:

> The position of England among the nations is the position of a dog with a bone in the midst of a hungry pack. (Hear, hear.) Plenty of other dogs would like to share that bone, lots of dogs would like to borrow it just to take care of it for a little while – (laughter) – and there are one or two of the larger and fiercer dogs who would take that bone by force were it not for the fact that the dog who holds the bone is a British bulldog. (Laughter and cheers.)[5]

When war broke out in 1914 Churchill, then First Lord of the Admiralty, summoned up the animal again as an emblem of his country's pluck and grit. It enabled him not just to emphasize the power and purpose of the Royal Navy but to tweak the Kaiser's tail. 'By one of those dispensations of Providence, which appeals so strongly to the German Emperor,' he said, 'the nose of the bulldog has been slanted backwards so that he can breathe with comfort without letting go.'[6] According to the *Manchester Guardian*'s reporter, Churchill was able by some histrionic gift to suggest quite the bulldog as he spoke.

In peacetime he occasionally enlivened political debate by introducing bulldogs into the party political mêlée. During the 1930s he urged Tories to deal with the Liberal and Labour dogs by showing them a little of the snarl, growl and bite of the British bulldog. Later he slated the Socialists for making the British bulldog chase his own tail until it was dizzy and then wonder why it could not keep the wolf from the door. The Second World War, though, sealed Churchill's identification with the bulldog.

He was made for the part: the gruff voice, the prognathous jaw, the pendulous jowls and the stocky frame. As the epitome of pugnacity and tenacity he symbolized and invoked the bulldog spirit. In November 1939 he told the Russian ambassador, 'In peacetime the British often look like pampered, gluttonous sybarites, but in times of war and extremity they turn into vicious bulldogs, trapping their prey in a death grip.'[7] During the Dunkirk evacuation he was, according to the head of the Foreign Office, Sir Alexander Cadogan, 'theatrically bulldoggish'.[8] After the fall of France, Churchill personified Britain's determination to fight and its will to win, being ever ready, wrote a junior minister, with a bulldog growl and snap. A young diarist who witnessed him touring the City during the Blitz said that Churchill looked invincible: 'Tough, bulldogged, piercing.'[9] Seeing him in 1942, broad-shouldered, thickset, his head obstinately lowered, Ivan Maisky concluded that he was 'a real English bulldog'.[10] Later in the war Harold Nicolson had exactly the same impression.

So in popular iconography – in cartoons, posters, plaques, plates, figurines and so on[11] – Churchill was frequently represented as some kind of a bulldog. He was likened to a bulldog in the press and on the wireless, in public rhetoric and private conversation. He reminded a guest at the White House of a big English bulldog who had been taught to give his paw. Observing him at close quarters, one of his private secretaries wrote that he had the face of a good-humoured bulldog. In 1952 a Mrs Doris Whitehorn told Churchill about Roger, her 'almost human' Boston Bull Terrier who, equipped with a wing collar, bow tie and cigar, did an impressive imitation of the Prime Minister. At one children's party the animal had performed for royalty and, wrote Mrs Whitehorn, 'afterwards Prince Charles came to me and enquired if Roger was really smoking Mr Churchill's cigar!'[12] Churchill said that he was amused to hear about her gifted dog.

Many people tried to give him presents reflecting his alter ego, everything from bulldog ties to bulldog puppies. In October 1944 the British ambassador in Belgium reported that he had been visited by a man with a large performing bulldog 'stuck in various parts of his body with the flags of the Allies. In his mouth he held a Swastika flag.'[13]

The man insisted that the ambassador should dispatch a picture of this quadruped to 10 Downing Street, which he did. A more welcome gift was the painting of a beautiful bulldog by Charles Montag, an artist friend of Churchill's, which he hung in his London sitting room where it could be generally admired.

Churchill was so concerned that he himself should be correctly portrayed that he clashed with two of the most eminent artists of his day. When the Croatian sculptor Oscar Nemon fashioned a bronze bust of Churchill for Windsor Castle in 1952 he initially roused his subject's ire. 'You think I look like a crafty, shifty war-monger, do you?' Churchill asked. Nemon protested that he had tried to bring out the Prime Minister's determination and purpose. Whereupon Churchill 'gave further vent to his wrath with some explanatory remarks about his "bulldog" image, an attitude he struck for the morale of the nation, saying that he was not just a ferocious watchdog but a man compounded of many qualities including about fifty per cent humour'. Later in the day Churchill changed his mind completely and hailed Nemon as a genius. He even turned his own hand to producing a bust of the sculptor, but the experiment was fraught with difficulty. As Nemon recorded, 'His cigar began to come to pieces in his mouth and soon he was roaring like a lion over its prey.'[14]

No rapprochement occurred between Churchill and Graham Sutherland, whom parliament commissioned to paint his portrait as its eightieth birthday present to him in 1954. The Prime Minister asked the artist, 'Are you going to paint me as a bulldog or a cherub?'[15] As Sutherland told Lord Beaverbrook, Churchill consistently 'showed me the Bull Dog'.[16] But the sitter felt, when shown the finished work, that he had been depicted as a sot, gross and decrepit. 'I never looked like that,' he declared. Clementine, who at first thought the resemblance alarmingly good, disagreed. 'I once saw you look like that,' she replied. 'It was during the war, after the fall of Crete.'[17] However, when she realized how much he hated the portrait, Clementine came to share her husband's feelings and had it destroyed – not her first act of pictorial purgation. All the same, Sutherland did capture something of his subject's stubborn fortitude and it was this image that prevailed to the last. Observing a very aged Churchill in the Commons, the future Labour minister Tony Benn noted the bulldog expression on his face.

BUTTERFLIES

A ll his life Winston Churchill was fascinated by butterflies. While at prep school he was given a net and encouraged to compete with other boys in catching different species and pinning them to boards. Years later he regretted the massacre of tortoiseshells, red admirals and peacocks, but at the time he enjoyed collecting them immensely. In the country he was never at a loss for anything to do since he was so preoccupied by these creatures. At Harrow he attended a lecture about butterflies, which taught him the rudiments of evolution:

> A nasty tasting butterfly has gaudy colouring to warn the bird
> not to eat it. A succulent, juicy-tasting butterfly protects himself
> by making himself exactly like his usual branch or leaf. But
> this takes them millions of years to do; and in the meanwhile
> the more backward ones get eaten and die out. That is why the
> survivors are marked and coloured as they are.[1]

As a subaltern on India's North West Frontier Churchill contrasted the harshness of the landscape with the splendour of the butterflies, whose blue-and-green wings were as iridescent as shot silk. In Bangalore, where his garden coruscated with purple emperors, white admirals, swallowtails and other beautiful insects, he amassed and mounted so many specimens that his fellow officer, Reggie Barnes, complained that their bungalow was degenerating into a taxidermist's shop. Churchill was mortified when a rat destroyed his collection. 'I have however caught the brute,' he told his brother Jack, 'and had him killed by "Winston" the terrier.'[2]

The young Churchill was well aware of the symbolic significance of the butterfly. A blaze of glory between the chrysalis and the sepulchre, it is nature's most vivid image of the transience of life. When visiting the Temple of Luxor en route to the Sudan in 1898, Churchill was struck by the contrast between the living minute and centuries long dead, and he was 'reminded of the bright butterfly on the tomb'.[3] During the war in South Africa eighteen months later, when his fate once more depended on the caprice of a bullet, he also dwelt on this metaphor of mortality. 'Existence is never so sweet as when it is at hazard,' he wrote. 'The bright butterfly flutters in the sunshine, the expression of the philosophy of Omar Khayyám, without the potations.'[4] Of course, Churchill did enjoy the potations. With no religion save faith in his star he also believed, like the author of the *Rubáiyát*, which he knew virtually by heart, that time flies and one must seize the moment.

In 1907 Churchill was prompted to further philosophical reflections during his journey through Uganda, where he found 'butterflies beyond imagination'. Some were as big as birds, others as ethereal as gossamer:

> Never were seen such flying fairies. They flaunted their splendid liveries in inconceivable varieties of colour and pattern …
> Swallow-tails, fritillaries, admirals, tortoise-shells, peacocks, orange-tips – all executed in at least a dozen novel and contrasted styles, with many even more beautiful, but bearing no resemblance to our British species.[5]

He was struck by the perversity of butterflies, gleaming in the sunshine then vanishing in the shades of the forest, flitting between fragrant flowers then clustering around putrescent filth. The vagaries of their appearance provided a lesson in perception, a demonstration that shifting perspectives altered one's world view. Facts were subject to interpretation. Everything was relative. A butterfly's wings might change from 'the deepest russet brown to the most brilliant blue,' Churchill wrote, 'according to the angle from which you saw them'.[6]

Churchill continued to conjure with, and focus on, butterflies. In 1924 he dismissed the rich and promiscuous Sir Oswald Mosley, an ex-Tory who had just defected to the Labour Party and would eventually lead the British Union of Fascists, as a gilded butterfly. Travelling across North America in 1929 he told Clementine that the only butterflies he had seen were the Camberwell beauty, as common in the Canadian Rockies as it was rare in England, the clouded yellow, the larger tortoiseshell and several kinds of fritillaries. Churchill was more impressed by the butterflies at San Simeon, the private game reserve of the Californian press magnate William Randolph Hearst. He urged his son Randolph and his nephew Johnny to catch specimens but they were too busy chasing women. In mature years Churchill himself liked to dwell on the sexual habits of butterflies, speculating about 'the length of their love lives and whether they had penes'.[7]

Before 1939 Churchill proposed to breed butterflies at Chartwell. During the war he was sometimes accused of resembling a butterfly himself, picturesque, erratic, a creature of whim and fancy. Alan Brooke grumbled in his diary that the Prime Minister never seemed to reason anything out, instead simply flitting from one idea to another like a butterfly in a garden. But after victory over Germany and defeat at the polls Churchill persevered with his plan. He aimed to swathe Chartwell in clouds of butterflies. Their numbers had declined recently, he told his doctor, and the 'love of flowers and affection for animals were two of the noblest qualities of our race'.[8]

In the spring of 1946 Churchill sought advice from L. Hugh Newman, a commercial entomologist who ran a butterfly farm in Bexley. Together they strolled round the Chartwell estate and Churchill asked him 'to give me the means to multiply the common butterflies in my garden so that they will fly out among the flowers'.[9] Churchill waxed eloquent about the project and Newman was not sure 'if he was serious when he suggested laying on "fountains of honey and water" in the rose garden to feed the butterflies which I was to release'.[10] He was serious enough to convert an old summer house, formerly a game larder, into a butterfly cage. Newman recommended the installation of a skylight and provided mosquito netting to protect the pupae from mice and earwigs. In June 1947 he brought 500 half-grown peacock caterpillars to Chartwell, telling Churchill: 'Unlike the swallowtails, which I consider a "luxury" butterfly, peacocks hibernate and you will see them again, or rather a percentage of them, next spring.'[11] Newman supplied other varieties – white admirals, scarlet tigers, green-veined whites, speckled woods, painted ladies – as well as privet and elephant hawk-moth caterpillars. He also instituted the planting of vegetation attractive to butterflies – buddleia, fennel, thistles and nettles – which caused conflict with the head gardener. On sunny days Churchill loved to sit at his butterfly nursery and watch young ones palpitate into life. These he let out, shimmering flakes of freedom to brighten nature's palette.

Newman, however, was not a scientifically trained lepidopterist but an enthusiast – he contributed to *Nature Parliament* on BBC radio's *Children's Hour*. It was his ambition to establish alien colonies of butterflies at Chartwell, among them the swallowtail, the clouded yellow and the black-veined white. Newman persuaded Churchill to back the scheme, using the martial language that appealed to him: Chartwell should become 'the new headquarters of the black-veined white, as Kent was previously its last [English] stronghold'.[12] Actually these imports were unsuited to their new habitat. The large, rare, yellow-and-black swallowtail, for example, only flourished in the fenlands of Norfolk which sustained its food plant, milk parsley. All those sent to Chartwell died and the whole experiment (of a kind banned in 1981) was a failure. Churchill was unfairly blamed: he could defeat the Nazis, it was said, but he 'could not play God with butterflies'.[13]

Churchill had no such pretensions for he had always believed that Mother Nature's rule was absolute and arbitrary. She set no store by the sanctity of life: 'Think of a beautiful butterfly – 12 million feathers on its wings, 16,000 lenses in its eye – a mouthful for a bird.'[14] After 1950, however, perhaps disheartened and certainly preoccupied, he let the butterfly house fall into abeyance. Six decades later the National Trust, which acquired Chartwell on Churchill's death in 1965, recreated it. Today, reflecting his fancy, home-bred peacocks and painted ladies flutter into the gardens, perpetual emblems of evanescence.

CAMELS

Churchill did not share the common view that camels were invincible ships of the desert. He saw a lot of these ungulates in India in 1897 and during the Sudan campaign the following year. On the North West Frontier they proved less hardy than mules and slower over rough terrain. But Pathan tribesmen, as active as cats and as fierce as tigers in Churchill's estimation, targeted all British beasts of burden, without which 'a brigade is as helpless as a locomotive without coal'.[1] In the Sudan, needless to say, humpbacked mounts carried the Camel Corps or camelry, which he described as chocolate-coloured men on cream-coloured camels. Kilted Seaforth Highlanders also tried to ride camels though, Churchill noted wryly, it was 'an experience for which neither their training nor their clothes had prepared them'.[2]

Camel caravans played a vital role in complementing the rail and river transport on which General Kitchener's army depended and Churchill once found himself in command of a 'strange procession' of weary pack animals. It confirmed his view that camels were less resilient than mules. The rocks of the desert cut camels' soft feet and the uneven ground broke their toenails, he wrote, and even their famed capacity for enduring without drinking was limited. On long journeys they were sometimes driven to death. Churchill recorded that on one occasion a 'young camel, though not apparently exhausted, refused to proceed, and even when a fire was lighted round him remained stubborn and motionless; so that, after being terribly scorched, he had to be shot'.

In response to harsh treatment, Churchill said, many 'tales of woe came from the camels'.[3] But their weird groans and obscene gurgles, their vile smells and hideous grimaces, were not endearing traits and he seems to have felt little sympathy for them. He might not have gone as far as the *Times* correspondent who characterized the 'Devil's steed'[4] thus: 'He will bite the hand that feeds and tends him; he knows no gratitude, is bereft of softer passions and looks upon whomsoever approaches him – for whatever purpose – as a bitter enemy.'[5] But probably Churchill did endorse the standard British opinion that 'the horse is a gentleman and the camel is a boor'.[6]

Of course, he did not condone cruelty. Just as sore-backed,

Churchill astride what Kipling called a 'cameelious hump', with Clementine on his right and Gertrude Bell and T. E. Lawrence on his left, 1921.

girth-galled horses developed bursitis, a severe form of ulceration, weary camels got fist-sized, maggot-filled calluses which British marines were known to caulk with oakum, as though they really were ships of the desert. Churchill criticized the ill-loading of camels, which inflicted unnecessary suffering on them. And he was horrified by the heaps of mangled camels and donkeys among the human carnage of the battlefield, the ghastly results of shellfire. However, he had no qualms about sacrificing camels to military needs. In war, he wrote, 'the miseries of animals cannot be considered; their capacity for work alone concerns the commander'.[7]

When appropriate, Churchill was prepared – even determined – to straddle a camel rather than a horse. Returning to Egypt in 1902, he arranged a 70-mile camel ride across the desert to the oasis of Fayoum. Later he was apparently kicked off by a bad-tempered camel, which he kicked in turn to enforce docility. At the Cairo Conference in 1921 he went on a camel-borne excursion to the pyramids and the Sphinx with T. E. Lawrence, Gertrude Bell and others. Once again he was unseated. Lawrence could hardly contain his laughter, telling Churchill:

> It was only to be expected you know. The old camel blew himself out when he heard that he was to have the honour of carrying such a great man, but when he saw the way you ride he decided that he must have been misinformed. He deflated himself and the saddle girth slipped round, throwing you.[8]

With a growl, Churchill refused the offer of a horse: 'I started on a camel and I will finish on a camel.'[9] Clementine joked about how easily the mighty were fallen.

In Cairo again in February 1945, Churchill insisted on stopping and minutely inspecting a parade of Haganah troops mounted on Bishareen camels, whose unusual strength and endurance he recalled from the time of the River War. But as years advanced and troubles accumulated, Churchill soured on all inhabitants of the Middle East. Forgetting his Kiplingesque feelings of admiration for the Dervishes as first-class fighting men, he once expostulated that 'the Arabs were barbaric hordes who ate little but camels' dung'.[10]

CATERPILLARS

fter Lord Randolph Churchill's death Winston emerged, wrote his cousin Shane Leslie, 'like a strong-winged being that had been hitherto a caterpillar'.[1] And as early as 1902 he was caricatured as a caterpillar. Churchill appeared in a parody of Lewis Carroll's *Alice in Wonderland* entitled *Clara in Blunderland*, penned by the pseudonymous Caroline Lewis to satirize Britain's bungling during the Boer War. Arthur Balfour starred as Clara, the equivalent of Alice, and other prominent figures were given lesser parts; Joseph Chamberlain, for example, featured as the Red Queen. Early in the novel Clara encounters Churchill, 'a very green Caterpillar' sitting on a mushroom. He is wearing a topee, inhaling gas from a hookah, writing copiously for the *Morning Post* and telling all and sundry that they are wrong about everything. This bumptious insect, Clara finds, belonged to the species *Winstoniensis Vulgaris*. She and the Caterpillar spar verbally and each produces a neat pastiche of Carrollian verse. Clara infuriates him with this sally:

> How doth the arm-chair strategist
> Improve each censored cable,
> Converting it by natty twist,
> Into egregious fable.[2]

This was unfair in the sense that Churchill liked to be in the thick of any action on which he reported. On the other hand, he was far from being a slave to veracity. And he was clearly destined to mutate from journalistic caterpillar to political butterfly.

Churchill himself was drawn to the caterpillar for what it offered in the way of metaphor as well as metamorphosis. In South Africa he described the long chain of soldiers linking arms in order to cross the

The larval stage in a long process whereby cartoonists transformed
Churchill into a fantastic variety of creatures.

Tugela River at Waggon Drift as a sort of human caterpillar. Writing about the battle of the Marne, he said that enemy airmen saw British columns advancing into the gap between the German armies as five dark 15-mile-long caterpillars eating up the white roads. Even more memorably the creature wriggles through the pages of Churchill's biography of his great ancestor, the first Duke of Marlborough. Churchill dubbed the army which Marlborough marched from north Germany to the Danube in 1704 'the scarlet caterpillar'. It took its colour from 'the variety of tints in red, scarlet and crimson prevailing in the British uniforms of the period'.[3] And its transfiguration occurred at Blenheim, a brilliant victory over the forces of Louis XIV which altered the balance of power in Europe. This glorious feat haunted Churchill's imagination and his visions of military masterstrokes took wing when he himself became a warlord.

He also continued to conjure with images of the humble caterpillar. On a visit to Turkey in January 1943 he observed that the President's train crawled through the snow-capped Taurus Mountains like 'an enamelled caterpillar'.[4] He savoured the expression, repeating it several times and later working it into a speech in the House of Commons.

The seemingly miraculous transformation from creeping grub to flying gem prompted Churchill to exercise his fabulous capacities for the benefit of his young nephew Johnny and he fashioned something akin to the parable of the talents. Caterpillars could be good or bad, he said. The bad ones were greedy, never stopped eating and grew indolent. They were punished in their next world, becoming drab meadow browns or common heaths and living miserable lives for only a day or two. 'If on the other hand a caterpillar behaves himself and is not greedy,' Churchill continued, 'he will emerge as a gorgeous swallowtail, or a painted lady, or even a Camberwell beauty. He will live for many days and may be allowed to hibernate for the winter and enjoy the spring the following year.'[5] Zoologically unsound though this account was, it was also, as a juvenile reincarnation myth, morally persuasive.

More practically, as First Lord of the Admiralty at the outbreak of the Great War, Churchill gave a crucial impetus to the evolution of the caterpillar-tracked tank. This vehicle had many pioneers but H. G. Wells's science-fiction short story 'The Land Ironclads' (1903) was Churchill's original inspiration. Inevitably the vehicles developed by 1915 were more sophisticated than Wells's steam-driven, pedrail-wheeled, rifle-toting leviathans. The new land-ships, which Churchill regarded as sisters of naval monitors, both being instruments of offence, were not only bulletproof but well-armed, petrol-powered and shod with a rotating steel-linked belt designed to crush barbed wire, straddle trenches and traverse muddy shell holes. He was disappointed that Arthur Balfour, his successor at the Admiralty, did not pursue his experimental work with vigour. 'My "caterpillar" was tried before the old tabby and performed miracles,' he told Clementine. 'Foolish slugs & dawdlers ....'[6]

He also lamented the fact that, against his advice, General Haig put tanks to premature and piecemeal use on the Somme. Had they been further improved and employed en masse, these 'mechanical elephants'[7] might have achieved some sort of breakthrough. They certainly demonstrated that capacity during the Second World War, though in 1938, belying his earlier foresight, Churchill assumed that modern anti-tank guns would force them underground. He envisaged that the tank would become 'a mechanical mole, which will make trenches with incredible rapidity, or which will burrow right on through hostile trenches while remaining perfectly safe itself'.[8]

As these images suggest, Churchill was not only apt to see animals in human terms but machines in animal terms. He once told his brother Jack that his (Winston's) typewriter sent him its love, as though it were a domestic pet. Referring to the automatic digger which got bogged down while excavating the lake at Chartwell, he wrote: 'The animal is very strong with his hands but very weak with his caterpillar legs.'[9] He hoped it would waddle away soon.

CATS

Among the birthday cards the Prime Minister received on 30 November 1951 was one from his black cat, to which he replied: 'Thank you so much dear Nelson for your card and greetings, WINSTON CHURCHILL.'[1] Churchill had adopted this cat and named him after England's paramount naval hero because of his courage in chasing a big dog out of the Admiralty in 1939. The following year Nelson moved with his master into 10 Downing Street. He evicted the resident cat, Treasury Bill, known to the Churchill family as the 'Munich Mouser', who continued to prowl around his old home, may have sought refuge with Neville Chamberlain and eventually found sanctuary in the Foreign Office, where he died in July 1943. (The Prime Minister, who feared that his corpse had been thrown into a dustbin and would have been willing to give him burial in the grounds of No. 10, said that he had 'died of remorse and chose his deathbed accordingly'.)[2] Anyway, Nelson quickly established himself as the PM's familiar. On 27 June 1940 Jock Colville described a typical scene: Churchill in bed wearing a red dressing gown, surrounded by boxes and dictating to a secretary, while smoking a large cigar, dropping the ash into a vast chromium-plated cuspidor, and every now and then gazing affectionately at Nelson, who snoozed at his feet, and saying, 'Cat, darling.'[3]

Nelson was spoilt – fed on cream and given titbits such as pheasant and smoked salmon. He was also flattered. Churchill told R. A. Butler, who was responsible for the 1944 Education Act, that the cat did more for the war effort than he did – by acting as the PM's hot-water bottle. The Prime Minister included Nelson in his family's arrangements to move from Downing Street should enemy action make that necessary. In consequence, perhaps, the animal got ideas above his station and his temper became as uncertain as his bladder. Churchill's vet Leslie Pugh once swept Nelson off the bed before he relieved himself on the Prime Minister;[4] and President Roosevelt's emissary Harry Hopkins, who tried to play with Nelson, found him 'very ill-natured'.[5]

Furthermore Nelson's reputation for bravery was impaired when he hid under a chest of drawers during an air raid. Churchill was indignant. 'Come out, Nelson!' he commanded. 'Shame on you, bearing a name such as yours, to skulk there while the enemy is overhead!'[6] By ill chance, though, Nelson was wounded during the Blitz, whereupon he was honourably discharged to Chequers. Like other evacuees he evidently resented the move, becoming still more snappish and assaulting any dog that showed its face. However, he remained in this privileged billet after the war and in 1948 Churchill's former secretary, Kathleen Hill, reported: 'Your black cat, Nelson, is still here and flourishing. He haunts the kitchen, but indulges in a good deal of hunting.'[7]

Nelson's place in No. 10 was taken by a large, dark, fluffy Persian called Smoky, who was promoted from kitchen to bedroom. He too was mollycoddled, received ceremoniously, fed on the Prime Minister's bed and embraced by its brocade cover. This Smoky sometimes clawed and, when gently rebuked, he nipped his master's feet – or, disconsolate when Churchill was away, those of Clementine. Like Nelson, he grew wilder with time, scratching the legs of visitors, laddering secretaries' stockings and sometimes drawing blood. On one memorable occasion he attacked Churchill's wriggling toes while he was speaking to Alan Brooke on the telephone. Churchill roared, 'Get off, you fool!' It required some diplomacy to convince the general that the Prime Minister had been addressing the cat. Having kicked Smoky off the bed, Churchill then had to mollify him, crying, 'Poor little thing.'[8] On another occasion Smoky's loyalty was called in question. After a serious Cabinet leak the Prime Minister summoned Sir Stewart Menzies, head of MI6, to a meeting in his bedroom. Smoky at once jumped onto the window-sill and Churchill said to Menzies, 'You see it is as I thought – my cat is signalling with his tail to the pelicans in the Park.'[9]

At Chartwell Churchill's favourite cat was a fine marmalade tom called Tango, because of his tangerine colour. Despite his gender, reinforced by the nickname Mr Kat, Churchill invariably referred to him as her. Esteemed above more plebeian moggies, Tango was, Mary Churchill said, 'the apple of my father's eye'.[10] Delicacies were lavished on him. Like the Prophet Muhammad's cat Muezza, Tango rested undisturbed. When he scratched at the door at night, Churchill got up to let him in, curling up in bed to give him room. Tango was even immortalized in art. Churchill told a correspondent that he himself had 'never made a painting or a drawing of a cat, although I am very fond of them', but that Sir William Nicholson had produced 'some very beautiful black-and-white studies of my yellow cat'.[11] No doubt these were sketches for Nicholson's imaginative conversation piece of Winston and Clementine at breakfast, with Mr Kat demurely sitting on the table.

Churchill making friends with Blackie, the ship's cat on HMS *Prince of Wales*, at Placentia Bay, Newfoundland, August 1941.

Tango did not always behave impeccably at meal times. During one Chartwell dinner, after the ladies had left, he brought in a mouse and started to play with it. Viewing such a scene, as the fourteenth-century theologian Arnold of Liège had memorably observed, was like watching the Devil toying with a human soul. Some guests, including his warm-hearted friend Brendan Bracken and his vegetarian scientific adviser Professor Lindemann, were shocked, but Churchill remarked on how interesting it was to see the cat exercising control over his victim. 'Now is the time,' he urged, as Tango prepared to execute the *coup de grâce*. And in the stricken silence which followed Mr Kat's swallowing the mouse head-first in a single gulp and beginning to clean his whiskers, Churchill said, 'You see, a whole army destroyed in one move!'[12]

During the war Churchill visited Chartwell infrequently but he did make time to read a long report from Leslie Pugh about an operation to remove a tumour from Tango in December 1940. The Prime Minister was doubtless gratified to learn that Mr Kat had been a model patient with a great sense of dignity, though he hardly needed the vet to point out 'the analogy which exists between Nazism and malignant growth characteristics'.[13] Still, after this ordeal Churchill evidently doted all the more on Tango. On 3 June 1941, at a time when the PM was perturbed by setbacks in the Mediterranean, he had lunch with Jock Colville and Mr Kat, who sat on a chair to his right and occupied most of his attention. Colville recorded that 'he kept up a running conversation with the cat, cleaning its eyes with a napkin, offering it mutton and expressing regret that it could not have cream in war-time'.[14] Just over a year later, during the week when Tobruk fell, Tango died. Churchill was not told until the war news improved.

The war, indeed, prompted astonishing expressions of devotion to the feline tribe. Churchill's American friend Kay Halle witnessed an occasion when the Prime Minister was moved to tears while describing the saturation bombing of Germany. 'Ten thousands of lives were extinguished in one night,' he said. 'Old men, old women, little children, yes, yes, children about to be born – and – and pushie cats.' The lisping delivery combined with the bathetic conclusion provoked nervous mirth among his auditors. When Churchill detected it he turned like a flash and said in deadly earnest, 'When I mentioned "pushie cats" I would not have you think I take them lightly.'[15] Nor did he take lightly their fate in Hiroshima and Nagasaki. As his research assistant Denis Kelly wrote, a lachrymose Churchill later declared: '"The worst thing Truman and I did was to throw that bloody bomb. And think of all the poor little dogs and pussy-cats." It was said with such passionate sincerity that none of us even smiled.'[16]

Yet Churchill's relations with cats were not always harmonious. He resented sulky and snooty felines, slashing at one Chartwell cat with his papers when it refused to respond to his polite 'Good morning'. But he felt remorse when it ran away and had a card put in the window saying that if it returned 'all is forgiven'.[17] This seemed to do the trick and the cat was welcomed home with fresh salmon and cream. Churchill's brindled tom Mickey, whom he described as an 'awful old Turkey cat', also walked by himself. He was a semi-feral farm cat who roamed the Chartwell estate catching rabbits and rodents. And although Churchill's valet sometimes brought him in, pretending that he had come to call on his master (who was much gratified by the visits), Mickey disliked the heat of Churchill's bedroom, which was kept at 70 degrees Fahrenheit. 'I could never get that cat to like me,' Churchill said, 'though I tried so hard.'[18]

The feline imagery which so often sprang to Churchill's lips was likewise not invariably amiable. Churchill regarded the former Tory Prime Minister Arthur Balfour as a pampered grimalkin – suave, cunning, lazy, fastidious, sybaritic and probably (like Tango) neutered. When Balfour took over from him at the Admiralty after the Dardanelles fiasco, Churchill called him an 'old grey tabby'.[19] (Clementine said, more precisely, that he resembled 'a shabby maiden aunt's tabby cat.')[20] Describing Balfour's Machiavellian move from Asquith's ministry to Lloyd George's in 1916, Churchill likened him to 'a powerful graceful cat walking delicately and unsoiled across a rather muddy street'.[21] In a less well-known but equally telling analogy, Stanley Baldwin turned the tables on the Chartwell Chancellor: he said that when up to mischief Churchill resembled a cat stealing out of a dairy. Churchill might not have challenged the analogy. He told the journalist Charles Eade, 'One of my ancestors must have been a cat because I like cream ... I like cats too.'[22] Like cats, too, he had a remarkable ability to catnap.

Cats, sometimes disagreeable ones, persistently crept into his discourse. A few days before the Japanese bombed Pearl Harbor, Churchill compared himself to a dead cat floating on the sea, who would eventually be washed up on the shores of victory. Later he proposed to inveigle the Turks into the war with cat-like wiles, 'treating them purry purry, puss puss'.[23] Hearing that Labour ministers were misbehaving in Attlee's absence, Churchill smirked, 'When the mouse is away the cats will play.'[24] Annoyed by an independent woman in the Cabinet during the early 1950s, Churchill instructed his private secretary to 'tell the old cat to do what I say or I'll sling her up by the tail'.[25] Apocryphal, alas, is the story that when unable to get hold of Lord Catto, Governor of the Bank of England, he said, 'Lord Catto is lying doggo.'[26]

In general, of course, Churchill found cats irresistible. He associated them with marital bliss. Rejoicing in Clementine's presence, he wrote on their wedding anniversary: 'Ten years ago my beautiful white pussy cat you came to me.'[27] He pined when they were apart, saying that a cat purring on the bed reminded him of her and even taking to verse:

> One thing lack these banks of green –
> The Pussy Cat who is their Queen.[28]

Yet even when they were together Clementine remained a territorial creature. When the Prime Minister took colleagues into her parlour at Chequers in 1954 she submitted a 'Petition from the CAT' requesting privacy, to which he replied over the drawing of a mouse: 'I was only trying to catch a fat mouse for the Cat. I will not trespass again.'[29]

If Churchill saw cats as the fulfilment of family and domestic life, he was also inclined to give them precedence at official functions. At one reception, graced by a cat basking near a window, he commanded a female guest to stand aside. She was nonplussed. 'Stand aside, won't you,' he repeated. She remained uncomprehending. 'Can't you see,' said Churchill, 'you're keeping all the sun off the cat?'[30]

As well as treating felines with anthropomorphic indulgence, he made them the focus of comic grandiloquence. One cat he termed 'jocund'.[31] Another he fed on 'matutinal grouse'.[32] A kitten he adopted behaved with its 'customary punctilio'.[33] At Chartwell relations between Clementine's exquisite Siamese Gabriel and his yellow rival could best be described, he said, as an armed neutrality. Gabriel was apt to be 'saucy' to Churchill himself. Undaunted by his impertinence, the Prime Minister would look him straight in the eye and say firmly, 'I am your Father and 'tis a great honour!'[34]

Churchill was a soft touch for strays: when a strange black-and-white cat pounded at his window in July 1944 the Prime Minister admitted him, settled him down in an armchair and, a witness recorded, 'kept making sucking noises at the sleeping mog'.[35] Aware of his tastes, well-wishers tried to deluge him with pets and Churchill had to protect himself from a rain of cats and dogs, complaining that 'I could literally be petted to death.'[36] One secretary wrote, 'It *hurts* me to turn down so many cat offers!'[37] Another secretary brought him a basket of white kittens with red bows presented by a Chartwell neighbour. They at once made themselves at home, chasing round the room, burrowing under the bedclothes and tearing up his papers. After an hour Churchill could bear it no more. 'Take these kittens away,' he thundered, 'before I fall in love with them.'[38]

One gift, though, was an enduring object of worship. It was an eighteenth-dynasty Egyptian cat, sent to him by Jacqueline Lampson, socialite wife of the British ambassador in Cairo, with the cryptic injunction: 'Feed on gin to keep small.'[39] Probably Churchill was superstitious about cats, as about other things. Certainly he honoured Kaspar, a large, black, wooden cat carved by the sculptor Basil Ionides for the Savoy Hotel, who sat at table during meetings of the Other Club when the diners would otherwise have numbered an unlucky thirteen. A napkin was placed around Kaspar's neck and he was served the full menu.

In the natural world Churchill saw fauna where others saw flora. When he looked at trees and shrubs he often perceived the shapes of creatures. Pointing to one lot of foliage, he told Lord Moran that it resembled a yellow-bellied animal pawing the air, like a crouching cat.[40] Just as Montaigne could not tell whether he was playing with his cat or it was playing with him, it is impossible to know what cats made of Churchill. He himself credited them with refined responses and enjoyed repeating the story of one cat saying to another, 'These humans are very intelligent: I believe they understand a lot of what we say.'[41] And maybe cats did return his affection. Perhaps wishing to augment the diet of a fellow carnivore, the white cat at Lord Beaverbrook's French villa La Capponcina once killed a beautiful rat, Churchill reported, and brought it to him at the dinner table. When Churchill died in 1965 his ginger cat Jock came into his bedroom, jumped into the coffin, peered at the still face and went away never to re-enter that room.

Colville had given Jock to Churchill as an eighty-eighth birthday present – a marmalade kitten with white chest and paws which he had obtained from the RSPCA. Clementine told her daughter Mary, 'It is a lovely little beast and Papa is delighted with it.'[42] Jock was grossly spoilt: Churchill thought nothing of pouring cream directly onto his polished dining-room table for the cat to lap up.[43] Since Jock's death in 1975 the National Trust, at the behest of the Churchill family, has supplied successors with similar markings to live at Chartwell. In 2014, earning global publicity, Jock entered his sixth incarnation.

CATTLE

During his safari in South Africa Lord Randolph Churchill used one of his trek oxen for target practice, first wounding and then killing it. As a boy Winston had a catapult for shooting green apples at a cow. As a man he attended bullfights abroad. Nor, apparently, was he discouraged by a particularly sanguinary incident he witnessed at Bayonne in 1923: a bull, stabbed in the neck with a sword and maddened with pain, shook its head so fiercely that the weapon flew out, whirled through the air and pierced a spectator in the heart, killing him instantly.

On the whole, though, Churchill cherished the bovine race. As a young Cabinet minister he liked to quote the biblical injunction, 'Thou shalt not muzzle the ox that treadeth out the corn', interpreting it to mean that effort deserved a due reward and that genius should be given a special licence. After the Great War he supported a parliamentary measure to prevent imported cattle from being ill-treated or landed in a damaged and broken condition. And he began to accumulate a treasured dairy herd, acquiring a cow and a four-day-old calf from his cousin Sunny, the ninth Duke of Marlborough, in August 1918. Clementine told Winston that the 'cow is most handsome, dark red in colour, a shorthorn. We fetched the calf in the farm cart & the cow ambled behind. She was milked last night and much resented the outrage.' When the animal kicked over the milking stool Clementine desired the cowman 'to soothe her poor tits with linseed'.

Clementine had qualms about farming in general, telling her husband that it was 'really a very brutal occupation – one is always killing some animal or mating it without consulting its inclination, or separating it from its child, or putting a ring in its nose, or clipping its wing'. However, she concluded pragmatically, 'the result of all this barbarism is that we shall be adequately supplied with milk & butter.'[1] Winston shared her ambivalence. He red-bloodedly professed to being a beefeater and considered butter fresh from the churn 'diilicious' [sic].[2] But when fed roasted strips of newly slaughtered ox as a prisoner of the Boers he felt a kind of cannibal. And he was upset by the idea of an abattoir. In a review of Upton Sinclair's novel *The Jungle* (1906), he expressed horror at Chicago's 'mighty slaughter machine' which hourly despatched hundreds of cattle as well as conducting 'a holocaust of hogs'.[3]

Churchill experienced a series of ups and downs with his own cattle. He farmed imaginatively rather than practically and spent more than he earned on ambitious schemes at Chartwell, once telling Lloyd George that he was determined to make agriculture pay, whatever it cost. Churchill also embarked on short-lived economy drives. Thus in 1926 he decided to give up producing milk and to dispense with the services of his cowman, attempting to find him employment elsewhere. Two years later Churchill announced the arrival of five new cows as big as elephants. The health of his animals was sometimes suspect and he once had to assure a neighbour that 'no addled cow will be allowed to approach your herd'.[4]

Propagation was not always straightforward, though Churchill was indulgent to the vagaries of his cattle. In 1935 he reported that one of his heifers had 'committed an indiscretion before she came to us and is about to have a calf. I propose however to treat it as a daughter.'[5] The following year Churchill had problems with Eagle, a bull belonging to his old comrade General Sir Ian Hamilton, a pioneer breeder of Belted Galloway cattle, known as Belties. Eagle twice failed to impregnate a cow called Lullenden Helen, which Hamilton had sold to Churchill – whose cowman denounced her as wild and expressed the hope that he'd never see her again. Churchill wrote to Hamilton: 'I am vexed that one of my men should have been so churlish. I value most highly your beautiful cow. She has adorned our pastures during the summer, and if only her family affairs can be satisfactorily adjusted will be an unfailing source of interest in the coming year.'[6]

This contretemps did not mar their friendship, though Hamilton was being optimistic when, in the middle of the Second World War, he invited Churchill to come and see a calf christened Winnie. The Prime Minister replied, 'How lovely about the calf. Alas, I cannot make any plans, being tied by the leg and both ears.'[7] After 1945, however, Churchill was free to revive and expand the Chartwell estate. He bought neighbouring farms and cattle to go with them, welcoming the first six Belties in 1947 with a great shout. Within a few years he had two milking herds which he valued for their financial worth, their ornamental character and their pedigree quality. In 1949 Mary Soames told her mother that a beautiful Chartwell cow called Beatrice had 'triumphed again at Edenbridge. I bet she's intolerable to be tethered next to in the cowshed now!'[8] But Churchill also appreciated that cattle were meat on the hoof. He once telegraphed Randolph, who was abroad: 'Everyone except the fatted calf is looking forward to your return.'[9]

Churchill found both amusement and instruction in cattle. Considering a case of bestiality as Home Secretary, he quipped, 'I do not think I am ever likely to let my virginity suffer from a cow!'[10] In 1914 he blithely dismissed Swiss complaints about British aviators flying over their neutral territory, saying that they should be told to go and milk their cows. In 1924 he blamed Liberals for keeping the minority Labour government in power and said that he could only do justice to Asquith's generosity, 'the generosity of the cat which lent its paw to the monkey to take the chestnuts out of the fire', in verse:

> How shall I deal with this horrible cow?
> I will sit on the stile
> And continue to smile,
> Which may soften the heart of the cow.[11]

Ten years later, warning parliament of Nazi Germany's growing strength in the air, he described London as 'the greatest target in the world, a kind of tremendous, fat, valuable cow tied up to attract the beast of prey'.[12] Arriving in Normandy soon after the D-Day landings, and observing lovely red-and-white cows basking in the sunshine, he coined a richly bucolic image to express his joy: 'We are surrounded by fat cattle lying in luscious pastures with their paws crossed.'[13]

After the war he would not retire, refusing to be exhibited like a prize bull whose chief attraction is his lost prowess. Instead he attacked the Socialists at home for squeezing the country's udders dry. Drawing on his own experience, he likened rich men to exceptionally productive milch cows: these were 'greatly valued in any well-conducted dairy, and anyone would be thought very foolish who boasted he had got rid of all the best milkers, just as he would be thought very foolish if he did not milk them to the utmost limit of capacity, compatible with the maintenance of their numbers'.[14] Perhaps modifying his attitude towards taxation as his own fortune waxed, he later added that private enterprise was not a cow to be milked, let alone a tiger to be shot, but the strong and willing horse that pulls the whole cart along.

Abroad, as Prime Minister, he pursued the will-o'-the-wisp of détente with the Soviet Union, now armed with atomic weapons. That quest was impeded by President Dwight D. Eisenhower and his lumbering Secretary of State John Foster Dulles who, terrified by the McCarthyite Red Scare in the United States, would not support anything that might be interpreted as appeasement. Churchill was quoted as saying that Dulles was the only case he knew of a bull who carried around his own china shop.

Churchill himself was sometimes likened to a bull rather than a bulldog. The British ambassador to Russia, a ribald figure called Sir Archibald Clark Kerr, vividly described Churchill's arrival in Moscow for his first encounter with Stalin. Bringing with him the unwelcome news that there would be no second front in 1942, the Prime Minister emerged from his Liberator aircraft

> like a bull at the corrida when it first comes out of its dark pen and stands dazzled and bewildered and glares at the crowd. Like the bull's, the PM's eyes were bloodshot and defiant and like the bull he stood and swayed as if uncertain where to make his first charge.[15]

The confrontation in the Kremlin was fraught and Churchill's doctor recorded that, after contending with Stalin, the Prime Minister resembled a bull in the ring maddened by the pricks of the picadors.

The socialite MP 'Chips' Channon (whom Clementine thought 'wormish but harmless')[16] described a similar scene that took place in the Smoking Room of the House of Commons. Offended by a hostile question concerning his scientific adviser Lord Cherwell (formerly Frederick Lindemann), put to him in the chamber by the diehard Tory backbencher Sir Waldron Smithers, Churchill, 'bellowing at him like an infuriated bull, roared: "Why in Hell did you ask that Question? Don't you know that he is one of my oldest and greatest friends?"' Elsewhere Channon noted the way in which Churchill, when meeting someone he disliked, seemed suddenly to contract and 'his famous charm is overclouded by an angry taurine look'.[17]

CHICKENS

Churchill reared chickens as a boy and later kept them at Chartwell. Here he dignified their residence as Chickenham Palace, its surroundings, a well-scratched patch of mud, being known as Chickenham Palace Gardens. These birds were hardly pets, though bantams were sometimes to be seen pecking for scraps in the Chartwell dining room. But they were not indulged like the chicken in the domestic menagerie of Churchill's friend Maxine Elliott, which was allowed to parade from one end of the dining table to the other, taking its pick of the guests' food. Quite uninterested in the type of his birds, Churchill simply bred poultry for eggs and meat. He did, though, have occasional qualms about eating members of his own clutch. Once he hesitated in front of a large roast chicken until Clementine said, 'What are you waiting for? Get on with the carving.' In a voice fraught with emotion, Churchill replied, 'I'm just wondering if this is Ethel.'[1]

Churchill hesitating over whether to leave the Tory chicken coop for the Liberal henhouse (with leader Campbell-Bannerman inside), March 1904.

Like his other attempts at animal husbandry, poultry-breeding at Chartwell was prone to disaster, especially when Chickenham Palace became infested with vermin and red mite. Friends tried to help and in 1945 Lord Beaverbrook supplied more chickens. Churchill feared that Clementine, who said the press baron was a microbe that should be purged from her husband's blood, would object to the taste of their eggs. During the Second World War Churchill attached particular importance to egg production on a national scale, particularly when he learned that hens were better than cattle as converters of protein from a mixed diet. He was also concerned about the effects of poultry rationing on rural well-being. Keen to dispense nutritional treats, he maintained that the hen had been 'part and parcel of the country cottager's life since history began'.[2]

Of course chicken was more of a delicacy than it became after the introduction of battery rearing. That development Churchill failed to foresee though in 1936 he did read a book by a Danish poultry expert about collective chicken farms in the Soviet Union. It revealed such incompetence, squalor and starvation as to make Churchill suspect that Russian strength was simply a façade.[3] However he continued to have faith in what science might achieve and in one of his essays on that subject he made this prediction: 'We shall escape the absurdity of growing a whole chicken in order to eat the breast or wing, by growing these parts separately under a suitable medium.'[4] It's hard to imagine Churchill enjoying synthetic food but he certainly found free-range chicken toothsome. He even told transatlantic readers that he preferred the substantial English fowl to the diminutive American variety: 'I am on the side of the big chicken as regularly as Providence is on the side of the big battalions.' He thought it strange indeed that such a large country as the United States should produce such small chickens. 'Conscious, perhaps, of their inferiority, the inhabitants call them "squabs". What an insulting title for a capon!'[5]

Chickens, whether as strutting roosters or cackling hens, also served Churchill well rhetorically. On the voyage to India in 1896 he performed well in a mock debate with brother officers despite his speech impediment. 'I came like a Duckling among chickens,' he wrote. 'I don't know whether I or they were most astonished to find I could swim.'[6] He felt entitled to crow about his exploits during the Boer War, when he sported the cock's feather cockade of the South African Light Horse (known as the Cockyolibirds) in his hat and twitted regiments who lacked that distinction for their miserable jealousy.[7] As a war leader he was nothing if not flamboyant. In September 1940 an official at the Home Office passed on a proposal about air-raid sirens (made by an eccentric patriot) to 10 Downing Street on the grounds that it would appeal to the Prime Minister: 'Why not use the signal of one note which from time immemorial has meant defiance and triumph, viz., "cock-a-doodle-doo", instead of the demoralizing wail of the amorous gargantuan tom cat, so much disliked by the public at present?'[8] Although Churchill might not want the sirens to crow, he promptly called for a reduction in their 'banshee howlings'.[9] Furthermore, attaching great importance to martial panache, he admired the fabulous Chanticleer from crest to spurs. At the end of the conflict he remarked that France without an army was a cock without a comb.

If roosters symbolized bold virility, hens embodied ruffled timidity[10] and Churchill toyed with them to great comic effect. Having been broody at the Home Office, he was happy with his new hutch at the Admiralty in 1911 'because I can now lay eggs instead of scratching around in the dust and clucking. It is a more satisfactory occupation. I am at present in the process of laying a great number of eggs – "good eggs", every one of them. And there will be many more clutches to follow.'[11] Among them was a huge wire-netting 'hen-coop' to protect battleships against submarines, an undertaking assisted by two septuagenarian admirals, Jackie Fisher and Arthur Wilson, whom he described as 'well-plucked chickens'.[12] During the late 1930s Churchill insisted that Spain had been hopelessly enfeebled by the Civil War and when someone argued otherwise he retorted, 'You are talking of something which has no existence – as of a chicken that barks.'[13] Still more piquant was Churchill's speech to the Canadian parliament on 30 December 1941, reporting his pledge to the French government in May the previous year that, whatever France did, Britain would fight on. French generals had then warned their Cabinet that in three weeks England would have her neck wrung like a chicken. 'Some chicken!' he famously quipped, 'Some neck!'[14]

CRANES

In 1935 Churchill was given a pair of Stanley cranes by his old friend Sir Abe Bailey, the wealthy Randlord whose son John was briefly married to Winston's daughter Diana. The birds came complete with samples of their food and instructions about their care. As ground-dwellers, they had been penned up together and 'it would not be safe to let them loose until one wing of each bird is cut. They require to be kept in at night, and in a fairly warm place in the winter.'[1] However these beautiful grey-blue South African birds were ill-suited to the English climate and otherwise accident prone. In May 1937, Churchill wrote, 'the female crane fell into a small pool and most stupidly drowned herself'.[2] He at once sought a replacement from G. B. Chapman Ltd in London's Tottenham Court Road, which advertised itself as the world's largest animal dealer, able to supply anything from an elephant to a boxing kangaroo. But Chapman wanted £37 10s for a Stanley crane, an offer Churchill turned down as too expensive. Instead, always happy to exploit amenable plutocrats, he applied to Bailey:

> The male bird is magnificent, but seems restless and fretful now that Spring is here and he has got no mate. Do you think it would be possible for you to get me another female from Africa? They walk about most agreeably around the bathing pool and in the gardens, and I think it is rather hard on his [sic] having to remain a widower.[3]

Bailey sent two more birds. Churchill telegraphed a 'thousand thanks' and said that 'we are building them a dugout'.[4] Plainly this new home did not give them enough protection, and by January 1939 Churchill's daughter Mary informed him that the one surviving crane 'stalks about and looks a little draggled by the wind and rain'.[5] Whatever their fate, Bailey punningly prophesied that it would be Churchill's abilities and not 'the *cranes* that will lift you into your proper place in the government'.[6] In 1965 his achievements as Prime Minister were saluted by mechanical cranes, operated by London dockers who famously dipped their jibs to salute Churchill as his coffin journeyed down the Thames on its way to interment at Bladon churchyard, near Blenheim.

CROCODILES

'I avow, with what regrets may be necessary, an active hatred of these brutes and a desire to kill them.' So wrote Churchill about crocodiles, having seen many in the Sudan and more on his East African safari in 1907. It was then that he shot at least one of them. It 'gave a leap of mortal agony' and terrified hundreds more of its kind, he recorded, which 'sprang into hideous life' and rushed 'madly into the Nile'.[1] As the embodiments of primeval menace, armed to the teeth, clad with bony scales, and often half-submerged in the interests of aggression, these creatures usually put Churchill in mind of Communists. He identified the Bolshevik leaders as both subhuman and superhuman, 'crocodiles with master minds'.[2] When one of them, Mikhail Tomsky, spoke at a conference of British trade unionists in 1926 Churchill dismissed his address as barbaric nonsense and declared: 'We do not want this new-laid crocodile egg from Moscow put upon our breakfast table.'[3] Uncomfortably allied to the Russian Communists during the war, the Prime Minister told Anthony Eden never to forget that they were crocodiles, and crocodiles who had to be fed.

Churchill had long been prepared, though, to adapt the image to the equal but opposite barbarism of the Nazis, and during the 1930s he denounced the policy of appeasement as cowardice in the face of saurian hostility. In January 1940, having praised the sublime resistance of Finland, caught in the Soviet 'jaws of peril', he famously said of countries trying to stay neutral: 'Each one hopes that if he feeds the crocodile enough, the crocodile will eat him last.'[4] When Hitler's panzer crocodile attacked Russia, Stalin in turn expressed scepticism about the British will to fight, only to be mollified for a time when Churchill sketched him a picture of a crocodile and showed that it was better to rip open its soft stomach than to bash its solid snout. This echoed the strategy he had advocated during the Great War but it was precisely the opposite of what he had argued in his biography of the first Duke of Marlborough, who was praised for fighting his foes where they were strongest. Moreover it was a completely misleading analogy since the underbelly of the Axis proved to be exceedingly hard.

A weapon that helped to destroy German resistance was a flame-throwing tank known as the Churchill Crocodile. This fire-breathing dragon, one of the innovative devices or 'funnies' developed under Churchill's auspices by Major-General Percy Hobart, was employed successfully after the D-Day invasion. It could squirt flammable liquid, towed behind it in a pressurized container, up to 150 yards and it was particularly adept at incinerating enemy pillboxes. In August 1944 Churchill told the minister in charge of the Petroleum Warfare Department, 'I am very glad that the Churchill Crocodile Flame Thrower has justified your hopes.'[5]

Despite the best efforts of Russia's western allies, however, Stalin remained rough, refractory and reptilian. Churchill expostulated, 'Trying to maintain good relations with a Communist is like wooing a crocodile, you do not know whether to tickle it under the chin or to beat it on the head. When it opens its mouth you cannot tell whether it is trying to smile, or preparing to eat you up.'[6]

CRUSTACEANS

As a young man Lord Randolph Churchill enjoyed 'deluding the wily lobster'.[1] He fished at Howth, north-east of Dublin, and sometimes cooked and ate his catch on the rocky shore. Winston shared his father's taste for such creatures, though he would hardly have attempted to act as chef, having never even boiled an egg. But he liked to feed himself and friends on lobster, so much so that before the Great War the right-wing *National Review* questioned the expenditure on his summer cruises aboard the Admiralty yacht *Enchantress*: 'How many lobsters have been eaten? How many magnums of champagne drunk?'[2]

Churchill was especially fond of transatlantic crustaceans, finding the soft-shelled crab by no means unpalatable and extolling the unrivalled American lobster: 'He has a succulence and a flavour that I have found nowhere else.'[3] In the United States during the Second World War he was quite capable of having Scotch whisky and cold lobster for breakfast, apparently thriving on the diet, which President Roosevelt's special envoy Averell Harriman thought 'a little rough'.[4]

With its powerful claws, armoured body and capacity to manoeuvre, the crab seemed designed for military metaphor and Churchill used it to particularly good effect in the fifth volume of *The World Crisis*. Here he described the immense pincer movement directed by the German military commanders Hindenburg and Ludendorff on the Eastern Front early in 1915: 'The Russian armies were to be seized, as it were, by a crab of monstrous size and gripped simultaneously with each of its two widely spread claws.'[5] 'The Crab' also served in the Second World War. It was the code name given to another of Churchill's 'funnies', a Sherman tank equipped with a flail to clear mines.

Recuperating from his major stroke in 1953 at Lord Beaverbrook's villa on the Côte d'Azur, Churchill went on a hunt for a remarkable crustacean called a sea-cricket. He had heard about it from Daisy Fellowes, the Singer sewing-machine heiress. She had once tried to seduce Winston – Clementine called her 'that witch'[6] – and was one of Europe's most notorious socialites, appropriately clad in shocking pink by Schiaparelli, whose Salvador Dalí-inspired lobster dress she also sometimes wore. As a source of information Daisy was unreliable but Churchill's curiosity about birds, beasts and fishes was insatiable. So Britain's Prime Minister set off in the rain, escorted by French police cars and accompanied by Jock Colville and his wife Meg (with whom Churchill had a flirtatious relationship), for the San Remo restaurant where this prodigy was supposedly to be found. As Colville recorded, they arrived at a dark, empty, ramshackle estaminet by the quayside. '"Where," asked Churchill, "is the sea-cuckoo?" "Sea-cricket," said Meg, by way of explanation. "I have come," said Churchill, quite unabashed, "to see the sea-cuckoo."'[7] But because of recent gales the establishment's glass tanks contained only a jaded langouste and a few prawns. A search was instituted but, to Churchill's chagrin, it produced nothing better than one ugly crustacean.

A final shellfish disappointment occurred five years later, when the tenth Duke of Marlborough gave a dinner at Blenheim to celebrate the fiftieth anniversary of Winston's engagement to Clementine. Churchill, now a very old man, sat through most of the meal with the Duchess's miniature dachshund on his lap trying to feed it lobster mousse. The animal rejected his offerings with every sign of disgust.

CUTTLEFISH

This mollusc has such a remarkable capacity to camouflage itself, both by changing colour and by squirting out repellent clouds of ink, that it is sometimes known as the chameleon of the sea. As such it appealed strongly to Churchill. His imagination may have been initially stimulated by his favourite science fiction author, H. G. Wells, whose novel *The War of the Worlds* (1898) featured an invasion force of cephalopod-like Martians equipped with toxic black smoke. However Churchill was always a champion of deception in warfare. Secrecy was not enough; stratagems had to be adopted by which Britain's enemies were positively misled. As the Prime Minister told Violet Bonham Carter in 1942, the duty of a democracy in wartime was not to conceal but to confuse, 'not the silence of the oyster serene in its grotto – but the smudge & blur of the cuttlefish'.[1] Of course Hitler appreciated this all too well, declaring that the most important soldier in the British Army was General Bluff. So too did Stalin, who endorsed Churchill's most famous pronouncement on the subject: 'In wartime, truth is so precious that she should always be attended by a bodyguard of lies.'[2]

Obfuscation was also an effective political weapon, as no one demonstrated more cogently than George Orwell, whose 'very remarkable' novel *Nineteen Eighty-Four* (1949) Churchill read twice.[3] Churchill himself, though a devotee of clear English, was adept at verbally muddying the waters. He, after all, had coined the classic euphemism for a lie: terminological inexactitude. But he was scathing about others who employed linguistic smokescreens, once telling a verbose Cabinet minister, 'You have clearly mastered the first rule of politics.... When you don't understand a subject, be obscure.'[4] In 1949 he administered a magisterial rebuke to the Labour Foreign Secretary, Ernest Bevin, for not giving de facto recognition to the new state of

Israel and for not saying whether he would do so. 'I regret that he has not had the manliness to tell us in plain terms tonight,' Churchill stated in the House of Commons, 'and that he preferred to retire under a cloud of inky water and vapour, like a cuttlefish, to some obscure retreat.'[5]

DOGS

Like most eminent Victorians, including the Queen herself, Winston Churchill's relations were extravagantly devoted to dogs. His paternal grandfather filled letters to his son with news about his own pack, which included everything from greyhounds to lapdogs. Gladys, the wife of Winston's cousin Sunny, Duke of Marlborough, walked round Blenheim Palace on a 'moving carpet of King Charles spaniels',[1] and Edith, the wife of his cousin Charlie, Marquess of Londonderry, dwelt amid a throng of pekes, chihuahuas and lurchers. His mother's father, Leonard Jerome, was keen on rare breeds, once telling Jennie that he was arranging to send an exotic Japanese dog to England, 'a tiny little beast with a long tongue'.[2] Lady Randolph herself adored dogs, and not just as fashion accessories or status symbols. When her black pug went missing in 1898 Winston made every effort to recover it, offering a £10 reward, printing 300 handbills and inserting an advertisement in the *Morning Post*. He told his mother, 'I am v[er]y sorry about it myself as I was fond of the little fellow.'[3]

In his youth Winston had several dogs of his own, all much indulged. The obverse of his thirst for the blood of wild animals was his tenderness towards domestic pets and he felt especially protective towards man's best friend. Cruising in the Sea of Marmara aboard the *Enchantress*,

Churchill was horrified to come across an island to which the Young Turks had shipped tens of thousands of Constantinople's pariah dogs. They were 'left there to devour one another and ultimately to starve', he wrote. 'I saw them with my own eyes, gathered in troops upon the rocky shores. The bones of these dogs whitened the inhospitable island and their memory noisomely pervaded the neighbourhood.'[4] At the Home Office he received a rare commendation from King George V, himself an ardent hunter and shooter who was profoundly sentimental about dogs, for the action he took over a case of cruelty to a dog at Walton in Surrey. Churchill had issued a 'sharp rebuke' to the magistrates, evidently for being too lenient, and the sovereign wanted them to know about his own concern.[5]

Once married, Winston and Clementine made dogs an integral part of their household. Actually she was unenthusiastic about them, her mother having accumulated animals indiscriminately, including mongrels as well as what George Eliot had called 'decent and "gentleman-like" dogs'.[6] Nevertheless the Chartwell dog population multiplied as the family grew, since the children also had dogs. Among them were Sarah's chocolate-coloured spaniel Trouble, Randolph's wire-haired terrier Harvey and Mary's licentious pug Punch. None seems to have been satisfactorily house-trained and on occasion Churchill banished the entire tribe from his domain. The pug was especially incontinent. Churchill complained to Clementine, 'He commits at least three indiscretions a day, and if his actions stain the carpets, his protests when chastised fill the air.'[7] When Punch fell ill, however, Churchill sympathized to the point of comforting Mary in, so to speak, doggerel:

> Oh, what is the matter with poor Puggy-wug?
> Pet him and kiss him and give him a hug.
> Run and fetch him a suitable drug,
> Wrap him up tenderly all in a rug,
> That is the way to cure Puggy-wug.[8]

Churchill was also concerned when his valet's dog injured its paw, paying for it to go to a dog's hospital for a fortnight because, he said, 'I can't bear to see it limping around.'[9]

At home, of course, Churchill played Mr Pug (in various guises, among them Amber Pug and Galloping Pug) to Clementine's Kat (occasionally Clem-Pussy-Bird). And elsewhere he adopted a canine persona, not necessarily that of the bulldog. As a prisoner of the Boers he likened himself to a whipped dog who must be thankful for the bone that is flung to him. During the abdication crisis he doggedly guarded the throne, whose feckless occupant he described as a poor little lamb – Robert Boothby had a premonition that Churchill would sacrifice his own prestige in a defence of the King when observing him at Chartwell, silent, restless, glancing into corners like a dog about to be sick. Soon afterwards Churchill visualized himself as the Blenheim Pup, in contrast to the German Eagle, Joachim von Ribbentrop. But

Winston and his younger brother Jack with a terrier – one of a diverse breed much favoured by their family.

when he was invited to an official lunch with Ribbentrop in 1938 he reckoned that Neville Chamberlain's ministers wanted to show the Nazi ambassador that 'if they couldn't bark themselves, they kept a dog who could bark and might bite'.[10] It was a role Churchill relished, comparable to that of the savage dog which protected the possessions of a gypsy known as Mrs Donkey Jack, who was allowed to camp on the Chartwell estate despite her habit of stealing potatoes. This animal, he wrote, taught a 'fine moral lesson to the baser breed of man!'.[11]

Other canine analogies, to which Churchill was irresistibly drawn, were less flattering. He described newspapermen who criticized his father as yapping curs hungry for their money bags. The Sudanese soldier whom he encountered during the River War possessed both the heart of a lion and 'the faithful loyalty of a dog', but he was, like the Muslim Pathan, prone to religious 'frenzy, which is as dangerous in a man as hydrophobia in a dog'.[12] At the Admiralty Churchill worried that the 'big dog',[13] Germany, would pose a threat in British home waters but claimed, soon after the outbreak of the Great War, that its fleet had been muzzled. (Lloyd George painted a somewhat different picture, saying that Winston reminded him of 'a dog sitting on the Dogger Bank with his tail between his legs, looking at the rat who has poked its nose out of the hole at the other side of the water'.[14]) After Mussolini invaded Ethiopia in 1935, Churchill accused the National Government of running away when the Fascist dog growled. As Hitler proceeded on his rabid course, Churchill told the German press attaché in London, 'If a mad dog makes a dash for my trousers, I shoot him down before he can bite.'[15]

Churchill also nipped and mauled his opponents in the domestic political fray. As a reforming Liberal minister in 1909 he alleged that Lord Curzon had been 'selected to follow me from place to place like a dog (laughter) – I mean with the fidelity and persistence of a dog (more laughter)'.[16] So violent were the outbursts of the Tory leader Andrew Bonar Law in 1913 that even members of his own party, according to Churchill, complained that he was not so much barking as howling. Consequently, Churchill claimed, Law had to hurry off and 'deliver a series of good, loud, raucous and unequivocal barks, and he certainly did his best'.[17] In 1923 Churchill attacked the Protectionist Prime Minister Stanley Baldwin for thinking that Britain was to live by taking in its own washing and feeding the dog on its own tail. As for Philip Snowden, Labour's Shadow Chancellor when Churchill himself was at the Treasury, he resembled the 'kind of fierce dog who would bite anyone and everyone for biting's sake'.[18]

While in opposition during the 1930s, Churchill was occasionally bested by his foes. 'Some of them are dirty dogs and their day will come,' he declared, 'though I thank God I am not a vindictive man.'[19] When a barking dog interrupted him at a 1935 election meeting in his Epping constituency, Churchill reviled it as a dirty, socialistic beast, only to receive an indignant protest from its owner, who said it was not only clean but Conservative, likely to sport a blue rosette when accompanying its master and mistress to the polling booth. In 1945 Churchill charged the Socialist Sir Stafford Cripps with jumping at office like a dog at a bone. And when Hugh Dalton slightly eased Labour's regulatory regime in 1950, Churchill accused him of doling out liberties as though he were giving biscuits to a prettily begging dog.

Since dogs loom so large in human life politicians exploit them for all they are worth, but Churchill's canine preoccupations seem to have been less calculating and more instinctive than those of, say, Franklin D. Roosevelt. Churchill's mind was a cornucopia of doggy maxims: every dog has its day; let sleeping dogs lie; don't keep a dog and bark yourself; never force little dogs to eat mutton; don't try to beat two dogs at one time; a living dog is better than a dead lion. When scorning visions of a brave new world in the aftermath of Armageddon, Churchill told Lloyd George that the old world was good enough for him: 'There's life in the old dog yet. It's going to sit up & wag its tail.'[20] When Lord Cherwell, Churchill's scientific adviser, came under fire from Sir Waldron Smithers in the Commons, the Prime Minister muttered furiously: 'Love me, love my dog, and if you don't love my dog you damn well can't love me.'[21] When denying that new technology could change human nature, Churchill asserted, 'It's the nature of the beast that counts. You may teach a dog all kinds of tricks … but you can't improve the breed of dog in a hurry.'[22] When characteristically mispronouncing General Badoglio's name, he put the emphasis on 'bad dog'. He nicknamed the Serbian leader Milan Stojadinović 'Son of a Bitch'. When inveighing against General de Gaulle's unmannerly behaviour in 1943, Churchill informed Attlee and Eden: 'I brought him up from a pup, but never got him properly trained to the house.'[23]

All his life Churchill was possessed by an overweening ambition, sparing no pains to climb to the top of the greasy pole and once even joking that megalomania was the only form of sanity. If he sometimes enjoyed hauling up underdogs, wrote Boothby, Churchill had no use for top dogs other than himself. According to one witness he admitted dismissing General Wavell from his Middle East command in order to show his power; according to another he enjoyed the game of 'general-hunting and like a pi-dog he goes looking for dirts in which to roll'.[24] In the struggle for ascendancy, success so elated him that he was said to resemble a 'dog with two cocks'.[25] Yet in acting as in speaking he was prone to distraction: Harold Nicolson once compared him to a spaniel who is diverted by the smell of a rabbit and dashes off wildly into the bracken.

However the will to win was not Churchill's sole driving force. He was compulsively animated, it seems, because he was pursued by the 'black dog' of depression.[26] The term is an ancient one whose origins are lost in the mists of time and the fog of folklore,[27] but it was evidently used by Winston's nanny, Mrs Everest, to describe what he called 'those terrible and reasonless depressions wh[ich] frighten me sometimes'.[28] There appeared to be no cure for a psychological condition which now and then plunged him into despair and even prompted thoughts of suicide. The black dog constantly prowled at Churchill's heels and occasionally jumped on his back. The only means of keeping it at bay was incessant activity.

DONKEYS

O ne of Churchill's earliest memories was of riding round
Dublin on a donkey. He was accompanied by his nanny
Mrs Everest, who saw a long, dark column of men marching
towards them. These were probably soldiers of the Rifle Brigade but
she became convinced that they were Fenian revolutionaries. Her alarm
communicated itself to the donkey which bucked, throwing Winston
to the ground. He suffered a slight concussion. This was, he liked to
say, his first introduction to Irish politics. The experience did not turn
him against donkeys. On holiday at Cromer in 1885 he could not
walk, swim or paddle because of 'irrespelas' (erysipelas, inflammation
of the skin) in the legs, but he told his mother, 'I am very happy on
the whole for I drive myself about in a little donkey carriage.'[1] At
Sandhurst he took part in donkey races, sending his brother Jack a
photograph of the Donkey Race Group.[2] He described Kitchener's
callous method of using donkeys to unwind spools of telegraph wire
during the Sudan campaign and deplored the sufferings of these
wretched beasts, remarking that in his own scheme of things animals
would always hold pride of place. In 1902, when crossed in love with
Pamela Plowden, Churchill was glimpsed 'pouting on a donkey around
the ruins of Luxor'.[3]

Of course donkeys, or asses, were frequently dragged into discussion
or debate as a means of ridiculing opponents or translating those at the
top into Bottom. Churchill was thus taunted since he was so prone to
mistake monologue for conversation, to talk the hind legs off a donkey
and to give gratuitous advice to his superiors. Asquith called him a
donkey and in November 1899 General Sir Redvers Buller, responding
to a lecture on strategy from the ex-Lieutenant of Hussars, told him
'not to be a young ass'.[4]

As a young politician Churchill himself could not refrain from such slurs. In 1902 he commended the British government for its calm response to the provocations of Irish MPs: 'There is an old saying to this effect: "The eagle suffers little birds to sing, and is not careful what they mean thereby." And in this case the lion suffers the little asses to bray, and is not careful what they mean by it.'[5] Later he hit back at the maverick radical cartoonist David Low: 'You cannot bridle the wild ass of the desert, still less prohibit its natural hee-haw.'[6] Yet he chided adversaries who employed similar raillery. Hearing that horses but not mules or donkeys were being purchased for the Army in 1919, one MP suggested that all the asses were in the War Office. Churchill, then presiding over this department, responded loftily: 'Observations like that carry one back to one's early schooldays, when jokes of the kind about the possession of asinine qualities by particular individuals were expected to pass muster.'[7]

In Churchill's (not uncommon) estimation, donkeys were versatile creatures. Like some other animals, they were rich in mythical and literary associations and could be objects of affection and compassion as well as derision and denigration. Thus, Churchill said, only the sensible little British donkey knew the way home from the Teheran Conference. At the same time he promised to operate on the Italian donkey at both ends, with a carrot and a stick.[8] Sometimes those who served him came into sharp contact with the stick. Before setting off to make a speech in Aachen (disliking that 'guttural expectoration' he preferred to call it Aix-la-Chapelle) in 1956, Churchill discovered that his private secretary could only speak a few phrases of German. '"That's no good," he snapped. "I can say 'Du bist ein Esel' ['You're a donkey'] perfectly well for myself."'[9]

DRAGONS

Lurking in the recesses of Churchill's imagination there were dragons, brought forth mainly for the purposes of entertainment. As a boy having to explore the mysteries of mathematics, he was especially apprehensive about 'dim chambers lighted by sullen, sulphurous fires … reputed to contain a dragon called the "Differential Calculus"'.[1] Campaigning with the Malakand Field Force a few years later, he found himself in the vicinity of a large rock where the Buddha had once converted a 'wicked dragon'. Churchill regarded both as figments of myth and he reported drily that since the Swat Valley was full of large rocks, he and his brother officers had been unable to pinpoint 'the scene of the dragon's repentance'.[2]

In the wake of the Great War, Churchill's attacks on the Communists were so inflammatory that one of them, Willie Gallacher, accused him of 'mouthing fire and brimstone like an inebriated dragon'.[3] Churchill was more inventive. A few weeks after Hitler came to power he updated the legend of St George and the Dragon for the amusement and edification of his compatriots. Churchill's target was England's current reliance on a 'vague internationalism' instead of its own imperial might. The modern

St George would arrive in Cappadocia, accompanied not by a horse, but by a secretariat. He would be armed not with a lance, but with several flexible formulas. He would, of course, be welcomed by the local branch of the League of Nations Union. He would propose a conference with the dragon – a Round Table Conference, no doubt – that would be more convenient for the dragon's tail. He would make a trade agreement with the dragon. He would lend the dragon a lot of money for the Cappadocian taxpayers. The maiden's release would be referred to Geneva, the dragon reserving all his rights meanwhile. Finally St George would be photographed with the dragon.[4]

Churchill was understandably pleased with this fable of national decadence, reprinting it and repeating it with minor variations.

At the end of 1934 Clementine set off for the Dutch East Indies on a quest for real dragons, or at any rate for the huge, flesh-eating monitor lizards known as Komodo dragons. She travelled on board the yacht of Churchill's friend Lord Moyne, who caught two live specimens for London Zoo. Churchill was thrilled to hear of their capture, cabling 'BRAVO DRAGONS' and saying how paltry his tales of Chartwell's heifers and nanny goats must seem 'compared to your dragons and tuataras'.[5] Oriental monsters leapt to his mind again in 1937 when Japan attacked China. As usual, he was chiefly concerned about the damage being done to British interests. 'The spectacle of the

Churchill at Carthage in his dragon dressing-gown, with Eisenhower and other Allied top brass, after lunch on Christmas Day 1943.

wounded frantic Chinese dragon, lashing out in the most senseless directions,' he wrote, 'is pitiful in the last degree.'[6] Later, of course, he was more sympathetic to the victim of Japanese aggression. But the famous Chinese-style outfit with which he dazzled visitors during the Second World War – a quilted green-and-gold silk dressing gown decorated with red dragons, and dragon-embroidered silk slippers – was not so much a reflection of allied solidarity as the expression of an extravagant personality.

Dragons entered Churchill's mind again after the Allies' victory, when he advocated the creation of a 'United Europe'.[7] What role Britain should play in this body remained unclear, since he was also committed to the unity of the English-speaking peoples. But Churchill extolled the idea as a means of reconciliation after the European civil war. It was a profoundly 'spiritual conception' calculated to prevent a regression to elemental savagery. Quoting Tennyson, whose poem *In Memoriam* contained anguished reflections about nature red in tooth and claw, Churchill asked rhetorically: 'Are we to sink through gradations of infinite suffering to primordial levels –

> "A discord. Dragons of the prime,
> That tare each other in their slime."

– or can we avoid our doom?'[8] The prospect of nuclear doom particularly exercised him.

Towards the end of his life the sometime subaltern of Hussars plainly felt that romance was an anachronism and the age of chivalry was dead. He remarked of the war memorial to the Cavalry of the Empire, which had been erected near Hyde Park Corner in 1924 and depicted St George slaying the dragon, 'It is entirely appropriate that an obsolete animal should commemorate an obsolete arm.'[9]

DUCKS

'Will the bloody duck swim?'[1] This was what Churchill said to himself on two occasions when accepting a prime-ministerial boon: first from Lord Salisbury, who in 1898 asked to meet the young author of *The Malakand Field Force*; and secondly from Stanley Baldwin, who invited him to become Chancellor of the Exchequer in 1924. The rhetorical question indicates that, well before Walt Disney, Churchill saw the funny side of ducks. Waddling, quacking, dipping and dabbling, they seemed to be nature's stooges. In 1927 Churchill deployed them effectively to lampoon the Socialist Shadow Chancellor, who had kept his head down during the General Strike:

> I have on my pond at home some little ducks, and I was watching one the other day. It is a diving duck, and whenever it is alarmed it plunges below the surface of the water. You see nothing at all until, when the coast is clear, suddenly up pops the little head and starts quacking again. This very accurately defines the attitude of that great statesman, Mr. Philip Snowden, during the great strike, for he has suddenly started quacking again.[2]

Equally droll was his response to Sir Philip Sassoon, a wealthy Jewish friend, who in 1934 sent him 'a very handsome pair of comb duck from India'.[3] Churchill, then campaigning to preserve the British Raj, telegraphed: 'Enchanted to receive comb duck from India. Hope by firm government [to] make them loyal subjects. All good wishes, Winston.'[4]

Churchill enjoyed eating and killing wild duck. As a Harrow schoolboy he annoyed his mother by ordering ducks as well as pheasants to be sent to him from home. And later he drew on the imagery of duck-hunting to enliven his speeches, accusing one opponent of acting as 'a quacking decoy duck' and asserting that to fire directly 'at an aeroplane in the air is like trying to shoot a flying duck with a pea-rifle'.[5] However Churchill populated Chartwell with a large number exotic ducks, all treated as honoured guests. He valued them for the colour and vitality they brought to his lake and he nurtured them with care, ensuring that they were not disturbed during the nesting season. Among them were Carolinas, mandarins, hand-reared tufted ducks and sociable South American Rosybills. Many of them were gifts from Sassoon. In 1936 Churchill apparently informed him that, since drakes outnumbered ducks, some of his waterfowl had been engaging in irregular sexual practices. Sassoon wrote, 'I will send you two lady Carolinas as soon as I can procure them. We must stop any abnormality on y[ou]r pond.'[6]

Churchill prided himself on having established an exclusive rapport with the Chartwell ducks. During the Second World War, as Lawrence Burgis, Assistant Secretary to the War Cabinet, later recalled, he attempted to demonstrate this to his Chief of Staff, General 'Pug' Ismay.

> 'They know me!' Churchill assured Sir Pug – and to prove it he stood by the bank uttering seductive cooing sounds until one solitary drake emerged from the reeds and swam slowly over to receive a reward of breadcrumbs at the Prime Minister's hand. Later Winston challenged Ismay to exercise the same influence over the birds. Armed with bread, Sir Pug imitated Mr Churchill's curious call and after a while the same drake paddled across towards him as had fed from the breadcrumbs thrown to it. Mr Churchill eyed it with the more in sorrow than in anger regard of a man whose valued friend had let him down, and then in a voice charged with emotion he said sadly 'I *do* wish he hadn't done that.'[7]

Churchill liked his relationships with animals to be unique.

'Duck' is a familiar appellation though Churchill himself played ducks and drakes with it. He called Clementine a 'sweet duck' and said that a letter from her was such a duck that 'I feel all over of a purr when I read it through', but he labelled the Iranian leader, Mohammad Mossadegh, 'Mussy Duck'.[8] Churchill's friends the Duff Coopers paid him back in his own coin, nicknaming him 'Duck' or 'Duckling'. This was not because of his devotion to ducks so much as his incessant quacking, though the alias could hardly have been less appropriate from a physical point of view. Diana Cooper acknowledged that fact when describing Churchill's appearance with General de Gaulle at the Armistice Day celebrations in liberated Paris on 11 November 1944 – 'the one so pink and benign, the other so sinister and elongated'. However, she noted, the two leaders seemed to have made up their differences by the evening, smiling and embarking on a 'Renaissance of Love Relations. The Giraffe shall lie down with the Duck.'[9]

She elaborated on the conceit after Churchill's defeat at the polls: 'Duckling quacked away energetically – and not bitterly – likes the subject of his fall, his meteoric rise and sudden nose dive.' Duff Cooper was now British ambassador to France and in November 1945 Churchill, accompanied by an immense baggage train, came to stay at the Paris embassy. Diana Cooper wrote:

> Duckling arrived at 5 yesterday – a picture of cherubic curves and glowing health – with boiler suit discarded in favour of civvies. He looked less porcine – in fact near elegant…. He undressed in front of me, trousers and all – no 'do you mind if I debag?' and got into bed.

The visit was a success. As his hostess recorded, Churchill visited the Louvre, revelling in the pictures and touching their surfaces gently with his delicate hands. He met French leaders, including de Gaulle, who was civil and 'looked less brontosaurus' than usual. He took afternoon naps: 'Duckling had put his head under his wing and was "not to be disturbed".'[10] By his own admission, moreover, Churchill 'got very drunk on their excellent wines … "Drunker than usual," he chuckled.'[11] A second visit in July 1946 gave him another, much-relished opportunity 'to air his atrocious & ingenious French'. He also quacked in English, as Diana Cooper observed. Addressing embassy guests 'gathered round him like the doctors around Christ', he denounced Communism abroad, Socialism at home and stressed the need for a strong France 'with always those enchanting slangs – "Half a mo" – Duff must come back to "bark at the bastards"'.[12]

One of Churchill's favourite pieces of light verse was a skit about the ducks in St James's Park which had appeared in *Punch* in 1895. It purported to be a soliloquy by a 'Socialistic Loafer' who complained in exaggerated Cockney that he could get no rest in the park because of the 'keckle, screech, an' squork' of ducks and 'sim'lar poultry'. To his annoyance they were, moreover, bursting with free cakes and buns:

> Whoy should the loikes o' them 'ave hall the luck,
> Whoile such as me ——? It's skendalus, I s'y 'tis,
> That – jest becos I ain't a bloomin' duck –
> Sercoiety don't grub and board me grytis![13]

Punch specialized in being facetious at the expense of the lower orders and Churchill, though imbued with a strong sense of *noblesse oblige*, obviously considered left-wing layabouts fair game. He also took a proprietorial interest in the feathered inhabitants of St James's Park, expressing particular concern for their welfare during the Blitz. Anyway, the sire of the Duckadilly (nickname for his daughter Marigold) was amused by *Punch*'s play on words, learned the poem by heart and recited it on all possible and some impossible occasions. Sixty years after its publication, just as he was preparing to announce his retirement as Prime Minister, Churchill declaimed it in front of the television cameras during a secret test. He disliked the medium and the result, and the film was never shown.

EAGLES

C hurchill's memories of parliament stretched back to the time of William Ewart Gladstone, whom he had seen defending his last ministry at the dispatch box 'like a great white eagle at once fierce and splendid'.[1] This was an inspired simile. The Grand Old Man possessed talon-like fingers, a beaky nose and, as the journalist W. T. Stead wrote, 'the eye of an eagle that gazes untroubled at the sun'.[2] (Years later Arthur Balfour told a group of officers that although they had witnessed fearsome sights during the Great War, they had never seen Mr Gladstone's eyes when he was angry.[3]) Once elected an MP, Churchill himself took on aquiline characteristics. His eyes glittered. He tore into his foes with carnivorous zest. He soared on wings of neoclassical magniloquence before making, as Harold Nicolson would observe, 'sudden swoops into the intimate and the conversational'.[4] In full flight Churchill was Jovian, remote from the world of ordinary mortals. Violet Bonham Carter wondered at his failure to appreciate mundane matters – his lack of antennae – until she recalled William Blake's lines:

> Does the Eagle know what is in the pit
> Or wilt thou go ask the Mole?[5]

Sometimes Churchill deployed aquiline imagery of his own. After his mother's marriage to George Cornwallis-West in 1900, he assured her, quite fallaciously as it turned out, that her husband's eventual inheritance would enable her 'to renew your youth like the eagle'.[6] As an adolescent Winston had seen the Kaiser wearing a helmet topped with a magnificent white eagle nearly six inches high and as First Lord of the Admiralty, appropriately enough, he adopted this martial motif for the uniform of the Royal Naval Air Service, replacing the anchor with an eagle on its buttons, cap badges, epaulettes and so on. When a German minelayer targeting Liverpool's trade routes sank the battleship *Audacious* in 1914 he said, rather less aptly, that the shot aimed at a crow brought down an eagle. Even while glorying in the heroics of the RAF during the Second World War he hankered for the romance of the cavalry charge, once expressing regret that man had parted company with his trusty friend the horse and sailed into the azure with the eagles. At the end of the conflict he was keen to prevent dissonant voices (notably Soviet ones) from upsetting allied harmony, asserting that often the eagles had been squalled down by the parrots. And he particularly resented the stridency of Marshal Tito and General de Gaulle: 'When the eagles are silent the parrots begin to jabber.'[7]

Since the eagle was the national bird of the United States, however, Churchill generally associated it with Americans and America. He nicknamed General Mark Clark the 'American Eagle'. He described the Secretary of State Cordell Hull as a gallant old eagle. And he advised the Russians, as the Red Army smashed its way through eastern Europe, not to provoke the avian avatar of the Great Republic:

> The American eagle sits on his perch, a large, strong bird with formidable beak and claws. There he sits motionless, and M. Gromyko [Soviet ambassador to the United States] is sent day after day to prod him with a sharp pointed stick, now his neck, now under his wings, now his tail feathers. All the time the eagle keeps quite still. But it would be a great mistake to suppose that nothing is going on inside the breast of the eagle.[8]

Well before the defeat of Nazi Germany, therefore, Churchill was contemplating the threat which a triumphant Soviet Union would pose to the western democracies. In his famous 'iron curtain' speech of 1946, delivered at Fulton, Missouri, he fired the first major salvo in the Cold War, warning about resurgent Communism and stressing the need to strengthen the special relationship between Britain and America. On board the train to Fulton, Harry Truman showed him the new Presidential Seal, which he had just re-designed so that the eagle faced the olive branches rather than the arrows. He asked what Churchill thought of it and got this reply: 'Mr. President, with the greatest respect, I would prefer the American eagle's neck to be on a swivel so that it could face the olive branches or the arrows, as the occasion might demand.'[9]

EELS

S uch was the galvanic power of Lord Randolph Churchill's sometime political ally Joseph Chamberlain that he put Winston in mind of an electric eel he had seen at London Zoo. 'You may put your hand in the tank and you get a slight shock from the electric eel,' he wrote. 'You can also see him kill the little fishes, which he afterwards eats. Joe Chamberlain gave one exactly this impression.'[1] Actually the electric eel, technically a knifefish, can deliver a severe shock to humans but perhaps Winston did not put it to the test. Anyway he was more interested in the analogy afforded by the unique endowment of this creature. Eels without voltage rather left him cold. In 1937 he was even rebuked by Bernard Shaw for failing to pay one proper attention. The playwright said that he (Shaw) had described the Red Flag, anthem of the Labour Party, as 'the funeral march of a fried eel, and not as Mr Churchill calls it the burial march of a monkey'.[2]

However Churchill did like to repeat a callous eely proverb much favoured by the Victorians. Complaining of being portrayed in cartoons as every kind of wretched animal, he remarked that just as eels are supposed to get used to skinning, so politicians get used to being caricatured. Addressing a secret session of parliament on 20 June 1940, the new Prime Minister uttered a grim exhortation to his compatriots about the incipient German bombing campaign: 'Learn to get used to it.' Then he added, in a characteristic descent from pathos to bathos, 'Eels get used to skinning.'[3] And in 1953 he tried to galvanize President Eisenhower's administration, paralysed by Senator Joe McCarthy's anti-Communist witch-hunt, into participating in a diplomatic dialogue with the Soviet leaders who had succeeded Stalin. Many people think that the best we can do is to get used to the Cold War like eels are said to get used to skinning, he declared, but life in a permanent state of big-power enmity was not worth living.

Although frustrated by American anxieties and Russian intransigence, as well as by his declining powers and the opposition of his own colleagues in government, Churchill pursued the goal of a parley at the summit with his usual pertinacity. He refused to be pinned down by the Foreign Office and he even wriggled out of Cabinet control, making a quite unauthorized overture to the Soviet Foreign Minister, Vyacheslav Molotov, in pursuit of détente. The manoeuvre was reminiscent of the slippery methods that Churchill had sometimes employed in attempting to get his own way over strategy during the Second World War. Alan Brooke called them 'eel-like tactics'.[4]

ELEPHANTS

When Winston was three his mother bought him a toy elephant; he had long demanded it and in the shop she only just stopped herself from asking for 'an ephelant'.[1] As Winston discovered when writing his father's biography, Lord Randolph also found elephants an unfailing source of interest and amusement. They were useful figuratively: Lord Randolph declared that the Earl of Durham had 'studied politics about as much as Barnum's new white elephant' and later said that he himself looked on his parliamentary colleagues as an elephant looked on its fleas. And in India elephants were a practical necessity. On his Himalayan hunting expedition in 1885 Lord Randolph employed no fewer than fifteen, extolling the strength, patience and sure-footedness of these 'most wonderful animals'.[2]

In 1896 Winston himself took to a howdah when showing the first great love of his life, Pamela Plowden, around the city of Hyderabad. He explained to his mother that it was essential to travel on elephant-back since the natives spat at Europeans, which provoked retaliation leading to riots. Elephants were a great feature of life in Hyderabad – one senior British official, Harcourt Butler, even enjoyed playing elephant to the Nizam's children – and Churchill witnessed a military parade in which twenty of these beasts were harnessed to colossal cannon. As he wrote in *My Early Life*:

> It was then the custom for the elephants to salute as they marched past by raising their trunks, and this they all did with exemplary precision. Later on the custom was abolished because vulgar people tittered and the dignity of the elephants or their mahouts was wounded. Later on still, the elephants themselves were abolished, and we now have clattering tractors drawing far larger and more destructive guns. Thus civilization advances. But I mourn the elephants and their salutations.[3]

Churchill naturally assumed that he himself was in the van of civilization and he managed to combine nostalgia for a romantic past with faith in a technological future. This was exemplified by his pioneering promotion of tanks, his mechanical elephants.

In Africa Churchill saw more elephants, regarding them with the characteristic ambivalence of the animal-loving huntsman. In the Sudan, where the Dervish advance was signalled by blasts on a war trombone made from elephant tusk, he noted that the wealth of the Equatorial Province was contained in the ivory of these 'valuable pachyderms'.[4] There were so many of them that they were considered pests and when

HIS MORNING EXERCISE.
THE LONE EX-MINISTER UPON HIS ELEPHANT.

More hostile to Gandhi than to Hitler for most of the 1930s, Churchill trumpeted and rampaged against plans to give India partial self-rule.

Churchill returned to the region on his 1907 safari, he was eager to add one to his big-game bag. He failed, though a member of his party did shoot an elephant and Churchill published a trophy photograph of its carcass. Yet he was plainly more impressed by the spectacle of living relations of the mammoth. From the top of an ant-bear hill, at a distance of 150 yards, he once watched a 'stately and awe-inspiring procession of eleven elephants'. They ambled along, a few bulls, several big females and two or three calves. Each bore on its back a beautiful white egret, sometimes more than one, which pecked at its corrugated hide for parasites or 'surveyed the scene with the consciousness of pomp'. Such sights were familiar to the African hunter, Churchill wrote:

> Those who dwell in the wilderness are the heirs of its wonders. But to me I confess it seemed a truly marvellous and thrilling experience to wander through a forest peopled by these noble Titans, to watch their mysterious, almost ghostly, march, to see around on every side, in large trees snapped off a few feet from the ground, in enormous branches torn down for sport, the evidences of their giant strength.[5]

These beasts occupied a jumbo-sized place in Churchill's mind. Such was his reorganization of the huge and cumbersome Ministry of Munitions in 1917, he recorded, that instead of 'struggling through the jungle on foot I rode comfortably on an elephant, whose trunk could pick up a pin or uproot a tree with equal ease, and from whose back a wide scene lay open'.[6] In 1921 he told Edwin Montagu, Secretary of State for India, that Gandhi 'ought to be laid, bound hand and foot, at the gates of Delhi and then trampled on by an enormous elephant with the new Viceroy seated on its back'.[7] Churchill depicted the Labour Party, which had formed a minority government for the first time in 1924, as a wild elephant flanked by two tame ones, Liberal and Conservative. As Baldwin's Chancellor he devised a scheme to boost industry by relieving it of rates, which were to be paid by general taxation, only to lament that the Treasury was empty because the rating elephant had eaten all his buns.

Churchill likened the progress of history to that of an elephant which would obliterate the rubbish in its path and thus vindicate his strategy over the Dardanelles. He asserted that Lloyd George had had a cardinal influence on the outcome of the Great War and had not 'merely scrambled on to the back of the elephant and clung on while the mighty beast blundered and trampled through the jungle into safety'.[8] He joked that everyone could recognize an elephant but no one could define it. And when asked how he liked reviewing Margot Asquith's memoirs he replied, 'Have you ever seen an elephant do an egg dance?'[9] In middle age he made a picture of circus elephants and late in life he was given two painted metal elephants by Aristotle Onassis, which sat on either side of the dining-room fireplace in his London house.

With his phenomenal memory, his fondness for bathing and an amiable temper periodically disrupted by attacks of musth, Churchill invited elephantine comparisons. Scrambling around the trenches or making forays into no-man's-land during the Great War, he was said to be as visible and voluble as a baby elephant. In 1933, when Churchill was at odds with the National Government over devolving power to India, a vivid *Punch* cartoon showed him riding an elephant and attracting a large body of support in the country. Later in the decade Tories were increasingly inclined to decry him as a rogue elephant.

Two days after Churchill became Prime Minister in May 1940, Lord Hankey, hitherto a member of the War Cabinet, said he feared a dictatorship and thought that the country's 'only hope lies in the solid core of Churchill, Chamberlain and Halifax, but whether the wise old elephants will ever be able to hold the Rogue Elephant, I doubt".[10] A year later Hankey hoped that Lloyd George and Sir Robert Menzies, the Australian Prime Minister, might be the wise old elephants to tame the rogue elephant. (Churchill said that Hankey's subsequent attempts to ingratiate himself resembled the caress of a worm.) Reckoning Churchill a genius as well as a bull elephant, his doctor rejoiced that he charged down everything that got in his way. Sometimes, however, his rampages were ill-judged. Finding a dearth of staff when he unexpectedly returned from Chequers to Downing Street in 1945, Churchill trumpeted with rage. At last one of his private secretaries, Anthony Bevir, said quietly but clearly, 'Prime Minister, you are behaving like a rogue elephant.'[11]

FABULOUS BEASTS

Needless to say, Churchill was by no means alone in using allegorical animals to make political points and appropriating familiar fables to illustrate them. In May 1941, when few could see any hope of winning the war against Hitler, the Prime Minister told the Swedish envoy, Björn Prytz, the tale of two frogs who had jumped into a large jar of milk. The pessimist, deciding that escape was impossible, allowed himself to drown. 'The optimist did not wish to perish disgracefully' and kept swimming until, quite unaware, he had churned the milk into butter and thereby saved his life. 'The same will happen,' Churchill concluded, 'to the British Empire.'[1]

Churchill was also a creative fabulist, attaining such mastery of the technique that he was able to turn it back on his foes. Thus a few months after his electoral defeat in 1945, a new Labour MP called Will Nally represented him as a noble but dying stag, the Socialist hounds at his throat and his own backbenchers no better than hogs. Despite 'the pathos and tragedy of the scene' that Nally had painted, Churchill replied, he was unworried by the howls of the curs opposite. He merely expressed the hope that longer experience of a Commons chamber allegedly divided between hounds and hogs would make Nally realize that 'both those branches of the animal kingdom have their virtues'.[2]

Inspired by parables in holy writ, to say nothing of a serpent and an ass scripturally endowed with the power of speech, clergymen were especially fond of animal analogies. William Inge, the 'gloomy Dean' of St Paul's, for example, mocked the efforts of the League of Nations to achieve peace between the wars: 'It is useless for the sheep to pass resolutions in favour of vegetarianism while the wolf remains of a different opinion.'[3] But no ecclesiastic could match the wit and ingenuity of Churchill's allegory in a similar vein. Designed to expose the folly of interwar disarmament, it epitomized the problem, as the historian David Reynolds has recently said, that what was for one country 'a legitimate means of defence was, for others, a blatant instrument of aggression'.[4] Churchill himself described his *jeu d'esprit* as a parable but, with animals as actors, it was really a fable – a classic of its kind:

> Once upon a time all the animals in the Zoo decided that they would disarm, and they arranged to have a conference to arrange the matter. So the Rhinoceros said when he opened the proceedings that the use of teeth was barbarous and horrible and ought to be strictly prohibited by general consent. Horns, which were mainly defensive weapons, would, of course, have to be allowed. The Buffalo, the Stag, the Porcupine, and even the little Hedgehog all said they would vote with the Rhino, but the Lion and the Tiger took a different view. They defended teeth and even claws, which they described as honourable weapons of immemorial antiquity. The Panther, the Leopard, the Puma, and the whole tribe of small cats all supported the Lion and the Tiger. Then the Bear spoke. He proposed that both teeth and horns should be banned and never used again for fighting by any animal. It would be quite enough if animals were allowed to give each other a good hug when they quarrelled. No one could object to that. It was so fraternal, and that would be a great step towards peace. However, all the other animals were very offended with the Bear, and the Turkey fell into a perfect panic. The discussion got so hot and angry, and all those animals began thinking so much about horns and teeth and hugging when they argued about the peaceful intentions that had brought them together that they began to look at one another in a very nasty way. Luckily the keepers were able to calm them down and persuade them to go back quietly to their cages, and they began to feel quite friendly with one another again.[5]

Fables expose foibles and seldom have fabulous beasts been made to give such a brilliant insight into the quirks and infirmities of human nature.

FERRETS, STOATS AND WEASELS

As a boy of sixteen Churchill kept ferrets as pets, once telling his mother that they sent her their love. He clearly liked these lithe carnivores and later admiringly described Lord Beaverbrook, who unearthed secrets with rare sinuosity, as a little ferret. However, ferrets and their mustelid relations had a poor press in Edwardian England. The ferrets, stoats and weasels in *The Wind in the Willows* represented a raucous revolutionary proletariat invading the property of the landed gentry, Toad Hall. And H. G. Wells's novel *Ann Veronica* (1909), a scandalous study of the New Woman, was denounced by the editor of the *Spectator* for describing 'a community of scuffling stoats and ferrets'.[1] Eventually Churchill himself seemed to regard these creatures as vermin.

In 1934 he hoped to nail the bad behaviour of political enemies such as Sir Samuel Hoare 'upon a board, as stoats and weasels are nailed up by gamekeepers'.[2] And in April 1943, as Allied troops finally drove Rommel from North Africa, Churchill delivered this magisterial rebuke to A. P. Herbert, who was an Independent MP for Oxford as well as a pillar of *Punch*:

> I must say that I think 'Punch', in the cartoon this week, pays the Eighth Army a very back-handed compliment by representing it as a squirming little ferret. Considering that the intention was to do them honour, the shot was a very poor one. Nor is the proportion of Montgomery to his Army that between a man and a ferret, and he would be the first to resent it. As a constant reader of 'Punch' over so many years, I think I must tell you that this is the biggest flop since the cartoon of John Bull waking from his wartime nightmare on the very day the Germans marched on Prague.[3]

Actually the cartoon, which was entitled THE DESERT FERRET and did depict a large General Montgomery putting a small ferret labelled '8th Army'[4] down a hole to flush out the remaining forces of the Desert Fox, would almost certainly have flattered Monty's 'peacock vanity'.[5] Perhaps this added to Churchill's annoyance. He did, after all, memorably remark of Montgomery: 'In defeat, unbeatable: in victory, unbearable.'[6]

FISH

C hurchill developed a quite unusual passion for the denizens of his ponds and aquaria, as will be seen, yet he was brought up to be a keen fisherman. Lord Randolph had devoted far more time to angling than appears in his son's biography. He filled his letters with copious accounts of the 'sport', often complaining of what 'bad luck I do have fishing always'[1] but supplying his wife with details of what he did catch. In 1877 he went so far as to send her a telegram with the important news that his father, the Duke of Marlborough, had killed a 25 lb fish. A few months later the infant Winston had his first piscine experience which, as he later wrote, 'made a scar on my mind'.[2] Having almost witnessed the sinking of the naval training ship *Eurydice*, which capsized off Ventnor in a sudden squall with the loss of more than three hundred lives, he was shocked to hear that some of the divers had fainted with terror at seeing fish eating the corpses. Aged eight he struck back, telling his mother that he had caught his first fish by himself.

It was the first of many, as Winston conformed to the customs of his caste and followed in his father's footsteps. Like Lord Randolph, he also grumbled about his lack of success with rod and line. In the autumn of 1927, for example, he cast flies for six wearisome hours without getting a single bite, exclaiming to Clementine: 'Curious creatures of caprice, these salmon!'[3] Churchill did better off California a couple of years later, speedily securing a swordfish weighing 188 lbs. But at Nassau in 1932, he recorded, the fishing was not remarkable though he greatly enjoyed it. And the gift from a well-wisher of the beautiful fishing rod that had once belonged to his 'illustrious ancestor'[4] the Duke of Marlborough, which Churchill accepted with very great pleasure in 1934, scarcely improved his piscatorial fortunes.

At the TRIDENT conference in Washington in 1943, he was pictured with Roosevelt on a fishing expedition at the President's rustic retreat Shangri-La. Roosevelt wrote that the photographs didn't turn out well but at least they proved that 'you and I tried to catch a fish. Better luck next time!'[5] Churchill cared little about this failure since outside the door of his luxury log cabin was a fountain and a pool of clear water 'in which swam a number of large trout, newly caught in a neighbouring stream and awaiting the consummation of their existence'.[6] In any case he was not really angling for fish but for strategic advantage. Churchill wanted the continuation of the Allied assault on the soft underbelly of Europe, though without General Eisenhower's irrelevant designs on Sardinia – 'I absolutely refuse to be fobbed off with a sardine.'[7]

During the war he was sometimes urged to relax from such cares by taking a fishing holiday. Loch Dionard was 'full of unsophisticated salmon and large trout', wrote one enthusiast, and 'it's impossible to think of anything else when fishing'.[8] As another correspondent acknowledged, however, 'Unlike me I'm afraid you get no time to catch a salmon or shoot a grouse – but your bigger game must be much more exciting.'[9] This was true and it pointed to the further truth that Churchill was by no means a complete angler and far from being addicted to what Lord Byron had called that solitary vice.[10]

It was insufficiently creative. Soon after discovering the joys of painting he told Clementine that he was off to the river to catch pictures, which was much better fun than catching salmon. He preferred making a pun to baiting a hook: when his daughter Diana spotted a

Provoking the envy of Californian fishermen, Churchill caught this
swordfish off Catalina Island in just 45 minutes.

turbot he told her not to disturb it. He was more stimulated by being a fisher of men, once holding out two imaginary rods to demonstrate his contention that General Wavell was a tired fish and General Auckinleck a lively one. Churchill was too impatient for riparian recreation. Less trouble than catching fish, he found, was to receive them as gifts in the aristocratic manner – the Duke of Westminster sent one salmon with a note saying, 'His facial expression resembles some of our Hebrew friends that should be undoubtedly taxed in the near future.'[11] There are hints, too, that the mature Churchill, besotted with his domestic fish, was more inclined to empathize with those in the wild. When told that an angler permitted to fish on his lake had lost the only one he had hooked, Churchill commented, 'Well, in that case I am very pleased for the fish.'[12]

All his life, however, he aimed for dramatic results. On vacation while First Lord of the Admiralty before the Great War, he dropped depth charges off the Adriatic coast and directed sailors to drag the bay with a huge net for killed or stunned fish. At Admiralty House, where his berth was a gigantic four-poster bed rising from a sea of gold dolphins and tritons, Churchill engaged in an epic struggle with Lloyd George, Chancellor of the Exchequer, over the naval estimates. The Welsh Wizard, who had earlier invited him to Criccieth for sea-fishing, now accused Churchill, already notorious for immersing body and soul in a single issue, of having become a water creature: 'You think we all live in the sea, and all your thoughts are devoted to sea life, fishes and other aquatic creatures. You forget that most of us live on land.'[13] Churchill won the battle for more warships but lost his job over the Dardanelles disaster. Describing his sensations at being deprived of intensive activity at the Admiralty, he too employed thalassic imagery: 'Like a sea-beast fished up from the depths, or a diver too suddenly hoisted, my veins threatened to burst from the fall in pressure.'[14]

Much marine life Churchill regarded as alien, if not menacing. During the South African war he anticipated Mao Tse-tung's aphorism about guerrillas swimming in the sea of the population by describing the Boer fighter as a fish which lives in the water and belongs to the element. Between the world wars Churchill represented Japan as being caught between the great growling Russian bear and China, an enormous jellyfish stinging poisonously. The latter was both too large and too amorphous to yield to coercion. Echoing Finley Peter Dunne's comic Irish–American character Mr Dooley, Churchill declared that punishing China was like flogging a jellyfish. During the war he complained to the government's chief whip that his huge parliamentary majority behaved like a helpless whale attacked by swordfish, never even giving a lash of its tail. And more than once he equated Britain's foes with the most feared oceanic predator. Faced with unrest on the North West Frontier, he warned, 'To go into the mountains to fight an Afridi is like going into the water to fight a shark.'[15] Faced with a still more powerful enemy in Burma, he elaborated:

> Going into the swampy jungles to fight the Japanese is like going into the water to fight a shark. It is better to entice him into a trap or catch him on a hook and then demolish him with axes after hauling him out on to dry land. How then to deceive and entrap the shark?[16]

In person Churchill was wary of such beasts, though he loved swimming or rather, as described by his daughter Mary, 'floating peacefully like a charming porpoise washed by lucent waves'.[17] When assured that he had only encountered a harmless sand shark at Palm Beach, where he also sported in the water like a porpoise, Churchill replied, 'I want to see his identity card before I trust myself to him.'[18]

On the other hand, Neptune's subjects could be Britannia's allies. Broadcasting to France in October 1940, Churchill memorably remarked, 'We are waiting for the long-promised invasion. So are the fishes.'[19] The fishes also benefited humanity in general. He lauded them for eating mosquito larvae. Even the most exotic species provided food: beside the Nile during the Omdurman campaign Churchill observed that soldiers caught and ate as a great delicacy 'weird-looking creatures with long gelatinous appendages hanging from their jaws and gills, and red and blue flushes on their fins'.[20]

Cod, herring, mackerel and sardines were more prosaic but more vital, and when supplies dwindled during the Second World War

Churchill was much concerned, muttering to himself, 'I shall never eat another sardine.'[21] He wanted trawlers to be released from mine-sweeping duties and gave the order to implement a policy of 'utmost fish'.[22] Yet in the struggle against Nazism he himself reckoned fish insufficiently fortifying. Sent a salmon, he first said, 'That is indeed a magnificent fish: I must have "some of him".' Then he changed his mind: 'No! No! I will have meat. Carnivores will win this war!'[23]

Still, fish clearly nourished the spirit. After the war Churchill aimed to improve the amenities of the south London poor by creating a fountain-filled park for children with lots of ponds full of sticklebacks. Flying fish in particular gladdened the heart of man. Churchill waxed lyrical about a school he saw en route to South Africa in 1899 – 'a flight of glittering birds that, flushed by the sudden approach of the vessel, skim away over the waters and turn in the cover of a white-topped wave'.[24] Over sixty years later he insisted that a flying fish which landed on the deck of Aristotle Onassis's yacht should be quickly returned to the sea, 'or it will die'.[25]

FLIES AND OTHER FLYING INSECTS

C hurchill reckoned flies to be among the 'accessories of martyrdom'.[1] In North Africa, where they teemed in such multitudes as almost to constitute a biblical plague, his repugnance was understandable. It was also general. Of course he could hardly have been expected to manifest the indulgence of Shakespeare's Titus Andronicus towards a poor harmless fly with 'slender gilded wings' and 'pretty buzzing melody';[2] or the sentiment of Laurence

Sterne's Uncle Toby, who released a fly because the world was wide enough for both of them; let alone the idealism of William Blake, for whom a fly's life was as sacred as that of a man. However, like the cruel Emperor Domitian and the gentle philosopher Spinoza, Churchill positively relished killing flies.

Pestered by them in Egypt when he wanted to talk strategy over lunch in December 1943, he swatted a large number with his whisk, each small corpse being conveyed to the mortuary he established near the corner of the table. Irritated again when dining beside Lake Como during a painting holiday in September 1945, Churchill resumed the offensive. As Lord Moran recorded, 'He rose from the table with a mischievous glint in his eyes; then, biting his lip as if he was about to spring on some animal, he raised his napkin and for a moment stood poised, ready to strike, before with a smack he destroyed a fly on the wall.'[3] His companions joined in the hunt and soon there were thirty dead flies laid out in a line. This was an emphatic way of fulfilling one of Churchill's favourite maxims, drolly employed in varying circumstances, to keep the flies off the meat. It hardly comported, though, with his contemptuous dismissal of one general as a useless pupstick who should be swatting flies in his wife's boudoir. Nor was it consistent with his ironical self-characterization when Eden advised him against intruding into the troubled Middle Eastern arena in 1942: 'You mean like a great blue-bottle buzzing over a huge cowpat!'[4]

Churchill was serious about eradicating the tsetse fly, an operation so problematic that he compared it to laying a vampire. This insect, which resembled a horsefly, caused sleeping sickness throughout large swathes of central Africa and, for the benefit of King Edward VII, Churchill gave a melodramatic account of the approved contemporary means of dealing with it. The disease was 'like an old-time wizard's curse. In order that the spell may work, five separate conditions must be present: water, trees, bushes, the tsetse fly & one infected person. Remove any of these, & the charm is broken.' Churchill reported that the Governor of Uganda had undertaken energetic and effective work to destroy the tsetse's leafy habitat and thus eliminate the scourge, which had killed 20,000 people around Lake Victoria alone. Unless a cure could be found for the sickness, however, all those infected would die. 'But when this melancholy harvest has been reaped,' he concluded, 'the field will be clear.'[5]

He was unduly optimistic. Indeed, it is arguable that the remedy he canvassed, the ecologically harmful clearing of trees and shrubs, was worse than the disease; subsequently medical advances have reduced the incidence of sleeping sickness and a more sophisticated campaign has been waged against the tsetse fly. But it has no more been defeated than has the strident-voiced and fever-bearing mosquito, clouds of which disturbed Churchill in Africa with their chorus of ferocious buzzing. He thought that cutting down the bush had also proved effective against these fierce-biting vectors of malaria. Moreover he hoped and expected that the 'police of science',[6] armed with chemical weapons and perhaps assisted by natural allies such as voracious birds and larvae-hungry fish, would eventually triumph over such loathsome little harpies.

Still, they and their ilk did inspire a swarm of vivid images. As a subaltern in Cuba, where Churchill first came under fire, he likened the sound of bullets to the buzz of an offended hornet. As a young Tory MP he compared the opposition to a hornet, 'with the head biting the tail and the tail stinging the head. The brains of the Liberal Party were all in the tail.'[7] Less fancifully he said that the main defence against Zeppelins during the Great War was British aircraft, formidable squadrons of hornets. Irritated by hostile press comments in October 1941, Churchill told Beaverbrook that he had trouble in restraining his combative instincts amid the gadflies of criticism. At the end of March 1943 Churchill commended General George Patton's fine advance, after the Allied invasion of North Africa, on the waist of the Tunisian wasp. Uncompromising aggression was essential, he reckoned, since Britain was fighting a foe who would think as little of obliterating every soul in the country as a gardener would think of smoking out a wasps' nest. Equally ruthless were warriors inspired by religious fanaticism: 'what the sting is to the wasp, the Mohammedan faith was to the Arabs of the Soudan – a faculty of offence or defence'.[8]

He himself was as ruthless with wasps as with flies. Clementine was afraid of wasps and when, soon after their marriage, one settled on her sleeve Winston took it by the wings and thrust it into the ashes of a fire. In 1924 he himself was bothered by a wasp on his plate at Chartwell. '"What!" he cried, "shall I, who advocate beheading Gandhi, be unable to deal with a wasp!" and slew it.'[9] But such creatures were not always hostile. When the American aircraft-carrier USS *Wasp* ferried two batches of Spitfires to the beleaguered island of Malta in 1942, Churchill thanked her Captain and company by telegram: 'Who said a wasp couldn't sting twice?'[10]

FOXES

Like his parents and his clan, Winston Churchill was ardently devoted to fox-hunting. This had become by the time of his birth not just the national sport but a neo-feudal cult, enshrining values of bravery and hierarchy, by which the aristocracy disseminated its influence throughout society. Occasional critics attacked a pastime that fostered snobbery, involved cruelty and was 'founded on a morbid love of slaughter'.[1] It was also imbued with hypocrisy, since landowners justified hunting as pest control but preserved foxes in order to enjoy the chase. But few patricians questioned this rural orthodoxy, certainly not Lord Randolph Churchill, whose sole reading was said to be R. S. Surtees and who would have agreed with the Irish playwright Lord Dunsany that not to hunt the vixen and her mate was 'the certain sign of a fool or an ass'.[2] In early childhood Winston learned to sing 'A-hunting we will go'.

Advancing from donkeys to ponies to horses, he became a bold rider to hounds. Shortly before his twentieth birthday he told his mother

Clementine cuddles a fox cub at Chartwell, though she sometimes wore a fox stole complete with head and paws.

that there was nothing in the world he would 'rather do than hunt – I mean so far as pleasure is concerned'.[3] He was particularly exhilarated by view-hallooing over the springy turf of Leicestershire with the Quorn Hunt on his cousin Sunny's magnificent horses. Having faith in his star, Churchill braved all hazards and never worried about breaking his neck. But he took plenty of tumbles in his eagerness to be in at the death. This was the consummation and climax of the chase – hunting without killing, as Montaigne had said, was like having sexual intercourse without an orgasm. Churchill was not squeamish about the bloodshed. He kept trophies of the sport, thanking his mother for having a brush mounted for him and winning on the toss of a coin 'the sole remaining pad of a very gallant fox' that had given him 'a great gallop of 35–40 minutes'.[4]

Subalterns in the 4th Hussars were encouraged to hunt during the winter months, their superiors echoing the Duke of Wellington's maxim that fox-hunters made the best cavalry officers. But rather than engage in synthetic military exercises, Churchill crossed the Atlantic in 1895 to experience genuine combat with the Spanish Army in Cuba. And although he later hunted foxes in both India and South Africa, he was more excited by the pursuit of human quarry, Pathans and Boers. The latter were far more mobile than the British, as Churchill discovered when they bagged him in Natal in 1899 during the ambush of an armoured train. 'I held up my hand,' Churchill wrote, 'and like Mr. Jorrocks's foxes, cried "Capivy".'[5] After his escape he appealed in the *Morning Post* for more irregular horsemen to catch the elusive foe and demanded to know whether the gentlemen of England were all fox-hunting. His impertinence outraged Clubland and he received a telegram saying, 'Best friends here hope you will not continue making further ass of yourself.'[6] His patrician friends had further cause for complaint before the First World War, when Churchill, in his most radical phase, lamented that the land was monopolized by so few and that so much of it was 'fooled away for foxes and pheasants'.[7]

Revelling in risk, Churchill was delighted to find that the Westminster arena provided him with as many thrills and spills as the battlefield or the hunting field. As the journalist A. G. Gardiner observed, 'He is out for adventure and follows politics as he would follow the hounds. He has no animus against the fox, but he wants to be in "at the kill".'[8] In full rhetorical cry he was willing to mock the sport: adapting (or misquoting) Oscar Wilde's famous epigram about English gentlemen galloping after a fox, he described Lord Curzon's demand to punish the Kaiser in 1918 as 'the inexpressible in pursuit of the uneatable'.[9] He also mocked the High Church master of foxhounds Lord Halifax, who appeased Gandhi as well as Hitler: Churchill said that he was the kind of Christian who deserved to be thrown to the lions and called him 'The Holy Fox'.[10] However, Churchill was seriously opposed to a parliamentary attempt to abolish hunting in 1949, plainly regarding it as a piece of left-wing faddishness that deserved its defeat.[11] The private member responsible for the bill was the Labour representative for Broxtowe, Seymour Cocks – a name positively inviting the comment '… and hear more balls'.[12]

For geo-political reasons, though, Churchill was quite prepared to suppress fox-hunting in West Germany. There it was illegal for horsemen to hunt game with hounds, a prohibition imposed by the Nazis, who deemed the torture of animals (though not, of course, the slaughter of *Untermenschen*) ignoble. But the ban did not apply to British forces after the war and by 1952 they had some fourteen packs hunting in their zone of occupation. Local objections to their activities prompted the Bundestag to propose a new law. The British High Command protested to the War Office and its complaint was backed up by the Dukes of Beaufort and Marlborough, the latter telling Churchill that German shooting interests were being bloody-minded. However this 'grave matter',[13] as Churchill ironically called it, was trivial beside the vital concern of securing full German support for the defence of Europe in the Cold War. 'Do the Germans really object to fox-hunting by British troops in Lower Saxony?' Churchill asked. 'If they do, it should be stopped. You may occupy a country but that does not give you unlimited freedom to indulge in sports which annoy the inhabitants.'[14]

If Hitler, the homicidal opponent of hunting, was a paradox, so too was Churchill, the humane sentimentalist who followed the hounds well into his seventies. It is true that Churchill was a recognizable type not a malign freak of nature. He belonged to what one historian of fox-hunting, Raymond Carr, called 'that strange, peculiarly English, breed: the animal-loving sportsman'.[15]

But Churchill had more affection for Reynard than most. He kept tame fox cubs at Chartwell before the Second World War. After it he refused to trap or shoot wild foxes responsible for slaying many of his beloved black swans, preferring to invest in fox-proof fences, which were ineffective. Of course his self-denying ordinance was a matter of upholding the traditional taboo against vulpicide (killing a fox by means other than the hunt, to which it was consecrated), such a rural abomination that it reduced M'Turk, in Kipling's *Stalky & Co.* (1899), to incoherent fury. Nevertheless Churchill was tender-hearted to a fault: 'I couldn't bear to think the foxes were being hurt.'[16] Contemplating the animal kingdom during the myxomatosis epidemic in 1954, he was inconsolable. He told Clementine, 'All the Chartwell rabbits are dead & now the poor foxes have nothing to eat, so they attack the little pigs and of course have eaten a few pheasants. It is said they will perish & migrate & that then there will be no one to cope with the beetles & rats.'[17] Life without foxes was a gloomy prospect.

FROGS

The frog was a transmuted tadpole with a legendary capacity to turn into a prince, but according to Archie Clark Kerr, Britain's ambassador in Moscow in 1942, Winston Churchill rivalled it in his gift for metamorphosis. He had a priceless ability, even rarer than his mastery of the English language, to transform his features from 'the most laughing, dimpled and mischievous baby's bottom into the face of an angry, an outraged bullfrog'.[1]

Actually Churchill was attracted to these leggy amphibians, though on the Upper Nile he did complain about the 'croaking of innumerable frog armies'.[2] He generally referred to the Gallic race as 'Frogs', to the pain of the occasional anglophone Frenchman who overheard him, but his use of the term, even when preceded by the adjective 'bloody', did not invalidate his essential Francophilia. During the Christmas festivities at Chartwell in 1945, he sat in the front row of a children's marionette show, giving a running commentary on the action and concluding that he had enjoyed the item about a frog and a duck best 'because the frog got away'.[3]

Furthermore one of the most intriguing letters sent to him, preserved among his papers but hitherto unpublished, suggests that he used the word 'frog' as a term of endearment. The letter, a valedictory billet-doux, is dated 1906, two years before Churchill married Clementine Hozier. It was despatched from 9 Air Street, the short passage linking London's Regent Street to Piccadilly, just before the Circus. As the 1911 census shows, this building was an all-female boarding house whose inmates were mostly young hotel staff (perhaps employed by the nearby, newly opened Ritz), among them two chambermaids, a linen maid, a bar attendant, three cashiers and a bookkeeper. It is possible that Churchill's unknown correspondent, who wrote in a good hand and addressed him as 'Dearie', had a similar occupation. Indeed, Winston may have shared his father's opinion about illicit liaisons with servants, which the latter confided to Lady Randolph: 'What does an occasional cook or housemaid matter.'[4]

To be sure, Winston was a romantic not a libertine like Lord Randolph, whose fate he was obviously anxious to avoid. By his own account Winston did not keep concubines in India and he was plainly joking when he described the French château allocated to him in 1918 as 'a little maison tolere' [sic].[5] But it is hard to believe that he came to the altar a virgin. Like many young men of his caste and profession, he probably went through some more or less commercial form of sexual initiation and indulged in one or two discreet *de haut en bas* pre-marital affairs. Certainly Churchill took a robustly Regency view of carnal peccadilloes. He was always partial to women of experience such as Maxine Elliott, Daisy Fellowes and Doris Castlerosse (though the recently revived rumour that the last of these became his 'secret mistress'[6] during the 1930s is ill-founded). Conversely Churchill hated purity campaigners like Mrs Ormiston Chant and in 1894 he led a contingent of Sandhurst cadets to destroy the screens she had erected outside the Empire music hall in Leicester Square in order to segregate playgoers from streetwalkers. Moreover, like other patrician stage-door Johnnies, he fell for a number of beauties on the boards, notably Ethel Barrymore and the dancer Mabel Love. So it seems quite likely that his 1906 correspondent was a demi-mondaine or an actress.

Her note is suggestive though not, alas, conclusive. She expressed the hope of seeing him later in the week because she was going out of town for some time and would probably soon be married:

> ... so this will be the last opportunity of bidding you goodbye. If you cannot see me this week I wonder if you would send me some little keepsake to remind me of the very pleasant hours we have spent together. I have thought so much about you lately and I am about half way through 'Coniston' [the then bestselling novel written, intriguingly, by the American author Winston Churchill, with whom she may have confused his English namesake] which I am enjoying immensely. I had no idea you wrote books, except of course the life of your father, but I am getting all your books now which I shall keep a special place for in my new home. Please let me hear from you as soon as possible and perhaps for the last time.

With his penchant for identifying intimates (and others) as animals, Churchill himself was surely responsible for the subscription of this letter. It was signed, 'Your loving pink frog. M.'[7]

GEESE

lthough geese saved Rome's Capitol, the goose was generally regarded as a silly bird, not least by Winston Churchill. He labelled inept political opponents as geese and in 1954, having inadvertently revealed in a speech to his constituents that he had been prepared to re-arm Germans to fight against the Russians before the end of the Second World War, he acknowledged privately that he had made a goose of himself. During an off-the-record interview in 1943 he took sharp exception to vacillations of the liberal *News Chronicle*: 'It's all over the place! Geese! Geese!'[1] And he habitually referred to the geese he kept at Chartwell as flying fools. What is more, despite his fondness for wildfowl, he did not scruple to foment hostilities between them. As Diana Cooper recorded in 1934: 'The basket of bread on his arm is used first to lure & coax & then as ammunition. The great aim is to get them all fighting. "We must make a policy," he says. "You stone them & we will get the 5 flying fools on their right flank."'[2]

However Churchill did endeavour to fend off alien invaders. From his Chartwell dining-room table during the late 1930s, he witnessed the arrival on the lake of a flight of Embden geese, distinguished by their long necks and large white bodies. '"Oh!" he said indignantly, "Look at those frightful Nazi geese molesting the peace of the swans! This must be stopped at once. Come on."' Grabbing a stick and accompanied by his nephew Johnny, Churchill ran down to the lake. '"You horrible Nazis, get out!" he shouted. "Fetch the gardener, Johnny, and tell him to make a concentration camp for them."'[3] So, amid much hissing and pecking and goose-stepping, the Embden insurgents were rounded up and put in an enclosure.

Churchill demonstrated a proprietorial partiality to his own gaggle in other ways. Evidently he started keeping them at Chartwell in

1928, having received a pair from his cousin's wife Flora Guest, who found geese intensely fascinating and agreed with Churchill's view that these uxorious birds were '*very* modest and very shy, as well as moral'. He acquired additional breeds and gave them appropriate names, christening two Canadian geese Lord and Lady Beaverbrook, and designating another goose his naval aide-de-camp. Churchill grieved when, as often happened, they fell victim to foxes. He took the geese food and treated them as pets. Thus they were not, despite Flora Guest's avowal that 'goslings are *delicious* to eat',[4] for the table – a rule sometimes broken, though Churchill famously refused to carve a goose whom he'd looked on as a friend. During ceremonial visits to the lake he would make a strange honking call which, wrote a witness, attracted 'a bar-headed Canadian goose known to the family as the Flag Lieutenant. Waddling hurriedly across the valley the goose would fall in two or three paces behind his master and march proudly round as he made his tour of the estate.'[5]

Churchill peppered his discourse with anserine allusions: wild goose chases, cooking people's goose, games of Fox and Geese, sauce for the goose being sauce for the gander. He opposed giving too much German territory to Poland in 1945, telling Stalin, 'It would be a great pity to stuff the Polish goose so full of German food that it died of indigestion.'[6] Geese also wandered into the debating chamber. When the opposition booed Churchill during a Commons spat in December 1952, he asked whether booing was in order, prompting a Scottish Labour MP, William Ross, to respond, 'What else can you say to a goose?'[7] The Prime Minister retorted that he had been called worse things than that, afterwards chiding himself for not having thought to reply that he did not object to being called a goose – even at Christmastime.

However, since the word 'goose' had not been deemed unparliamentary language, Churchill opened a second terminological front. He wrote to Ross claiming that he had been guilty of misquotation and citing Swift to show that the correct 'expression is "to say Bo (as in Bo-Peep) to a goose", and not "Boo"'. This was an old bugbear of Churchill's, though he had been known to say 'Boo' himself, and he concluded by asserting that in any case he ought to have been called a gander. Ignoring that weighty point, Ross defended himself with spirit. He quoted earlier authors and Scottish dictionaries which showed that 'Boo', uttered to excite terror, was commonly used. Churchill answered gracefully: 'Your kind letter leaves me in your debt. We shall certainly not quarrel on the differing usage of "Boo" and "Bo" north and south of the Tweed.'[8]

Characteristically Churchill had the last word on the subject of geese. He paid the code-breakers of Bletchley Park, who made such a vital contribution to winning the war, an immortal tribute. They were 'the geese who laid the golden eggs and never cackled'.[9]

GIRAFFES

I n the wild and in captivity the tallest living terrestrial creature naturally attracted Churchill's gaze. He saw the fleet giraffe in the Sudan and observed many of them 'lollopping'[1] [sic] through the bush in Kenya. And he could not miss them in London Zoo or in William Randolph Hearst's private menagerie at San Simeon in California. But, surprisingly, Churchill seems to have found little of personal interest or rhetorical stimulus in these prodigies, which had occupied an elevated place in popular imagination from the time of Julius Caesar, who first introduced one to Rome where it was torn to pieces by lions in the arena, to the reign of George IV, who owned the first live one to land in England, a subject of much curiosity and satire.

Indeed giraffes seem to have appealed to Churchill mainly because of their classical name, camelopards – Romans had regarded them as a hybrid between the ungainly camel and the dappled leopard – and the use his literary hero T. B. Macaulay had made of this exotic word. Leopold von Ranke's *History of the Popes*, Macaulay had famously written, carried one's 'mind back to the times when the smoke of sacrifice rose from the Pantheon, and when camelopards and tigers bounded in the Flavian amphitheatre'.[2] Fascinated by the conceit, Churchill conjured with it more than once: first when he saw the ruins of an ancient civilization in India's Sarai Valley, which prompted the further Macaulayesque consideration that the British Raj itself might eventually be reduced to a 'few scraps of stone and iron';[3] and again when he discovered that Californian redwood trees were old when camelopards first bounded into the Colosseum and might remain vigorous when Macaulay's future traveller from New Zealand stood upon 'a broken arch of London Bridge to sketch the ruins of St Paul's'.[4]

Otherwise Churchill ignored giraffes, which he might have used to illustrate the height of absurdity. Perhaps this was too obvious. Lord Moran, for example, employed the standard simile to describe General de Gaulle: 'an improbable creature, like a human giraffe, sniffing down his nose at mortals beneath his gaze'. Churchill found a more original analogy, one so ludicrous that he denied to a sceptical Moran that he had coined it. He apparently likened the General to 'a female llama who had been surprised in her bath'.[5]

GOATS

With their satanic associations, their priapic reputation and their habit of eating everything in sight, goats have not always been popular. George Orwell, who was inclined towards masochism, once urged the writer V. S. Pritchett to keep these capricious creatures, saying that they would be certain to cause him a lot of trouble and to lose him a lot of money, and getting 'quite carried away as he expounded the "alluring disadvantages" of the scheme'.[1] Churchill himself was initially doubtful about admitting goats to Chartwell, wondering whether they would get on with the other animals, particularly the wallabies, and fearing that it would be almost as complicated as politics. Certainly the political connotations were unfortunate: Lloyd George was nicknamed 'the Goat' because of his satyr-like propensities and Churchill often complained of having been made the scapegoat for the Dardanelles disaster. When he left office at the end of 1915 to fight on the Western Front, Churchill described himself as 'the escaped scapegoat'.[2]

Nevertheless in 1935 he bought two pregnant nanny goats for a pound each from a nearby gypsy encampment: a brown one called Sarah and a white one called Mary. He stationed them around his pool on nibbling duty. Unluckily they nibbled ammonia, used as fertilizer, and Sarah died, but Mary was saved thanks, Churchill said, to a timely dose of castor oil. She flourished, eating the cherry trees to Clementine's annoyance, and produced two kids. They multiplied and before long Chartwell could boast a small brigade of goats. Churchill became extremely fond of these nimble, inquisitive and sociable beasts. But he did not confine his affections to his own herd.

During a writing and painting holiday in Marrakech in December 1950, Churchill ventured into the foothills of the Atlas Mountains where, having settled down in front of a suitable subject for his canvas, he was quickly surrounded by a bevy of goats in the charge of an Arab boy. Since Churchill hated being interrupted at his easel, everyone expected an explosion. Instead he made a fuss of the intrusive

Eisenhower praised Billy's 'soldierly deportment' when Churchill explained that the goat had refused Ike's proffered cigarette since smoking was forbidden on parade.

ruminants, petting them and giving them titbits from his lavish picnic. Over the next few days this became a routine and one amiable black goat emerged as his favourite. By mischance this animal was killed and Churchill's worried entourage felt bound to engage a substitute. But the lookalike refused to act the part and tried to bite the hand that fed it. 'What's wrong with my dear little goat?' Churchill cried. 'We did not dare tell him,' wrote his valet. 'It would have broken his heart.'[3]

In fact he seems to have lost his heart to a cashmere goat, predictably called Billy, a magnificent creature with curving horns and a full beard who was the mascot of the Royal Welch Fusiliers. Due to join President Eisenhower for a summit meeting in Bermuda in 1953, Churchill went to elaborate lengths to ensure that Billy was among those present. Indeed he evidently valued the goat's attendance more highly than that of the third person in the tripartite talks, the French premier. The Prime Minister telephoned his Secretary of State for War, Antony Head, to remind him that he would shortly be attending the conference and the conversation continued as follows:

'You will probably send some troops there for Guards of Honour.'
'Yes.'
'The Welch Fusiliers perhaps.'
'Yes.'
'Ah, I hoped so.'
Pause. Throat clearing.
'They have a very attractive goat with whom I made friends in Jamaica.'
'Yes, Prime Minister.'
'I'd very much like him to come to Bermuda. I would be so much obliged if you could do this for me.'
'Of course, Prime Minister.'
'But he mustn't fly. He should go in a ship, I think.'
'That may be difficult.'
'Well, please try.'
'Of course.'
'Thank you so much my dear boy.'[4]

In the event Churchill had to postpone his departure because on 23 June he suffered a major stroke. Informing Eisenhower, the Prime Minister wrote that in his current state he would be unable to inspect the Welch Fusiliers' Guard of Honour, 'complete with their beautiful white goat, whose salute I am sure you would have acknowledged'.[5]

Churchill slowly recovered and the Bermuda conference was reconvened in December. But it was not possible for Billy to go by sea and the Prime Minister authorized speedier transport as well as cavalier treatment of the quarantine regulations: 'Fumigate the goat and fly it.'[6] Churchill himself made the journey by air, reading during the flight, rather ominously, C. S. Forester's novel *Death to the French* (1932). On arrival he sent Clementine a telegram saying, 'EXCELLENT JOURNEY. ALL WELL. GOAT SPLENDID. LOVE. W.'[7] However his partiality to Billy almost caused a diplomatic incident. Waiting to greet Eisenhower at the airport, the Prime Minister virtually ignored the French premier Joseph Laniel and, it was reported, ostentatiously spent his time caressing the goat.

Churchill was equally disrespectful to Laniel during the summit itself, which proved to be a disappointment. Bitterly conscious of his waning powers and deeply concerned that the post-Stalin Soviet Union possessed the hydrogen bomb, the Prime Minister failed to persuade the President and his Secretary of State Dulles to seek an end to the Cold War. But with the help of Billy he mollified his transatlantic allies, who perhaps recalled Abraham Lincoln's liking for goats. At any rate the Americans were much amused by Churchill's devotion to Billy, especially when he had the animal ceremonially paraded around the dining table during a banquet at Government House. The Prime Minister rewarded his cloven-hoofed friend with a glass of champagne, while the President offered Billy a cigarette, which he rejected. Laniel might have deplored such Anglo-Saxon levity and immaturity. And Dulles clearly regarded Churchill as a case of arrested development: 'In many ways he's just a little Peter Pan.'[8] But Churchill's playing the goat was an expression of urchin mischief that charmed friends and disarmed foes, a gaminerie that defied the years. When the Labour MP Edith Summerskill wished him a happy seventy-fifth birthday, Churchill told her, 'I have never grown up so of course I don't feel old.'[9]

GOLDFISH AND GOLDEN ORFE

As a boy Churchill acquired two goldfish in a bowl and as a man he prized equally their glittering cousins, golden orfe, describing them as wonderful fish. Churchill began to breed both varieties at Chartwell before the Second World War, finding out about 'silver goldfish',[1] taking expert advice, and greeting small fry warmly – 'I told them to eat all that they wish.'[2] In 1938 he stocked his round pond with 1,000 little golden orfe, pale yellow in colour with the occasional dash of red, some of which grew to be well over a foot long. He was very excited about them and correspondingly grateful to Lindemann, who gave him a pair of polaroid glasses so that he could see them better under water. Churchill told his daughter Mary that they owed their existence to the killing of 'the horrible common tenches, pike etc, which would prey on them'.[3]

Evidently golden fish occupied an elevated place in the piscine social hierarchy and in due course Churchill ensured that they were fed on 'high-class maggots'.[4] He had personally encountered a more uncouth strain in 1909 at the Queen's Hotel in his Dundee constituency: 'Yesterday morning I had half-eaten a kipper when a huge maggot crept out & flashed its teeth at me!'[5] But the superior maggots he eventually selected for his fish were sent by rail from Yorkshire in fibre-packed tins at a cost of 22s and 6d a week. '"Aristocratic maggots, these are," he sometimes said. "Look how well the fish are doing on them."'[6]

So keen was Churchill on his new hobby that in September 1939 he rather surprisingly agreed to the request of Stanley Plater, who supplied the decorative fish sold by Harrods, to give 1,000 of them sanctuary at Chartwell while hostilities lasted. Plater said this would afford them a chance to live. And he delivered a mixed variety, mostly different types of goldfish with picturesque names: lionheads, orandas, celestials, calicoes, fantails, veiltails, fringetails, shubunkins, blackmoors, golden comets and golden orfe. Churchill wanted some of the prettiest ones put in the top pool. Plater gave publicity to the whole undertaking, reporting that Churchill called some of his fish by name and burnishing his reputation as a fish fancier.

In August 1942 Churchill had a suggestive misunderstanding with Stalin over goldfish. Visiting Moscow to explain why there would be no second front that year, the Prime Minister was lodged in State Villa No. 7. This was a luxurious, heavily-guarded dacha surrounded by fir trees which was sometimes occupied by Stalin himself, and it contained, among other things, a large glass tank filled with different kinds of goldfish. Churchill assumed that they had been put there as a friendly gesture to him and wondered if he could get food for them. Attempting under difficult circumstances to establish a personal accord with the Soviet leader, he thanked him for the attention and said that he was very fond of goldfish. Obviously baffled, Stalin told Churchill that he was 'welcome to take some for your breakfast'.[7]

This hospitable offer is a piquant illustration of the gulf between the soft-hearted western democrat and the bloodthirsty oriental despot. The former adored those angels of the watery world which, as the poet Harold Monro wrote, moved on golden fins and filled 'their paradise with fire'.[8] The latter saw them as trifles to be snapped up. Apparently, however, goldfish are edible, though when cooked they are said to turn black with surprise. Whatever the truth of this, Churchill continued to treasure his golden fish throughout the war. And he plainly reckoned that the disruption to their lives was yet another count against Nazi Germany. In a letter (marked 'not sent') to the West Country magnate Sir Richard Acland MP, Churchill wrote:

> ... you saw the pains I took to get rid of all the black fish in my
> pool, but this war has upset everything and there are now as
> many black fish as there are red, or perhaps even more. I shall
> have very heavy work after the war to get this pool properly
> cleaned out. On the whole however the fish have done very well,

This affectionate study of Churchill absorbed by his golden horde at feeding time was painted by his nephew Johnny.

considering they get nothing but what they can find on their own. The above is in no way allegorical.[9]

The final sentence was an ironic tilt against the Common Wealth Party, a briefly successful movement favouring public ownership over private enterprise, which Acland had co-founded.

As Prime Minister Churchill took little exercise but occasionally, feeling the need for movement, he did go out to feed his golden fish during the war. And even at its climax they were not far from his thoughts. A couple of weeks before the D-Day landings in Normandy he gave orders that Stanley Plater should 'go down to Chartwell on a hot day and look at the fish. He should be able to get out in the canoe on the middle pool.'[10] On 2 June 1944 Plater reported that the fish were still doing well despite lack of nourishment, though he did warn about the presence of adders around the top pool. Worse than adders were otters, whose depredations in April 1945 left Churchill with but a single goldfish. He was inclined to exonerate the otters, despite the evidence of their tracks, and to blame local gypsies. Much upset, he called in Scotland Yard, which failed to identify the culprits.

After his defeat at the polls three months later, Churchill set about restoring Chartwell's grounds and restocking its waters with fish. As an obvious target for bombers or invaders during the war, the estate had been camouflaged and guarded by barbed-wire entanglements, which had become choked with weeds, briars, brushwood and debris. Ironically, Churchill employed two German prisoners of war to do much of the clearing work around the two pools and the lake, the last of which had been drained for the duration. As they were cleaned up he gave elaborate orders about the disposition of the remaining fish, which he supervised in person, as well as their care, protection and feeding 'till they go to sleep for the winter'.[11] He instructed the head gardener to 'keep a sharp look-out for herons, both at the lake and in the garden pool, and if any appear drive them away'.[12]

Churchill acquired new supplies of golden orfe from Douglas Parbury, who had also worked for Harrods before the war. Satisfying Churchill's taste for brilliant hues, he provided higoi (red carp) and multi-tinted shubunkins as well as large numbers of golden orfe. In 1949, for example, he sold Churchill 150 baby fish for £27 and soon Mary Soames was telling her father that his pool was teeming with them, all eager to bask in his affection – 'at a rough estimate they look like *trillions*!'.[13] Parbury assisted in various other ways. He advised about preserving maggots and obtaining mealworms. Their acquisition was problematic. Churchill apparently refused the offer of free worms from a Dutch supplier who had secretly listened to his broadcasts during the war. But he was understandably dissatisfied with those sold to him by Stanley Plater: 'The worms, which cost more than caviar, are rotting.'[14] Parbury also warned against the use of the insecticide DDT, suggested the purchase of an air pump and helped to segregate predators from prey, part of Churchill's sustained effort to prevent cannibalism in his fishponds.

Furthermore Parbury gave Churchill guidance about breeding and feeding: golden orfe eggs were 'about the size of sago balls.

Other eggs, such as newts, roach, and other vermin, are about a third of this size.'[15] Hatchlings, he said, should not be overcrowded but distributed in about eight available tanks and fed on minute insects (infusoria) and powdered egg. With growth they increased in value, from a few shillings to as much as £6, an accretion about which, as the journalist Malcolm Muggeridge observed, Churchill seemed to wax quite sentimental. Over spawning he invoked the aid of London Zoo: it approved his having waterweeds planted in shallow shingle which, he informed Clementine, offered fish 'attractive glades for their approaching honeymoon'.[16]

Churchill was, in the words of a valet, 'crazy about his fish'.[17] It was a mark of the value he attached to them that he presented Roosevelt with two male and four female golden orfe from the top pool at Chartwell, sending them by air three months before the President's death. And when drought dried up the Chart well, which fed his pools and gave the house its name, he seemed to feel, according to his research assistant Denis Kelly, 'that the spring of his own home life was drying up too'.[18] Churchill was also much upset when his golden orfe became infected with a fungal disease. Each fish had to be caught individually and rubbed with a chemical solution. Churchill mobilized family and workmen, supervised their laborious task and complained that it was taking so long. This was because the nets kept breaking and he was amused when one of his assistants said, 'Give us the tools and we'll finish the job.'[19]

By the 1950s golden fish had become such a key part of Churchill's life as often to divert him from serious work. Going to see them was an established ritual, as visitors who were bidden to accompany him observed. After lunch he would stroll down to summon the gleaming horde, rapping his stick on the paved path and calling out 'Hike, Hike – Hike, Hike'. 'See, they can hear me,' Churchill would exclaim. 'Look how they're all coming towards me.'[20] He would feed them by hand, addressing them as 'Darlings'.[21] Or sometimes, resting on a garden seat, he would throw them the well-bred grubs. Churchill explained to Muggeridge that 'his whole standing with the goldfish depended on their associating the sound of his voice with the provision of maggots'.[22]

'You mustn't give them too many,' he told Denis Kelly, 'because it upsets their insides. It's too rich for them.'[23] When the artist Graham Sutherland pointed out that Churchill was feeding the fish closest to him and neglecting the ones at the back, he drew a characteristic moral: 'Well, that's life, you see. We can't all be communists, we can't all be equal … Their turn will come if they try hard enough.'[24]

Churchill was offered many gifts that were fishy in more senses than one. Anxious not to be exploited, especially for the purposes of advertisement, he accepted only a few, but one that he could not resist was made, a month after his final retirement as Prime Minister, by the owners of the Valetta Fish Hatcheries in north Devon. They had bred 'a scaled fantail goldfish which is now in its third year. The body and fins are pearl coloured except for red-rimmed eyes and a perfect "V for Victory" sign clearly defined in red-gold on its dorsal fin.'[25] In thanking them, Churchill said that he was sure that this goldfish, when put on show in London Zoo, to which he had lent most of his collection, would give great pleasure. As late as 1961 he himself derived pleasure from the present of 'a splendid and virile mate, if that is the word, for my other placid goldfish … he sits beside her on the table in the drawing room'.[26]

Golden fish darted through the flux of Churchill's imagination. One of his best paintings, according to the artist Sir William Rothenstein, was *The Goldfish Pool at Chartwell*. At a portentous moment in Churchill's novel *Savrola*, the dictator Antonio Molara stared into 'the water in which the fat, lazy, goldfish swam placidly'.[27] To write a book at all, Churchill reflected, was to build 'an impalpable crystal sphere' around one's interests and ideas so that 'one felt like a goldfish in a bowl'.[28] As for a speech, nothing enlivened it more than a flash of subaqueous wit. Loftily disregarding his own ancestry, Churchill mocked the great landed magnates who opposed the People's Budget in 1909, one of whom, the Duke of Beaufort, famously wanted to see him and Chancellor of the Exchequer Lloyd George in the middle of twenty couple of dog-hounds. Churchill said that he would not bandy words with dukes: 'It is poor sport, almost like catching goldfish. These ornamental creatures blunder on every hook they see.' Rather than being left gasping on the bank of public ridicule, however, they should be placed gently back in their fountains and if 'a few bright golden scales have been rubbed off … they will soon get over it. They have got plenty more.'[29]

HARES

While Lord Randolph Churchill was an undergraduate at Merton College, Oxford, he assembled his own pack of harriers, consisting of nine couple of hounds managed by a whip dressed in livery. As a sport Lord Randolph ranked harrying hares only just below pursuing foxes. And he gloried in the achievements of the so-called 'Blenheim Harriers', recording in his game book, for example, that in 1868 they killed twenty-nine brace of hare. Winston seems to have preferred shooting to hunting or coursing hares, particularly when he was in the Sudan. Here the leporid was a very different beast from 'our fine English hares', Churchill recorded, 'only, in fact, a dried-up rabbit with long bat ears'. But it was equally agile. One that became the target of officers' guns 'dodged swiftly in and out among the spurts of dust kicked up by the bullets, just like a man under similar circumstances, and so escaped, though without dignity'.[1]

Churchill doubtless witnessed many such skedaddles when shooting hares on the estates of rich friends such as Baron de Forest, another animal-loving hunter, with whom he stayed at Eichhorn in Moravia before the First World War. He certainly did so at Blenheim, where he once took a potshot at a hare some 80 yards away, causing fur to fly but the animal to flee with still greater celerity. A guest asked why he had fired when the hare was well out of range. 'Young man,' Churchill replied, 'I wished that hare to understand it was taking part in these proceedings.'[2]

Since this creature was so elusive, Churchill quite took the point of Admiral Fisher's characteristic maxim illustrating the need for British warships to be speedier than their prey: 'Do remember the receipt for jugged hare in Mrs. Glasse's Cookery Book! *First catch your hare!*'[3] Actually this old saw was apocryphal. But that did not stop Churchill repeating it on suitable occasions. He did so to Eden late in 1942, for example, in order to justify his refusal to consider the Foreign Office's 'speculative studies'[4] about global reconstruction after the defeat of Hitler. Churchill had a taste for potted wisdom as well as for jugged hare and the creature served him well rhetorically. During the 1922 controversy about selling honours he said that Lloyd George was as timid as a hare; in 1923 he dubbed a newly protectionist Stanley Baldwin the March Hare; and in 1926 he tried to demonstrate his own steadiness as Chancellor by conjuring with the race between the hare and the tortoise. Churchill's foes retaliated in kind, accusing him of initiating hare-brained schemes and following dialectical hares into the wilderness.

Frisky and frolicsome, hares make delightful pets – as no one revealed more charmingly than the poet William Cowper, who kept three of them, Puss, Bess and Tiney, in his house at Olney. While skiing in the Tyrol in 1937, Churchill's youngest daughter Mary became fascinated by the gambols of snow hares, which discarded their brown 'smoking suits' in winter for coats of 'pure white'. She told her father that it 'would be such fun to have a hare at Chartwell'.[5] There is no evidence that her aspiration was gratified or that Churchill's house became home to so much as a leveret.

HEDGEHOGS AND PORCUPINES

Churchill seldom made rhetorical use of these mammals, a surprising omission since their spiny armour invited sharp phrase-making. With a little help from Shakespeare he did show what could be done in 1927, asserting that Liberal parliamentary candidates would sprout from the Lloyd George Fund, which had grown fat on the sale of honours 'like quills upon a fretful porcupine'.[1] More memorably, in 1943, Churchill said that conquering Burma was 'like munching a porcupine quill by quill'.[2] The image was perhaps even more graphic than his similar simile – that taking on the Japanese Army in the Burmese jungle was like going into the water to fight a shark. Elaborating on the theme during the Cold War, Churchill stressed the need for barbed defences against airborne attacks: 'Our country should suggest to the mind of a potential paratrooper the back of a hedgehog rather than the paunch of a rabbit.'[3]

In person Clementine, who was once said to have no opinions only convictions, bristled easily, and she told her husband that if unloved she would 'become like the prickly porcupine'.[4] Churchill too was capable of impaling both friend and foe. But his disposition was much less spiky, more akin to that of Kipling's Stickly-Prickly Hedgehog or even Beatrix Potter's Mrs Tiggy-Winkle. Alan Brooke painted an endearing picture of him arriving at Besançon in the winter of 1944, 'completely frozen and almost rolled up on himself like a hedgehog'. Under the influence of brandy and hot-water bottles, the Prime Minister thawed out and went on to make a speech in his idiosyncratic French that was 'indescribably funny'.[5]

HIPPOPOTAMUSES

ippos, Churchill wrote, were the scourge and terror of the Nile. Aggressive and unpredictable, they wallowed in the water with only their noses, ears and eyes visible, peeping from the depths like giant cats. Being almost indistinguishable from floating pieces of vegetation, they caused many deaths among native fishermen, whose frail canoes were 'crumpled like eggshells in the snap of enormous jaws'. On his African journey in 1907 Churchill yearned to kill a hippopotamus, drifting downstream among the herds in his steam launch to get the chance of a shot. 'One great fellow,' he recorded, 'came up to breathe within five yards of the boat, and the look of astonishment, of alarm, of indignation in his large, expressive eyes – as with one vast snort he plunged below – was comical to see.' Churchill did fire at another, which sank 'with a harsh sort of scream and thud of striking bullet'.[1] But he was unable to find the carcass.

Churchill therefore regarded the river horse in its own realm as the embodiment of brutality, right down to its skin. From this was fashioned the kourbash, the hippo-hide whip freely employed in Egypt and elsewhere in the region as an instrument of tyranny. Although Churchill always favoured the use of the birch and even seemed to share General Smuts's penchant for the sjambok, he declared sententiously in youth that 'patriotism does not grow under the "Kourbash"'.[2] At home, however, he invoked the pachyderm as a symbol of strength rather than savagery. Thus on 9 May 1945 Churchill saluted the population of London which, when facing the Nazi onslaught, had proved indomitable, 'like a great rhinoceros, a great hippopotamus'.[3]

When swimming in later life Churchill himself irresistibly suggested a hippo. Seeing him in the warm, blue, Florida ocean in January 1942, his doctor wrote: 'Winston basks half-submerged in the water like a hippopotamus in a swamp.'[4] Observing him in the sea at Hendaye in July 1945, just after his defeat at the polls, Jock Colville noted that he floated 'like a benevolent hippo, in the middle of a large circle of protective French policemen who had duly donned bathing suits for the purpose'.[5]

HORSES

Winston Churchill's lifelong love of horses stemmed from both sides of his family. Leonard Jerome, his maternal grandfather, had a passion for mettlesome thoroughbreds and was 'an artist with the reins'.[1] The Blenheim stables contained magnificent beasts and both Winston's parents were ardent riders, for whom hunting was not so much a sport as a creed. Lord Randolph ensured that Winston grew up in the saddle, as befitted a scion of the nobility. He advanced from trotting donkey to cantering pony and aged ten he rode for an hour three days a week. Soon he straddled larger steeds, among them (in 1891) a French cob with a hogged mane, a taste for biscuit and 'lots of pluck'.[2] To augment the training at Sandhurst, his father paid for Winston to have extra riding lessons with the Royal Horse Guards at Knightsbridge Barracks, and he eventually came second in the Military College's riding examination. Being a skilled equestrian was, he later wrote, one of the most important things in the world.

At Sandhurst (1893–4) his greatest pleasure came from horses. With his fellows, he hired hacks from a local livery stable, organized point-to-points, rode in steeplechases and hunted whenever he could. A reckless cavalier, he was always happier to dig in the spurs than to tug on the bit. Fatalistic about the dangers, he reckoned that breaking one's neck at full tilt was a good way to die. He suffered a series of falls. In September 1894 he came to grief after cornering too fast during a paperchase, but he was not hurt despite being galloped over and told his mother how much he loved this kind of riding. A few months later he reported that 'I have had the misfortune to smash myself up, while trying a horse on a steeple chase course'.[3] The animal refused a jump and swerved, nearly breaking Winston's leg and leaving him bruised and sore. Characteristically, he made the most of such exploits. He informed his mother that they demonstrated his need for better mounts and solicited not only cash but harness, bridles, saddles and 'horse furniture of any kind'.[4] He was also gratified by the boost to his reputation for courage, remarking after the steeplechase mishap that he was sure he had made a very good impression.

Winston's prime motive for wanting to join a cavalry regiment was the 'increased interest of a "life among horses"'.[5] And although Lord Randolph opposed his son's preference on grounds of expense, one of his last remarks to Winston (before his premature death on 24 January 1895) was: 'Have you got your horses?'[6] He had indeed. For service in the 4th Hussars the new subaltern equipped himself with one horse, two official chargers, a couple of hunters and a string of polo ponies. At Aldershot with this centaur regiment he experienced a kind of equine apotheosis: 'One hears "horse" talked all day long, in his every form & use.'[7] Churchill was responsible for the feeding and grooming of all his squadron's mounts, nearly a hundred of them. He received instruction in 'hard, regular, machine-like' cavalry drill, delighting in the intricate evolutions of the 'strong, long-tailed chargers with their shell-bridles, their shabraques [decorated saddle cloths], and their plumes'.[8] He also underwent a still more rigorous equitation course, learning to mount and dismount a bare-backed horse at speed and to jump a high bar without saddle or stirrups or even hands. So stiff that he had to write lying down, Winston told his mother: 'The riding is very severe and I suffer a good deal of pain from the muscles of my legs being swollen.' There was no option but 'to go on and ride it off'.[9]

The expertise he gained stood him in good stead during his subsequent military adventures. In 1895 he saw action with a Spanish cavalry column attempting to crush a rebellion in Cuba. Posted to India, he raced his horses and became a champion polo player. Hunting for glory and for medals with the Malakand Field Force on the North West Frontier in 1897, Churchill rode his grey pony up and down the skirmish lines within range of Pathan *jezails* (long-barrelled muskets) while everyone else was taking cover. And at the battle of Omdurman the following year he participated, with the 21st Lancers, in the last great cavalry charge in English history. Here he witnessed not only human bloodshed but horses streaming and staggering from the dreadful gashes inflicted by Dervish spears and scimitars. In the mêlée riders clung to their saddles for dear life and Churchill realized that 'the first weapon of the cavalryman is his horse'.[10]

He had comparable hair-breadth escapes during the Boer War, in which he acted as well-paid correspondent of the *Morning Post*, later combining this role with that of unpaid lieutenant in the South African Light Horse, an irregular corps commanded by Colonel Julian Byng. The two roles were sometimes at odds. In print Churchill recorded that he joined two cavalry squadrons which brushed aside the last Boers besieging Ladysmith and, after a thrilling gallop across hills, over boulders and through scrub, met a score of tattered men on the picket line, some cheering, others weeping. In fact, he arrived some hours after Lieutenant-Colonel Gough, at the head of the main relief column, had entered the town and 'the public celebrations were over'.[11] But although Churchill's reporting was sometimes imaginative, the perils he faced were real. He often came under fire on the veldt. During one skirmish his brother Jack was wounded right beside him. On another occasion Churchill was unhorsed after losing a race with the Boers to capture a *kopje* (a small hill), only to be saved when a trooper gave him a stirrup and rode him to safety amid a hail of explosive bullets, one of which hit their 'gallant beast'.[12] Churchill was supremely exhilarated by this horseman's war, fought, he considered, against the finest mounted warriors since the Mongols.

Horses continued to play a key part in his life after he was elected to parliament in 1900. It is true that he then acquired a horseless carriage, a red 10-horsepower Mors. But although Churchill favoured the automobile as a vehicle of progress and soon came to regard horse-soldiering (with its antiquated ironmongery) as obsolete, he drove his own cars like a cavalryman, occasionally using the pavement to overtake slowcoaches, and regretted the triumph of the petrol engine over the noble quadruped.[13] He spent much of his leisure on horseback, hunting, playing polo, cantering about the countryside, jogging along Rotten Row in Hyde Park. He derived unparalleled

Churchill called this four-month-old filly 'Darling' and no image better captures his lifelong hippophilia.

excitement from pig-sticking in Africa. And he revelled in chasing wild boar in Normandy on the Duke of Westminster's splendid steeds. One of them, which Churchill rode down a precipice of sand, along the shore and into the surf up to his hocks, was an 'enormous black English hunter with a head and shoulder which made you feel as if you were on the bridge of a battle-cruiser'.[14]

The seventeenth-century traveller Fynes Moryson had described England as a 'hell for horses'[15] and cruelties remained in Churchill's time, which he attempted to alleviate. Before the Great War he helped to improve the lot of pit ponies. After it he expressed outrage at the plight of legions of British Army horses 'left in France under extremely disadvantageous conditions'.[16] He condemned the complete failure of the Ministry of Shipping to rescue them and got extra vessels allocated to the task, repatriating the warhorses at a rate of 9,000 a week. Moreover, the ills that horseflesh was heir to permeated Churchill's discourse. The world in 1938, he said, resembled a tired old horse trying to graze peacefully by the roadside only to find a new master to flog it a bit further along. Dictating into the small hours during the war, he told an exhausted secretary: 'We must go on like the gun-horses, till we drop.'[17] Thanks to the Socialist government, he remarked in 1947, the workhorse pulling the British economy out of the mire had been 'bitted and bridled and hobbled and haltered till he can hardly move'.[18]

Equine images and adages sprang from his brain like mustangs. In 1909 he devoted almost an entire speech to demonstrating that the very large stable of arguments in favour of tariff reform contained not a single winner. Appointed Minister of Munitions in 1917 despite the Dardanelles disaster, he was grateful to Lloyd George for 'bringing me a fresh horse when I was dismounted'.[19] Recruiting T. E. Lawrence to assist him at the Colonial Office in 1921, Churchill managed, as he put it, to saddle and bit the maverick war hero.[20] Having been urged by his father to work like a dray horse at military studies, Churchill afterwards lamented his lack of a university education and said in 1929 that he was 'a pack-horse that had to nibble and browse'.[21] In the 1930s he likened India under firm but benevolent British rule to a well-conducted team of coach horses which go along beautifully, happily and in a most elegant manner.

During the Second World War, he urged that cavalry regiments should be converted into armoured forces, saying that it was 'an insult to the Scots Greys and Household Cavalry to tether them to horses'.[22] But despite mechanization, which by no means entirely superseded horse power during this conflict, Churchill still thought in equine terms. He warned that consultation impeded action and that the Allies faced the well-known danger of having more harness than horse. Conversely, yet also to promote the offensive spirit, he extolled ancient warriors who slit the throats of their steeds before going into battle in order to remove the means of retreat. In October 1943 he told Roosevelt that commanders should be appointed to oversee preparations for the D-Day landings because 'The eye of the master maketh the horse fat.'[23] As late as 1948 the American journalist Stewart Alsop recorded this Churchillian pronouncement, made over lunch at Chartwell:

> 'America,' he said slowly, 'America is like a great and powerful
> horse in harness, pulling the rest of the world up the hill
> to peace and prosperity.' He paused, and puffed at his cigar.
> 'America – a great and noble country.' Then suddenly he turned
> and looked hard at me. His voice rose: 'But will she stay the
> course?'[24]

It was an innocuous analogy but Churchill would not allow Alsop to repeat his doubt in print.

Winston Churchill was a charger. Snorting and stamping and straining at the bit, he bestrode the world at war like a Bucephalus. During the first air raid on London he was seen staring 'up into the sky like a warhorse scenting battle'.[25] Later he was compared to the horse in Job: 'He paweth in the valley, and rejoiceth in *his* strength: he goeth on to meet the armed men.'[26] Stalin called him 'the old war-horse'.[27] As the years advanced, though, Churchill became less bellicose, more mellow. He took up racing as a serious hobby. He talked confidentially to his horses. He gave the old grey pony at Chartwell its daily bread.

He stroked the two sculpted horses in the alcove on the landing outside his study, a rampant stallion poised to cover an eager mare, saying appreciatively: 'Sex in bronze.'[28]

HYENAS

Churchill took the common view that hyenas were cowardly scavengers whose laughter was a hideous travesty of human mirth. Actually they are formidable predators, killing nearly all their prey, standing up to lions and leopards on occasion, and communicating with other members of their matriarchal clan by means of yelps, whoops and howls. During the South African war these sounds reminded British troops of the skirl of Boer machine-guns and Churchill overheard one Tommy warning another that '"we'll have that —— laughing hyena" (the Vickers-Maxim gun) "let off at us in a minute".'[1] On the savannah as on the veldt, he saw no reason to change his opinion that these brutes were loathsome vermin living off putrescent carcasses. Finding one at the scene of a kill carried out by a lion he was hunting, Churchill drew the stock contrast between the king of beasts and the filthy hyena.

With such a reputation hyenas became a staple of Communist vituperation, along with jackals and running dogs, not so much creatures of myth as figures of speech. Maybe for this reason Churchill seldom employed 'hyena' as a term of abuse, reserving it for the denunciation of quite exceptional foulness. He was indeed quite prepared to turn the insult back on the Bolsheviks after the Great War, arguing for aggressive measures since they became very 'dangerous the moment they think you fear them. It is like taming a tiger – or rather a mangy hyaena!'[2] He condemned Poland, which in October 1938 snapped up morsels of Czechoslovakia left by Nazi Germany, for its hyena appetite. Broadcasting soon after the victory at El Alamein in 1942, the Prime Minister said that he had tried to keep Mussolini neutral but the hyena in his nature broke all bounds of decency and even common sense. Writing to General MacArthur in July 1943, perhaps with a touch of irony, he reckoned that once Stalin had finished tearing the guts out of the German Army he would declare war on Japan, 'whose hyena attitude he has thoroughly understood'.[3]

Churchill also exploited the fabulous potential of hyenas. He illustrated the danger of counting chickens before they were hatched (a failing to which he himself was prone despite his belief that we are all puppets of fate) with the story of the 'man who sold the hyena's skin while the beast lived [and] was killed in hunting it'.[4] He also condemned mockery of the League of Nations for its vain endeavours to prevent war. The 'crazy glee' of one critic over the failure of international arbitration reminded Churchill of what Thomas Carlyle had described as 'the laugh of the hyena on being assured that, after all, the world is only carrion'.[5]

INSECTS OF THE CREEPING KIND

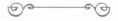

While inspecting British defences against a possible German invasion in 1940, Churchill was intrigued to see a platoon of Grenadier Guards constructing a sandbagged machine-gun post in one of the kiosks on Brighton Pier where, as a boy, he had admired the antics of performing fleas.

This nostalgic memory apart, he generally felt revulsion for fleas, lice, beetles, spiders, cockroaches, earwigs, centipedes, scorpions and 'other odious, crawling creatures'. He encountered many of them in the Sudan, where they 'held the ground against all comers'.[1] And in Uganda he took special care to protect himself against their onslaught, wearing long boots and shaking them out each morning in case they harboured a scorpion or 'a perfectly frightful kind of centipede'. Such precautions were especially needful to guard against the *Spirillum* tick, which waited in ambush beside paths 'like a tiny footpad'.[2] As Churchill told King Edward VII, many British colonial officers had been 'struck down by these tiny pests with an intermittent fever of the most cruel severity'.[3]

After his fall from grace over the Dardanelles, Churchill took command of the 6th Battalion Royal Scots Fusiliers on the Western Front in January 1916, promptly assembled his officers and declared war on lice. This announcement, wrote Captain A. D. Gibb, 'inaugurated such a discourse on *pulex Europaeus*, its origin, growth, and nature, its habitat and its importance as a factor in wars ancient and modern, as left one agape with wonder at the erudition and force of its author'.[4] Measures were duly taken for the extermination of these parasites which, though disagreeable, proved effective. Thereafter Churchill was not much troubled by lice, though a sow at Chartwell did suffer from an infestation and he attributed a certain itchiness he felt during the Second World War to lice or fleas he'd picked up in Egypt. But he did not scorn lousy verbal games. Churchill called Saint-Jean-de-Luz, a seaside resort he visited in south-west France, St John of Lice (though he might more aptly have termed it Saint-Jean-de-Puces). And using Pelmanism to aid his memory as an old man, he tried to fix the name of the Tory MP Charles Waterhouse in his mind by repeating 'water-louse'.[5] In the same vein he referred to the Liberal MP Walter Roch as 'Mr Cockroach'.[6]

Although the Sudan was plagued by all kinds of biting, crawling and stinging insects, Churchill recognized that none did so much damage as locusts. He wrote vividly about the successive swarms that had descended on that country's impoverished soil during the 1890s:

'The multitude of their red or yellow bodies veiled the sun and darkened the air, and although their flesh, tasting when roasted like fried fish, might afford a delicate meal to the natives, they took so heavy a toll of the crops that the famine was prolonged and scarcity became constant.'[7] Thus Churchill as Chancellor damned ministries keen to spend money on health and education for browsing onwards like a horde of injurious locusts. More judiciously, in 1936, he pounced on the biblical expression 'the years that the locust hath eaten', describing it as perhaps 'the most vivid of all metaphors',[8] to characterize the time wasted by the National Government when it should have been arming Britain against Nazi Germany. In a flaming parliamentary indictment of its barren record, Churchill said that he would not 'pry too closely in search of the locusts who have eaten these precious years'.[9] But he was clearly pointing at Ramsay MacDonald and Baldwin, whose administration had gnawed away the country's power and will to resist Hitler. Churchill was so enamoured of this insect analogy that he entitled his speech 'The Locust Years' and used the phrase not only as a chapter heading in the first volume of his account of *The Second World War* but also in his *History of the English-Speaking Peoples* – to describe the period after the battle of Waterloo. He was also drawn to the comparison when Hitler invaded Russia, depicting the 'dull, drilled, docile, brutish masses of the Hun soldiery plodding on like a swarm of crawling locusts'.[10]

Similarly, when facing opposition inside his constituency party in the spring of 1939 over his stand against appeasement, Churchill borrowed the famous image that Edmund Burke had used to denigrate English defenders of the French Revolution:

> Because half a dozen grasshoppers under a fern make the field
> ring with their importunate chink, whilst thousands of great
> cattle, reposed beneath the shade of the British oak, chew the
> cud and are silent, pray do not imagine that those who make
> the noise are the only inhabitants of the field ... or that, after
> all, they are other than the little, shrivelled, meagre, hopping,
> though loud and troublesome, insects of the hour.[11]

Later in the same year Churchill's chief local critic, Colin Thornton-Kemsley, wrote to him saying that Churchill had been right and that he himself was not proud of having made the field ring with his importunate chink – a mea culpa he later repeated in print.

Churchill had cheerfully likened distant British patrols in the Tugela Valley to beetles on a green baize cloth. He took a quizzical interest in exotica such as the praying mantis, describing it as the 'Kaffir God'. And he sometimes waxed light-hearted about creepy-crawlies. When rebuked by Lord Halifax early in the Second World War for speaking publicly about foreign affairs without consulting the Foreign Office, Churchill flicked a note to him across the Cabinet table saying, 'Asking me not to make a speech is like telling a centipede to get along and not to put a foot on the ground.'[12] However, he took seriously the prospect of 'entomological warfare'.[13] Warned in 1941 of unexplained (and almost certainly accidental) infestations of Colorado beetles, striped, fecund, voracious creatures which preyed on potatoes and might presage a six-legged Nazi invasion, he authorized a programme of defensive measures. The Germans suspected that these measures were offensive, which prompted them to start breeding their own Colorado beetles. Nothing eventuated in Europe thanks, perhaps, to Hitler's phobia about bacteria, but Churchill soon learned of Japan's disseminating cholera through China with bombs full of infected flies, which can only have increased his detestation of insects in general. He summoned them up to express repugnance. As a young man he had loathed being incarcerated by the Boers and said that in prison the hours crawled by like paralytic centipedes. Soon after becoming Prime Minister, Churchill confided to Jock Colville: 'I never hated the Germans in the last war, but now I hate them like … well, like an earwig.'[14]

JACKALS

During a comic but vitriolic parliamentary exchange in 1884, as Winston Churchill gleefully recorded in his biography of his father, Joseph Chamberlain described one of Lord Randolph's political allies, Sir Henry Drummond Wolff, as his jackal. Lord Randolph immediately asked whether it was in order for one member of the House to apply this term to another and the Speaker ruled it acceptable if used as a 'figurative expression'.[1] Lord Randolph took this as licence to indulge in beastly name-calling of his own and during the ensuing debate it was suggested that radicals might refer to their opponents as hyenas.

Certainly jackals and hyenas were linked in the public mind, an association reinforced by Kipling's *Jungle Book*, which classified both animals as despicable scavengers. Tabaqui the Jackal was especially obnoxious, prone to hydrophobia, rooting through village rubbish heaps for offal and fawning on Shere Khan the Tiger for scraps. Churchill, who hunted jackals with the Duke of Westminster's hounds in the shadow of Table Mountain, swallowed the stereotype whole. In the Sudan he defined the 'ragged crew of "friendlies"', irregular native forces lurking behind Kitchener's lines ready 'to turn a defeat into a rout or a victory into a massacre', as 'the jackals of an army'.[2] As a rising Edwardian politician, he attacked the jackal tribe of jingo newspapers and deplored election contests in which the Liberal candidate had to fight the Protectionist Tiger while a Socialist Jackal was snapping at his heels. In 1922 he damned the Industrial Workers of the World (IWW or 'Wobblies') for feeding off the Irish troubles: they were a jackal rabble, he said, preying on all the combatants in any disturbance or revolution. In 1942 he told Lord Selborne that it had been the genius of Britain over 400 years to align itself with the second-strongest Continental power, thus avoiding the fate of the jackal who goes hunting with the tiger.

Like American and Australian vilifications of, respectively, the coyote and the dingo, these were familiar shafts: conservatives identified jackals with jacquerie while radicals dubbed imperialists Union Jackals. However Mussolini, the jackal who did go hunting with the tiger, afforded Churchill the opportunity of injecting new verve and venom into the analogy. No doubt he was piqued because the Duce, by invading Ethiopia and allying with Nazi Germany, demonstrated that Churchill's initial admiration for him had been hopelessly misguided. But by attacking France in 1940, at the moment when Hitler seemed poised to devour the whole country, Mussolini displayed the classic attributes of the scavenger – greed and opportunism. Anyway Churchill several times deployed the image, doing so on 27 April 1941 with visible relish:

> This whipped jackal, Mussolini, who to save his own skin has made all Italy a vassal state of Hitler's Empire, comes frisking up at the side of the German tiger with yelpings not only of appetite – that can be understood – but even of triumph.[3]

The last day of the jackal, 28 April 1945, was suitably ignominious and Churchill's sole comment was, 'A bloody beast is dead.'[4]

JAGUARS

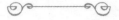

Despite their grace and strength, jaguars seldom stalked through the torrid zone of Churchill's imagination. They were indigenous to the New World and when depicting embodiments of ferocity he tended to fix on more familiar beasts from the jungles of the British Empire, such as tigers and leopards. However the American big cat did spring to his mind when his own Kat, Clementine, indulged in occasional bouts of savagery. She disliked Winston's friend F. E. Smith, a cavalier Tory who encouraged him to drink and gamble (not that he needed encouragement), and on one occasion she subjected Smith to 'a most fearful mauling'. With rueful admiration Churchill remarked, 'She dropped on him like a jaguar out of a tree!'[1]

More comically Churchill resorted to this animal analogy when praising R. A. Butler for having made significant economies as Chancellor of the Exchequer in July 1952. Butler was now 'a contented cat purring over a substantial meal', said Churchill, whereas after the Tories had come into office he had been a 'ravenous jaguar … prowling around our spending Departments in search of prey'.[2] Here was a wonderfully incongruous image, more fanciful even than Rebecca West's 'Jaguar' nickname for H. G. Wells. It concealed both the caution of the Prime Minister's current economic policy and the innate timidity of his Chancellor. Considering that Rab was an old appeaser whom he had reprimanded for favouring a compromise peace as late as June 1940, Churchill by no means regarded him as jaguar, always speaking of him as 'Rabbit Butler'.[3]

KANGAROOS

Churchill never went to Australia but he antagonized its populace in both world wars – by instigating the Gallipoli invasion and by sending Australian reinforcements to doomed Singapore – and he attempted several times to build bridges to the island continent via animal diplomacy. Actually he seems to have been more attracted to the weird creatures down under than to the colonial inhabitants, whose convict and Irish antecedents he dwelt on in his *History of the English-Speaking Peoples*. He gave a perfunctory account of their development in a single Antipodean chapter, remarking that its interest would be increased by referring to the unique character of the animals, such as the kangaroo and the platypus, and to the introduction of new species like the rabbit which 'played the devil with the balance of the local fauna'.[1]

Churchill was charmed when Clementine telegraphed him from New South Wales in 1935 with the news that she had purchased a pair of black swans, an opossum and two wallabies. He responded, 'MENAGERIE WELCOME.'[2] Still more welcome was the Australian gift of two white kangaroos after the Second World War. Deciding that their official presentation to him should receive wide publicity, Churchill bizarrely suggested that he might be photographed like a joey in a pouch. Certainly there should be newsreel cameras, he said, and 'I will make a short speech to the Kangaroos.'[3]

Churchill disregarded the warnings of his staff about the hazards of accepting these albino marsupials. He was gratified by the sentiments of the Livestock Owners' Association of South Australia, which offered them in May 1945 as 'a gesture of esteem and appreciation of his inspiring leadership of the Empire during the dark days of the threatened invasion of Britain by the Germans and during the war

Churchill was fascinated by Australia's exotic fauna and sketches of kangaroos exist which he apparently doodled during the war.

period since'.[4] He recognized that the kangaroo was emblematic of Australia and indeed referred to Australian leaders such as Dr Herbert Evatt as kangaroos. He also appreciated the rarity of this pair – they were said to be the only perfect white kangaroos in the world – and he hoped that they would settle down happily in Britain. However when the kangaroos arrived, in 1946, they were in poor condition because their steamship had broken down en route. At London Zoo they were housed in a 'warm sanatorium'[5] but within a few months the female, christened Matilda, was killed in a fight with another kangaroo. Churchill was much upset as he had not found an opportunity to meet the couple. Instead he was given the skin of the ill-fated Matilda, cured by the zoo's superintendent Dr Geoffrey Vevers, which had a very pleasant silky texture.

The male white kangaroo, who was called Digger, flourished for a time though its owner regretted that he had to live without a mate.

On 10 September 1947 Churchill was formally introduced to Digger during a presentation ceremony at the zoo and was afterwards filmed feeding him in a somewhat gingerly fashion. In April 1948 Vevers suggested that Digger might spend the summer at Chartwell, where it could subsist on a diet of hay, oat, carrots and a little bran. Churchill was delighted by the idea: 'It would be lovely to have it down here for a little. It could go in the orchard.'[6] However, Digger's health deteriorated in captivity and by February 1949 he was in such a parlous state that the zoo put him out of his misery, reporting to Churchill that 'as with all white albinos, your kangaroo was not very strong and was not a very good specimen'. 'I am grieved at the loss,' Churchill said. 'He is to have a burial – in Westminster Abbey.'[7]

No such interment took place and when the zoo proposed to cremate Digger's body, keeping his head for scientific research, Churchill said that they could do what they liked. Personally and politically, he was disappointed by the outcome of this promising initiative. Characteristically he made the best of it, extolling the achievement of the hopping prodigies. In a letter to Sir Charles McCann, Agent General and Trade Commissioner of South Australia, Churchill stated that the white kangaroos had died 'after giving a great deal of pleasure, as a great curiosity, to thousands of visitors to London Zoo'.[8]

LADYBIRDS

Churchill excluded the ladybird from his anathemas against insects, delighting in its infantile associations, its colourful livery and its auspicious reputation, to say nothing of its appetite for aphids. The nursery rhyme whirred into his head as he contemplated the difficulties of driving the Japanese out of Burma. As ever, he preferred an indirect method. Britain should wait until Russia declared war on its eastern neighbour and then establish airbases near Vladivostok from which to bomb Japan, meanwhile singing to her forces overseas, 'Ladybird, ladybird, fly away home, your house is on fire and your children at home!'[1]

In more kindly vein, Churchill supervised the liberation of a ladybird which Antony Head had rescued from the floor of the Commons' division lobby. He instructed Head to put it out of the window in the Chancellor's office and to let him know the outcome. Head returned to find the PM in conference with the French foreign minister, whose basest suspicions must have been aroused by his report: 'She escaped. I let her out through Macmillan's window. Nobody touched her.' 'Good, good!'[2] boomed Churchill.

He was equally benign on his seventy-fifth birthday. Lying in bed, surrounded by acolytes such as Generals Ismay and Pownall, Churchill observed that a ladybird had alighted on his nightclothes. He looked at it with admiration, apparently regarding it as a lucky omen, perhaps a present from Providence. 'Pownall,' he said, 'I'll be truly grateful if you will remove this exquisite and charming creature from my sleeve and allow it carefully to fly out of the window.'[3]

LEOPARDS

C hurchill regarded leopards as the embodiments of stealthy aggression and he frequently brought them into his discourses on war. The battle of the Marne, he wrote, was popularly but not accurately conceived as a French 'leopard spring at the throat of the invaders, as an onslaught carried forward on the wings of passion and ecstasy'.[1] While serving on the Western Front himself, Churchill admired General Louis Lipsett's tactic of making ferocious night-time descents on enemy trenches and extolled the Canadian soldiers who carried them out: 'Wonderful fellows: like leopards.'[2] In December 1917 he declared that the British Army was getting ready to spring like leopards upon the German hordes. In October 1940 he said that our armies must be maintained in reserve like leopards crouching to spring at the invader's throat.

More specifically, the Prime Minister proposed to repel any early landings on British shores after the evacuation from Dunkirk by means of a motorized corps of 20,000 Storm Troops, drawn from existing regiments, armed with the latest weapons and known as 'Leopards'. The Chiefs of Staff objected to the German term Storm Troops and to the creation of an elite force, though (with the Maginot Line in mind) they did favour a mobile defence. Churchill declared that the safety of the country depended on its ability to pounce on points of lodgement within four hours and in a few days nine special units had been formed, with six more in the pipeline. He called them '"Leopard" brigade-groups'.[3] Avid to employ them in an offensive role, he said that they should be trained as hunters. Soon Leopards became Commandos, mounting butcher-and-bolt raids on Nazi-occupied Europe.

The young Churchill, fresh from devouring the works of Gibbon and Macaulay in India, was also apt to associate leopards with barbaric splendour. In Cairo in 1899 he met the notorious slave trader Zubeir Rahamet, whose eyes glittered as he recalled the magnificent state in which he had once lived as 'the savage conqueror [of Darfur] before whose golden couch chained leopards walked'.[4] In East Africa in 1907 Churchill admired bronzed Masai warriors, who cast aside their ostrich-feather headdresses and leopard-skin karosses to dance naked in the dusk. He contrasted their sleek grace with the incongruous appearance of their chiefs, clad in European odds and ends – ragged trousers, cast-off khaki jackets, battered sun helmets. Paradoxically, though, he wanted Africans to adopt 'civilized attire', thus making them 'less crudely animal'[5] and, not incidentally, expanding the market for cotton goods produced in his Manchester constituency.

Moreover Churchill kept several leopard skins presented to him by local rulers, just as in 1943 he accepted a leopard skin from Archbishop (later Cardinal) Francis Spellman, a somewhat bizarre token of his esteem though not, the prelate confessed, 'any token of my ability as a marksman'.[6] Churchill, like his wife, was even prepared to don leopard skin. Having accepted the Kaiser's invitation to German Army manoeuvres in 1906, he followed King Edward VII's advice to attend in the uniform of the yeomanry regiment with which his family had long been associated, the Oxfordshire Hussars. A ceremonial adjunct to their frogged and plumed panoply was a leopard-skin cloak and, finding that his brother's had long served as a hearth-rug, Churchill had to borrow one from the Duke of Marlborough. In the event the Kaiser changed the sartorial order and, as Churchill told his private secretary Eddie Marsh, 'I did not wear the leopard – not even a whisker.'[7]

Churchill kept his eyes open for leopards in India and Egypt, and he observed that these fierce animals were especially numerous in regions of East Africa afflicted by sleeping sickness, where they 'preyed with daring and impunity upon the living, the dying and the dead'.[8] But although his father had shot and wounded a leopard, which escaped, Winston himself apparently never managed to kill one of these elusive beasts. In 1953, however, he did acquire a leopard of his own, a gift from Nuri al-Said, the pro-British strongman of Iraq. The cub arrived at 10

Despite Sheba's ferocity the press implausibly reported that Churchill petted
as well as fed the 21-month-old, 50-pound leopard, March 1955.

Downing Street in a crate which Churchill opened on the Cabinet
table. What emerged, as his private secretary Anthony Montague
Browne recorded, was 'an adorable fifteen-pound ball of fluff'. But it
had sharp claws and an angry glint in its eye. The Prime Minister said

to the secretary, 'Pray examine it and tell me its sex.' Browne politely suggested that since it was Churchill's leopard he should 'conduct this indelicate investigation himself. He declined.'[9] The leopard, a female as it happened, was sent to London Zoo where she quickly grew far too dangerous to handle, though Churchill fed her through the bars of her cage on later visits. He wondered what to call her, considering various names, among them Bermuda. At last he hit on a suitably exotic appellation for this superb desert creature – Sheba.

LIONS

From the lion rampant on the Marlborough coat of arms, via the lion's roar emanating from Downing Street during the Second World War, to *The Last Lion* of William Manchester's bestselling biography, Winston Churchill was always associated with the king of beasts. Of course that animal was ubiquitous in heraldry and many historical figures were identified, or sought identification, with this majestic embodiment of strength and valour. But no twentieth-century leader has been more lionized or has attracted more leonine imagery than Churchill.

The lion was chiefly distinguished by courage and this, in Churchill's view, was the cardinal virtue since it guaranteed all the other virtues. From an early age he himself earned a justified reputation for fearlessness. At prep school he was flogged by a sadistic headmaster and at Harrow he was caned more than any other boy, yet he put up an indomitable resistance. As a young soldier he took conspicuous risks, among them helping an intelligence officer to overawe Pathan villagers who refused to stand up and salute them: 'really things looked very black. But somehow they do recognize superiority of race – and at last they got up. It was like lion taming.'[1] The nerve he displayed on the battlefield was equally conspicuous in the political arena. As early as 1900 he declared that leaders must always be prepared to brave disaster: 'You must put your head in the lion's mouth if the performance is to be a success.'[2]

As his admirers proclaimed, Churchill did meet disaster, notably at Gallipoli, with lionhearted courage. Indeed, he was so often likened to the jungle monarch that, as he told Clementine in 1927, he proposed to subscribe himself as a Lion rather than a Pig in his letters to her. She replied from Venice, city of St Mark and his emblematic Lion, saying that this was the very place for his transfiguration. Consequently he depicted himself as a winged lion, like the ancient bronze beast in St Mark's Square. Ranging through the wilderness during the 1930s, a prey to thorns and barbs, Churchill needed all the fortitude he could muster. Back at the Admiralty in 1939 he was seen 'padding up and down his room like a caged lion'.[3]

Once free to direct the war against Hitler as he wanted, Churchill was frequently hailed as Britain's 'lionhearted premier'.[4] In fact the lion rivalled the bulldog as his animal avatar, not least in the minds of both Joseph Stalin and Harry Truman. But although Churchill kept a black, 3-foot-high iron lion at the top of the first-floor stairs at Chartwell, he did not boast about his leonine identity. On the contrary, after addressing troops in a ruined Roman amphitheatre near Carthage on 1 June 1943, he uttered this droll disclaimer: 'Yes, I was speaking from where the cries of Christian virgins rent the air whilst roaring lions devoured them, and yet I am no lion and certainly not a virgin!'[5] And after the war he modestly attributed the lion's heart to the nation and the race, claiming only to have given the roar.

Churchill continued to roar when he became Prime Minister for the last time and even after his serious stroke in 1953, as Clementine proudly remarked, 'The old lion could still issue from his den, and when he did so his growl was as frightening as ever.'[6] The following year, however, when Graham Sutherland was painting his portrait, Churchill was apt to be torpid after luncheon and the artist had to rally him: 'A little more of the old lion please, sir.'[7] Encountering a group of lions, themselves torpid after a kill, in a Kenyan game reserve in 1960, Randolph Churchill, also presumably well-lunched, paid the ultimate tribute to his father's leonine status. Randolph got out of his jeep and, to the horror of his guide, approached the lions bellowing: 'Do you know who my father is? He is a British lion. I know a British lion when I see one, and no self-respecting British lion lies down like you under attack. Get on your feet.'[8] They did.

At least since medieval times, of course, the lion had symbolized Britannia's might and majesty, and no one in the modern age exalted this icon more fervently than Churchill. The British lion was a glorious animal, he declared in 1910; but, perturbed by Edwardian social problems, he insisted that efforts must be made to heal its gangrened tail. The First World War, he said, proved that it had the strength and

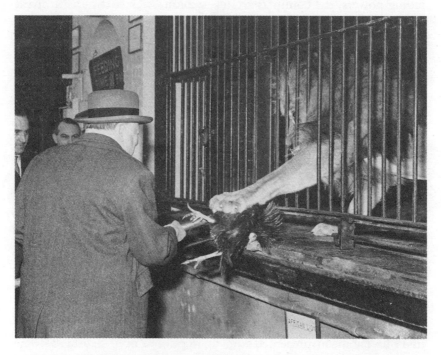

The expression of relish on Churchill's face as Rota grabbed his proffered snack was visible for all to see.

valour to defeat all comers. But as the imperial grip on India loosened, he changed his tune, asserting that the British lion could now be chased by rabbits from the fields and forests of his former glory. A sign of decay was its failure to challenge Mussolini's invasion of Ethiopia: when asked if it was not high time for the British lion to show its teeth, Churchill replied, 'It must go to the dentist first.'[9] But the lion's glory, further dimmed by Neville Chamberlain's appeasement policy, was restored during the struggle against Hitler. In a broadcast to the United States on 16 June 1941, Churchill declared that the old lion with her imperial cubs stood resolutely against the foe. And if sky-borne incursions took place, he added in 1943, the 'Nazi villains' would learn that they had 'not alighted in the poultry-run, or in the rabbit farm, or even in the sheepfold, but in the lion's den'.

After the war, evidently to counteract concerns about his own fading powers, the country's relative weakness and the decline of the British Empire, Churchill amplified his leonine rhetoric. Associating patriotism with Conservatism, he rallied his forces: 'Let us march forward with our sturdy lions, jaunty lions – yea, unconquerable lions.' Appropriating the lion rampant as the motif of revived Toryism, he proclaimed his enormous admiration for the character and the quality of this beast, as it advanced dauntlessly and victoriously through all trials. Humiliated by dependence on the United States, he reiterated that the United Kingdom must pay its way in the world and stand on its own feet since no one was 'going to keep the British lion as a pet'.[10] Churchill, though, did have his own pet lion and he made occasional visits to see it at London Zoo. However their relationship proved an awkward one and in due course the lion took him for a ride.

This lion was born in a circus in 1938. He was subsequently acquired by a man called George Thomson, who named him Rotaprince, soon shortened to Rota, and kept him in the back garden of his suburban house in Pinner. Rota was evidently a docile creature but the neighbours complained and when meat rationing was introduced in 1940 Thomson presented him to London Zoo. Here he became a star attraction. Thomson subsequently urged that Rota should be given to the lionhearted Prime Minister, which put the zoo in a quandary. On 27 January 1943 the Duke of Devonshire, a member of the zoo's Council, wrote to Churchill's parliamentary private secretary explaining that it did not wish 'either to be pilloried for churlishly withholding the lion, or on the other hand to embarrass the Prime Minister with an unwanted gift'. But the Prime Minister was not in the least embarrassed, telling the Duke on 13 February:

> I shall have much pleasure in becoming the possessor of the lion, on the condition that I do not have to feed it or take care of it, and that the Zoo makes sure that it does not get loose. You are quite right in your assumption that I do not want a lion at the moment either at Downing Street or Chequers, owing to the Ministerial calm which prevails there. But the Zoo is not far away, and situations may arise in which I shall have great need of it.[11]

Later in the war Churchill did, indeed, threaten to feed a diminutive private secretary to the lion, saying that 'Meat is very short now.'[12] More immediately he hoped to come and see Rota, well appreciating his propaganda value.

Churchill's visits to the Lion House certainly generated good coverage in both newspapers and cinema newsreels, particularly when he was pictured feeding Rota through the bars of his cage. On 1 August 1943 one of Churchill's staff, John Martin, recorded that the lion was

> given a bunch of catmint which it sniffed with obvious relish. There were large hot crowds which jostled us wherever we went. Inside the bars in the swan enclosure the PM turned to them and said 'I suppose you would like to feed me.'[13]

Equally cheering later that month was the news that the so-called Lion Squadron of the Royal Canadian Air Force, which flew Halifax heavy bombers, had got Churchill's permission to mark the achievements of the 8th Army in North Africa by adopting one of Rota's four cubs. It was called 'Mareth', the brother of 'Alamein' – their sisters were christened 'Tunis' and 'Bizerta'. Subsequently Churchill received several encouraging telegrams signed by Rota, though it is not clear who sent them. One exhorted him to 'GIVE THEM A BRITISH ROAR – ROTA'.[14] Another was written a few days after Churchill's stroke in 1953: 'MAY THE STRENGTH OF A LION BE SPEEDY [sic] RESTORED TO YOU – ROTA.'[15] Churchill gave special instructions that it should be acknowledged thus: 'The Prime Minister wishes to thank Rota very much for his telegram of good wishes. It was the first Sir Winston received and it gave him a great deal of pleasure.'[16]

Publicity, though, is a two-edged sword and it soon became clear that George Thomson was intent on exploiting Rota for his own purposes. In 1944 Churchill incautiously granted his request to keep the lion's skin as a souvenir when he died and thereafter Thomson did his best to keep Rota in the public eye. Not only did he appear on a Pathé newsreel fondling the lion through his cage bars but he also issued a series of statements to the press protesting about the poor conditions in which he was kept. The zoo's superintendent Geoffrey Vevers then informed Downing Street that before the war Thomson had been the British sales manager of a German company called Rotaprint, which manufactured offset printing presses and kept the lion as a mascot. Hence Rota's name. Vevers suggested that Churchill should change it in order to reduce Rota's 'advertising value'.[17] Evidently the Prime Minister thought this would draw more attention to the matter but MI5, the police and the Ministry of Economic Warfare were all asked to investigate Thomson. They found nothing against him and, to the regret of the Minister of Economic Warfare's private secretary, it proved unnecessary for officials to interrogate Rota himself.

Thomson therefore continued to make much of the lion. He kept complaining, seemingly with some justice, that the zoo was not looking after him properly. He informed Churchill that 'your noble beast' in its unloved state was 'no credit to you, Sir!'.[18] During the general election campaign in 1945 he told the *Daily Express* that 'Rota should be exhibited all over the country. His nobility would win the Prime Minister thousands of votes.'[19] The following year Thomson urged that the lion should march through London in the Victory Parade. During Rota's lifetime the zoo considered Thomson a 'daily nuisance'[20] and a 'publicity seeker in a big way'.[21] But when the aged sire of some sixty cubs had to be put down in 1955, his original owner seemed genuinely sorry, wiring Churchill: 'POOR OLD ROTA GOD BLESS HIM DEAR OLD CHAP.'[22]

Churchill himself was glad that 'dear Rota … ended his life so peacefully'[23] and wanted him to have a decent burial. However, Thomson claimed the lion's skin and insisted on having him 'preserved for posterity'.[24] Churchill faced what his private secretary called the 'unsavoury prospect' of Thomson's having Rota stuffed, 'mounted and exhibited for his financial gain, or sold abroad'.[25] This is exactly what happened. The lion was displayed in a Piccadilly showroom in roaring posture, though Churchill was able to veto the use of a plaque saying 'I'd provide the roar'.[26] Rota was bought by an American in 1956 and ended up in the Lightner Museum in St Augustine, Florida, where he can still be seen. Apparently Churchill was unworried by the outcome. Instead he looked forward to making friends with a new lion cub, named Rusty, presented to him by a Lions Club in the United States because 'a lion symbolizes great strength of heart, such as you have shown'.[27] Churchill showed a nice concern for his welfare. In 1959, for example, he refused a request from the Lions Club of Brighton to parade him through the town, explaining that Rusty would almost certainly become very alarmed and distressed by the proceedings.

Churchill honoured the king of beasts in captivity but treated him as 'royal vermin'[28] in the wild. Yet his account of lion-hunting, at which he had even less success than his father, reveals a wry sympathy for the prey as well as a gory relish for the combat. In fact Churchill gave a kind of commentary on the old French rhyme, '*Cet animal est très méchant: Quand on l'attaque, il se défend.*'[29] Lions were mild and gentle, he wrote after his East African safari in 1907, unless harried by hunters. Then they became vicious:

> When a lion, maddened with the agony of a bullet-wound,
> distressed by long and hard pursuit, or, most of all, a lioness in
> defence of her cubs, is definitely committed to the charge, death
> is the only possible conclusion. Broken limbs, broken jaws, a
> body raked from end to end, lungs pierced through and through,

entrails torn and protruding – none of these count. It must be death – instant and utter – for the lion, or down goes the man, mauled by septic claws and fetid teeth, crushed and crunched, and poisoned afterwards to make doubly sure. Such are the habits of this cowardly and wicked animal.[30]

Churchill's irony was directed against the beast in man. Hunters often claimed to exorcize this savage element by pursuing wild animals, killing the thing they loved and satiating their bloodlust in the interests of civilization.[31] Whatever Churchill thought about this, his ambivalence towards lions is unmistakable – and understandable in view of the multifarious part a large pride played in his life.

LIZARDS

Churchill shared the popular prejudice against lizards and the bigger they grew the less he liked them. Serving in the Himalayan foothills with the Malakand Field Force he encountered a particularly 'odious species of large lizard, nearly three feet long, which resembles a flabby-skinned crocodile and feeds on carrion'.[1] These were monitor lizards and, according to Churchill, they disputed their prey with other scavengers. Smaller and more elusive varieties quickened his innate spirit of the chase. Cruising in the Mediterranean aboard the Admiralty yacht *Enchantress* in the summer of 1912, Churchill organized a lizard hunt at Paestum, recruiting Admirals Beatty and Masterton-Smith as beaters. In this role they were plainly at sea. 'We must be more scientific about our strategy,' Churchill urged. 'There is a science in catching lizards and we must master it.'[2]

Lizards also scuttled into Churchill's mental parlour, prompting light-hearted banter – he likened a secretary squeezing through a door to a lizard – and at least one strikingly mischievous image. In *Great Contemporaries* he gave a character sketch of Philip Snowden, the vehement Socialist who succeeded him as Chancellor of the Exchequer in 1929, depicting him as an ideologue happy to succumb to departmental orthodoxy: 'The Treasury mind and the Snowden mind embraced each other with the fervour of two long-separated kindred lizards.'[3] Less suggestive but equally trenchant was Churchill's assertion that the leaders of the Soviet Union, making their first aggressive moves in the Cold War as early as 1945, were 'realist lizards'.[4] They all belonged to the crocodile family, he said, to whom sentiment and morality meant nothing.

In the South of France Churchill was sometimes entertained and sometimes appalled by the antics of different kinds of lizards. He found it diverting to watch chameleons and geckos catching flies 'before they went to bed'.[5] But in extreme old age he felt queasy when such reptiles caught and scrunched up moths on a large window pane at Lord Beaverbrook's villa. As his nurse Roy Howells recorded, Churchill 'gritted his teeth and winced at the gruesome exhibition'.[6] But when Howells suggested tapping the window to frighten the lizards away, Churchill was against it. He evidently reckoned that nature had to take its course.

MICE

From Aesop to Disney the mouse has been presented in a heroic light but Churchill usually regarded it as vermin or victim. In *The River War* he vividly described the millions of little red mice which plagued Egypt and the Sudan: 'So vast and immeasurable was the number of these tiny pests that after a heavy rain the whole country was strewn with, and almost tinted by, the squirrel-coloured corpses of the drowned.'[1] Mixing his metaphors in November 1914, he said of the German fleet: 'The swine are concentrating at Wilhelmshaven, & the situation is thoroughly "cat & mouse". Which will be the mouse?'[2] It was a question he asked more than once, but he had no doubt about the answer when it came to dealing with Italy after its surrender in 1943: Churchill told Stalin that he and Roosevelt would handle the Italians like a cat handling a mouse.[3]

To be sure, he was not always on the side of the cat. Referring to the leaders of Vichy France in 1941, he declared that 'Hitler plays from day to day a cat-and-mouse game with these tormented men.'[4] In 1950 he protested when West African convicts were several times brought to the scaffold and reprieved at the last moment: 'It is an act of inhumanity to "cat and mouse" human beings.'[5] But in general Churchill thought mice were for catching in traps baited with cheese or for use in scientific experiments – during the 1930s he was intrigued by the possibility of death rays able to kill mice. These little creatures were also serviceable for disparaging opponents or diminishing critics. Churchill declared that during the General Strike, a severe embarrassment to the Labour Party, Philip Snowden had been as mum as a mouse. Commenting on a press conference in January 1941 which at last satisfied journalists, Churchill said that 'starving mice appreciate a Stilton cheese when it is set before them'.[6]

And he represented Attlee as a wee, cowering, timorous beastie. This was a libel. But in 1950, according to Harold Nicolson, it reflected the view of the British people, who thought that Churchill could talk to Stalin on equal terms whereas Attlee 'would be like a mouse addressing a tiger'.[7]

Even in art Churchill was no respecter of mice. One evening during his final term as Prime Minister he became dissatisfied with the most famous painting at Chequers, *The Lion and the Mouse*, attributed to Rubens, because the small rodent gnawing at the net that ensnared the jungle monarch was almost invisible on the darkening canvas. Accordingly he called for a ladder and, taking up his brushes and palette, proceeded to 'highlight the mouse'.[8] Afterwards, apparently, more sober considerations prevailed and he expunged the embellishment. Incidentally, this was not Churchill's first such undertaking. Offended by a gloomy painting at his requisitioned Como villa in September 1945, he had 'improved' it with splurges of glorious colour. According to his daughter Sarah, 'it glowed brazenly like a bird of paradise and we were heartbroken when it was carried upstairs to have its face washed'. Far from showing remorse, Churchill took a mischievous delight in the act of what he called 'artistic rape'.[9]

Cheered by the behaviour of 'quite a good mouse' in the front line during the Great War, he reopened a letter to Clementine, written in his dugout, to tell her that he had been 'watching the little beast reconnoitring the floor of this cave with the utmost skill, daring & composure'.[10] Perhaps recollecting this moment, he later gave the mouse an enduring role as the incarnation of intellectual freedom. Delivering a vigorous attack on the fascist dictators in a broadcast to America in 1938, he said that despite surrounding themselves with bayonets, truncheons, cannons and aeroplanes, they nursed an unspoken fear:

> They are afraid of words and thoughts: words spoken abroad, thoughts stirring at home – all the more powerful because forbidden – terrify them. A little mouse, a tiny little mouse of thought appears in the room, and even the mightiest potentates are thrown into a panic.[11]

Mice scuttle everywhere in fancy, notably the mice of time in Guillaume Apollinaire's *Bestiary*, which nibble away at human life. But Churchill coined a conceit for the ages, at once comic and audacious: a mouse as the embodiment of the invincibility of ideas.

MONKEYS

Churchill encountered wild monkeys in India and Africa and he undoubtedly met Maxine Elliott's pet monkey – in fact a ring-tailed lemur – during his frequent holidays at her sumptuous villa, Château de l'Horizon, near Cannes. This creature was absurdly indulged, allowed to amble round the breakfast table upsetting crockery, and it occasionally got drunk on gin and bit women and attacked men. Indeed, as one guest noted, its owner so doted on it that she even permitted her favourite terrier, Christophe, to be 'humiliated by the caprices of the insufferable monkey'.[1] Churchill would surely have found in its antics confirmation that the Bandar-log were, as Kipling had portrayed them in *The Jungle Book*, a jabbering tribe of degraded outlaws. After all, as Winston noted in his biography of his father, one of the nastiest animal caricatures of Lord Randolph Churchill had taken the form of a ribald and vicious monkey.

Winston himself pilloried Mussolini as Hitler's monkey. When Chamberlain and Halifax made no concessions to the Axis on their visit to Rome in January 1939, Churchill was pleased that they had given 'nothing to the organ grinder or his monkey, not even to pay them to go into the next street'.[2] Similarly, when the Duce was totally subordinated to the Führer after the collapse of Fascist Italy, Churchill said, 'The organ-grinder has got his head in the monkey's collar.'[3]

However he was critical of the indiscriminate use of simian imagery, especially when it was applied to him – H. G. Wells once accused him of monkeying with British policy in the Middle East.

Such name-calling was particularly hazardous in wartime. On 20 July 1940 Churchill contemplated prosecuting the *Daily Mirror* for printing a cartoon by Zec linking the Japanese to monkeys, which he thought would help the war party in Tokyo. When the Second Sea Lord, Vice-Admiral Sir William Whitworth, publicly declared in March 1942 that 'the British Lion was having its tail twisted by "yellow monkeys"', Churchill sent him an informal rebuke, saying that the 'term cannot of course be limited to apply exclusively to the Japanese'.[4] In other words it might offend the Chinese, who were Britain's allies. Apparently the Prime Minister had no objection to the language, only to its application. His personal view, expressed in private, was that 'The Japs breed like vermin and die like heroes.'[5]

Churchill's own language was often quaintly dated and he amused his staff and colleagues by employing bits of Victorian slang such as 'monkey' (meaning £500) and 'mouse-trap' (meaning a sovereign). Excited by the prospect of a German bombing raid near Chequers in June 1940, he said to Jock Colville: 'I'll bet you a monkey to a mouse-trap they don't hit the house.'[6] According to Colville, when Hitler invaded the Soviet Union twelve months later Churchill proffered the same wager in the same terms to express his confidence that the Russians would be fighting, and fighting victoriously, in two years' time. Actually he feared that the odds were more like evens. But any ally was better than none and he was happy to put a monkey on the Bear.

NEWTS

Johhn Bullish though Churchill's French accent was, he would hardly have ordered in a restaurant, as did his self-educated wartime Minister of Labour Ernest Bevin, 'A bottle of Newts'[1] – meaning Nuits Saint Georges. Yet in sober truth Churchill did have an affinity with such amphibians. His political career nearly foundered on the failure of the waterborne attack on the Dardanelles in 1915 and, fighting to restore his reputation by literary means, he initially wanted to call his account of the use of sea power early in the First World War 'The Great Amphibian'.[2] His publishers insisted that this should be changed to *The World Crisis* – an appropriate title, as Arthur Balfour memorably quipped, for an enormous book about himself disguised as a history of the universe. Ever afterwards Churchill sought to vindicate warfare by land and sea and to advocate vehement offensive amphibious action. He made fanciful proposals to descend on alien shores from Scandinavia to Sarawak; he delighted in cockleshell heroism; he favoured attacks on such targets as Narvik, Dieppe and Anzio, all of which proved abortive; he backed the successful invasions of Sicily and (despite serious qualms) France.

Personally, too, Churchill was an aquatic terrestrial. He loved digging with his children on the beach and in developing the Chartwell estate he created an elemental compound of earth and water. He delighted in the construction of streams, dams, rivulets, cascades and lakes. His first swimming pool was so vast that he allowed it to revert to nature and become a large pond, a happy hunting ground for newts, toads and frogs. No Gussie Fink-Nottle he, but Churchill did suggest an amphibian image to Harold Nicolson, who observed him carefully during a lunch at Downing Street in 1942. While the Prime Minister was preoccupied his eyes were empty pools, glaucous, bored, blank, dead. When something caught his attention, however, Churchill's eyes would lighten with interest, pucker with amusement, blaze with anger, moisten with sympathy or darken with tragedy. 'Yet these passing moods and phases do not flash across each other,' Nicolson concluded, 'they move slowly and opaquely like newts in a rather dim glass tank.'[3]

OCTOPUSES

In Churchill's Ruritanian romance *Savrola* the eponymous hero, obviously based on the author, leads opposition to the dictatorial president of the fictional Mediterranean state of Laurania, who finds a suitable image to stigmatize the resistance. '"The octopus of Rebellion, Gentlemen," said the President to those around him, pointing to the Revolutionary proclamation, "has long arms. It will be necessary to cut off his head."'[1] With its prehensile limbs, its poisonous embrace, its jet-propelled evasiveness and its capacity for camouflage and inky obfuscation, the octopus was a gift to propagandists seeking a symbol of sinister conspiratorial power. During the first part of the twentieth century it was employed promiscuously to denigrate big corporations as well as authoritarian states, becoming a cliché, a slogan, and a metaphor so mixed that it was virtually meaningless, as in George Orwell's famous example: '*The Fascist octopus has sung its swan song.*'[2]

Probably for this reason, Churchill in his rhetoric kept the octopus at arm's length. But as a pro-Zionist anti-Nazi, he himself was memorably identified with this creature in Hitler's Germany. Shortly before the Second World War a virulently anti-Semitic cartoonist called Josef Plank, who signed himself 'Seppla', depicted Churchill as a huge octopus enveloping the globe with dripping tentacles under the Star of David.

Nazi propagandists portrayed Churchill (in many guises) as a drunken, demagogic warmonger, the puppet of Stalin, Roosevelt and international Jewry.

OSTRICHES

D uring his East African safari in 1907 Churchill witnessed wild ostriches parading sedately in twos and threes, and added at least one of these fleet creatures to his game bag. He also disparaged the fantastic ostrich-feather headdresses of the Kikuyu and the Masai. These he regarded as the trappings of savagery. A convinced sartorial imperialist, as already mentioned, he wanted to replace them with civilized garb manufactured on the looms of Lancashire. Ironically, however, at the very time when he was dismissing ostrich feathers as part of the grotesque 'frippery'[1] which marred the innate grace of nature's children, the fashion for such plumage was reaching its apogee in Britain.

Avian hats had waxed ever more extravagant and ostrich feathers were almost worth their weight in diamonds.[2] Pearly Queens sprouted them luxuriantly and they were an obligatory garnish to the outfits of debutantes being presented at court. Clementine herself, after marrying Winston at St Margaret's, Westminster, on 12 September 1908, embarked on their honeymoon wearing a grey costume topped with a large, black, satin hat lined with velvet and adorned with a long, sweeping ostrich plume. The Pearly Queens who saw them off (and favoured her husband for supporting costermongers' marketing rights as President of the Board of Trade) loved it. They cried, 'Ooh, wot a luv'ly fevver!'[3]

OWLS

In 1961 the Countess of Lytton, who as Pamela Plowden had refused to marry Winston some six decades earlier, gave him as a birthday present a copy of Edward Lear's poem 'The Owl and the Pussy-Cat'. The book was a favourite of hers, she told him, 'enchantingly translated into french [sic] with pictures!'.[1] What the gift signified can now only be guessed at. It might just have been a charming piece of whimsy calculated to tickle Churchill's anthropomorphic fancy. It could perhaps have recalled his owlish spectacles and his habit of turning night into day. But it may have been a nostalgic reminder of his fledgling courtship, which had foundered on lack of money – though the verse did not actually make clear which creature was the male, since the Owl wooed but the Pussy-Cat proposed.

However, this might be taken as a reflection of the perennial ambiguity of owls, which were sometimes reckoned birds of wisdom, sometimes harbingers of doom. The owl's ability to see in the dark made it the emblem of Athene, yet in medieval bestiaries Jews were depicted as owls because they supposedly preferred darkness to light. Owlishness can convey Merlin-like sagacity or Billy Bunterish obtuseness. Mortified that Winston had chosen to marry Clementine, Violet Asquith wondered if he would 'ultimately mind her being as stupid as an *owl*'.[2]

Churchill himself appreciated that dull solemnity often carried more oratorical conviction than sophisticated wit. Criticizing a draft of the chairman's speech introducing him at a huge meeting held on 18 March 1931 in defence of the British Raj in India, he wrote: 'I do not think it is at all easy to make small and rather refined jokes to a great Albert Hall audience. I suggest a grave, heavy style which runs no risks. Say it all very slowly with great impressiveness and an owl-like look, and all will be well.'[3]

OYSTERS

L ike the Walrus and the Carpenter in Lewis Carroll's poem, which Churchill happily quoted in parliament, he was an avid connoisseur of oysters. Once the fare of the poor (Dr Johnson famously fed them to his cat Hodge), these shellfish had become a delicacy of the rich by the late Victorian era and Churchill devoured them at every opportunity, usually accompanying them with champagne.

His papers contain many receipts from Wiltons, oyster purveyors to royalty. When he was First Lord of the Admiralty in 1913, the mess of the *Enchantress* gave him a birthday present of oysters specially flown in from Whitstable. At the Station Hotel, Hazebrouck, in January 1916, Churchill treated the officers of his new battalion to a sumptuous feast beginning with oysters and lots of champagne. Between the wars he sampled many different kinds, among them the American Blue Point oyster. This he thought too large, perhaps feeling with Thackeray that eating it was like swallowing a live baby. Instead he preferred the English variety, which would 'slide down the smallest gullet'.[1] As late as 1950 he discovered Marennes oysters in Marrakech, finding them excellent. He was also sent frozen Australian oysters, supplied by Theo Marmaras, the 'oyster king' of Melbourne. In Downing Street Churchill was served oysters and champagne in his bedroom. Crossing the Atlantic on board the *Queen Mary* in 1952, he had oysters for every lunch and every dinner apart from two, when he substituted caviar.

Possibly oysters do have the aphrodisiac qualities attributed to them by such as Casanova and Madame de Pompadour. At the very least they invigorated Churchill, particularly when washed down with Pol Roger. His metabolism was curious. He did not become lethargic under the influence of food and drink; instead the copious quantities he consumed acted as a stimulus, cheering him, buoying him up, convincing him that the world was his oyster.

PANDAS

On Christmas Eve 1938 London Zoo acquired its first giant pandas and Churchill, like many of his compatriots, was eager to see them. The star attraction was a cub called Ming, which means 'Brightness' in Mandarin, and she was greeted with a fanfare of publicity. This was partly generated by sympathy for China as the victim of Japanese aggression, foreshadowing the key part pandas were to play in diplomacy. But the animal's appeal stemmed mainly from its rarity, its delectable colouring – 'two lovely black eyes'[1] – and its furry, roly-poly good nature. Ming inspired panda mania: there were panda books, panda hats, panda toys, panda jokes, panda charms, panda wallpapers, panda cigarette cases. Furthermore, as *The Times* soon noted, 'one of the country's more benevolent elder politicians has been discreetly compared with a panda'.[2] This must surely have been Churchill.

He was given a private view of Ming, still being held in quarantine inside a large cage at the Lion House, by Julian Huxley, Secretary of the Zoological Society. An eminent biologist, Huxley was also a scientific popularizer whose ambition (subsequently frustrated) was to transform London Zoo from old-fashioned menagerie into a centre of 'popular interest in every aspect of animals and animal life'.[3] To that end he founded 'Pets' Corner' for children and welcomed influential visitors such as Churchill. He, as Huxley recorded, gazed for a long time at the exotic creature, which was 'lying supine and unaware of the honour done to it'. At last Churchill nodded his head appreciatively and said, 'It has exceeded all my expectations ... and they were *very* high!'[4] According to his daughter Mary, who recalled that her father had a much-loved panda hot-water-bottle cover, Churchill thought Ming amply satisfied 'the need for cuddleability'.[5]

Such was the giant panda's allure that it could even divert Churchill's thoughts from the prospect of war with Hitler. In June 1939 he attended a dinner party given by the art historian Kenneth Clark for the visiting American journalist Walter Lippmann. Among the guests were Julian Huxley and Harold Nicolson, who recorded Churchill's furious response to Lippmann's report that the US ambassador Joseph Kennedy had said Britain was bound to be 'licked' by Nazi Germany. In a crescendo of impromptu eloquence, orchestrated by the waving of his whisky-and-soda and the stubbing of his cigar, Churchill declared that it might well be true that 'steel and fire will rain down upon us day and night scattering death and destruction far and wide'. But this fierce ordeal would serve only to strengthen 'the resolution of the British people and to enhance our will to victory'. Eventually the dramatic monologue gave way to a bathetic dialogue. As Nicolson noted, 'We then change the subject and speak about the Giant Panda.'[6]

As a masterpiece of brute creation the panda was not just a political distraction but a stimulus to philosophical speculation. Churchill had no time for religion but he did hope for individual and social progress despite providential setbacks such as the Black Death. Of this scourge he wrote bitterly, in a passage later deleted from his *History of the English-Speaking Peoples*, 'when at length the Almighty, in his ineffable mercy, had used the process of harrowing and purging upon His creatures sufficiently to further His sublime purpose, the plague abated its force'.[7] A much greater catastrophe became possible with the development of nuclear weapons and, writing to Bernard Shaw in 1946, Churchill wondered whether the advance of humanity would be terminated for good. 'Do you think that the atomic bomb means that the architect of the universe has got tired of writing his non-stop scenario? There was a lot to be said for his stopping with the Panda.'[8]

PARROTS

Privately Winston Churchill liked parrots, with reservations, but in public he always represented them as vociferous and vacuous – typical, in fact, of his political opponents. Their arguments, he liked to say, were mere parrot cries. Protectionists squawked to no purpose. Socialists tried to make the complexities of modern civilization conform to 'a few barbarous formulas which any moderately intelligent parrot could repeat in a fortnight'. Critics of his conduct at the Admiralty were, he said, people whose brains are smaller than those of the smallest parakeet. Similarly, newspapers attacked his record at the Treasury in a raucous and repetitive manner. Between the wars his speeches were interrupted by hecklers making 'poll-parrot cries', one group being 'rehearsed beforehand, like a macaw on its perch'.[1]

However, from his early years Winston had been familiar with pet parrots and he knew that they were not only brilliant mimics but also charming, clever, dextrous, birds, though moody and prone to fits of pique. In 1891 Lady Wilton, a friend of his parents who was fond of their refractory older son, reminded him about her good-looking cockatoo which she carried about by hand to stop it from trying to destroy all the furniture. Having admired the gorgeous plumage of such birds in the wild, Churchill acquired a parrot of his own, a black-billed, red-tailed African grey, in about 1935. The gift of Daisy Fellowes, it was housed in a cage in the dining room at Chartwell. Here its new owner attempted to make friends with it, saying, 'Pretty polly! Pretty poll.' Unmoved by these overtures, the bird bit him on the thumb, whereupon Churchill unleashed a torrent of curses until the parrot released its grip. His nephew Johnny, who had been present at the scene, later acted it out for the amusement of his cousin Randolph and

Churchill with Clementine and their daughter Sarah in parrot heaven, Miami, 1946. One journalist remarked on his look of 'genial impishness'.

Churchill's research assistant Bill Deakin. But Churchill happened to witness this irreverent performance. He was furious.

The parrot, naturally called Polly, continued to be difficult. To show his dislike of the cold weather he made a nasty clucking noise which so irritated Churchill that he had to turn him out of the room. Nevertheless Churchill valued Polly's company, especially during Clementine's long absences abroad, though he had some reason to complain of the bird's cruelty. On one occasion he opened the cage to encourage Polly to sit on his hand: 'He gave me a frightful peck & got out. It took Edna [a housemaid] (& her young man) an hour to get him back. He is v[er]y naughty. But still a companion.'[2] Other members of the family also bore Polly's scars, including his daughter Mary, who once reported to her father that 'the parrot is in the highest spirits, and has bitten me once since you went away'.[3]

There is no truth in claims that before the war Churchill owned a splendid blue-and-gold macaw called Charlie who was trained to shout obscenities about the Nazis. But in 1938, at a cabaret staged for diners in the Monte Carlo casino, Churchill did encounter the loveliest parrot he had ever seen. This performing bird posed as a millionaire who kept a sailor to look after him. As Churchill told Clementine:

> The parrot first of all made speeches to the company using all kinds of French endearments such as 'Bon soir, coco', 'Au revoir, coco', 'Merde' etc. In addition he had a very cunning trick of whispering into the sailor's ear and then roaring with laughter. He imitated a cat with beautiful miaows, and also the drums of a military band marching off. Finally he sang like a prima donna, accompanied by the band, and really you would have thought it was a human voice. He was marvellous and not at all strident, and when he did the high notes, he brought the house down.[4]

It was a psittacine revelation.

Churchill's penchant for parrots may have inspired one of Neville Chamberlain's rare ventures into the realm of comedy. On 5 April 1940 Churchill, still First Lord of the Admiralty, crossed the Channel on a mission to convince the French government to support more aggressive action against Germany. Once in Paris, however, he himself was persuaded by the defeatist Minister of War, Édouard Daladier, that the French air force needed three months more to prepare itself to meet enemy retaliation. Churchill therefore concluded that it would be a great mistake to attempt to force their Gallic allies to fall in with British wishes. Chamberlain compared this unexpected conversion to 'the story of the pious parrot brought in to teach good language to the parrot which swore, that ended up learning to swear itself'.[5]

Churchill's interest in parrots did not wane after the war. Following his defeat at the general election in 1945, he went off to Italy on a painting holiday, staying at a villa requisitioned by Allied forces overlooking Lake Como. In the mirrored and marbled dining room of this small palace, he reported delightedly to Clementine, hung 'a large cage with a beautiful parrot of doubtful temper, and another in which twenty canaries chirrup or at night sleep in a long row on their perch'.[6] Four months later, in January 1946, Churchill crossed the Atlantic to deliver his 'iron curtain' speech, prior to which he enjoyed the hospitality of a rich Canadian friend, Colonel Frank W. Clarke, in Miami. Here he visited the Parrot

Jungle, a zoological park in which the birds flew about freely. They flocked around him, perching on his arms, shoulders and knees, 'quite undeterred by his cigar'.[7] He was photographed with several species, among them a military macaw and a sulphur-crested cockatoo. His face wore a particularly beatific expression.

PEACOCKS

The late Victorian Aesthetic Movement, symbolized by peacock feathers as well as green carnations, had long been satirized for arty self-indulgence, but by the time Winston Churchill reached adulthood it was, thanks largely to Oscar Wilde's trial, damned for moral decadence. Consequently, perhaps, Churchill never conjured with peacocks as images of beauty let alone as emblems of eternity – medieval bestiaries had perpetuated the ancient belief that the flesh of these birds did not decay after death. In Churchill's book the peacock was a vainglorious creature, a prancing poseur ridiculously proud of its garish livery. As a young lieutenant he was indignant about the open-handed profusion with which medals were awarded to Kitchener's officers in Egypt, many of whom had seen little or nothing of combat. In his account of the Sudan campaign he wrote, 'The irreverent British soldier, watching the bright-coloured ribbons which adorned so many breasts, was provoked to exclaim: "There goes another peacock!"'[1]

The ornamental preoccupations of the military continued to perturb Churchill during the Second World War. Then he constantly complained that generals were less concerned with teeth than with tail, less interested in bayonets than in decorative appendages – he asserted that Eisenhower's D-Day transports were filled with dental chairs, spare bootlaces and YMCA institutions.² Remaining in essence a subaltern of hussars, bent on attack at all costs, Churchill had little grasp of logistics and he always underestimated the supply train required to sustain the modern fighting man. 'The Army is like a peacock,' he insisted, 'nearly all tail.' Alan Brooke, whose hobby was birdwatching, replied, 'The peacock would be a very badly balanced bird without its tail.'³

This crushing rejoinder did not alter Churchill's derogatory view of the gorgeous fowl. In 1948 he derided the Labour government for making a show with borrowed plumage, for boasting about its welfare legislation while living on dollar loans. Here is Socialism, he declared, 'strutting around like some silly peacock spreading its plumes while all the time it has to be hand-fed and spoon-fed by capitalist America'.⁴

PIGS

'I am fond of pigs. Dogs look up to us. Cats look down on us. Pigs treat us as equals.'¹ But Churchill's celebrated pronouncement by no means told the whole story, even where domesticated pigs were concerned. From questing snout to curly tail these intelligent animals certainly attracted him and he wrote with special tenderness of those he encountered during the Great War. Some he saw foraging boldly among shell holes in the front line. Two red Tamworth pigs, he informed Clementine, 'having survived all the perils of these shot swept fields, & the risks incidental to their profession, have turned up at the mouth of my dugout on a visit of ceremony'.² In his first letter to the four-year-old Randolph he recorded with relish the presence near his billet of three large, fat, dirty pigs.

By 1918 Churchill was breeding such beasts himself, never passing their sties without greeting them and scratching their backs – according to Grace Hamblin, general factotum at Chartwell, 'he was never more pleased than when my father fixed a wire brush to a long stick and presented him with it as a back scratcher for his pigs.'[3] Twelve black pigs, all 'industrious rootlers',[4] Churchill christened the Apostles. He treasured his pedigree herd of Middle White pigs. In the early 1930s one of his sows won a prize and although he doubtless felt an Emsworthian pride in the achievement (a sentiment reflected in his subsequent purchase of four fine ivory pigs) he seemed mainly interested to know what the prize was worth.[5] Churchill concerned himself with buying and selling and propagating pigs, with pigmen and pigpens and pigswill, but his pig farming, like his other agricultural pursuits, met with mixed success. As late as 1954 he hoped in vain to make a fortune from starting a herd of Swedish Landrace pigs, telling Clementine that he would not sign himself with his usual portrait since he didn't want to compete with the new stock.

Winston delighted in his piggy persona and, wrote his valet, Clementine made the term '"Dear Pig" sound like an affectionate

Churchill's graphic portrait of his porcine avatar.

caress'.[6] But although she cherished her 'débonnaire [sic] pig',[7] Clementine did worry about his greediness. During the General Strike she said that although he was having a thrilling and engrossing time, 'which is what the Pig likes', he should allow one or two of his colleagues near the trough to 'have a tit-bit now & again'.[8] Her husband, though, was allergic to self-denial. A gourmand as well as a gourmet, he even indulged the appetite of his newborn son Randolph, saying that in a baby 'greediness and even swinishness at table are virtues'.[9] As Churchill himself grew stouter his resemblance to a porker became more pronounced. Seeing the Prime Minister wearing a silk vest in bed on 16 June 1940, Jock Colville said that he looked just like a rather nice pig. The similarity was further accentuated by the dungaree-style garments known as 'siren suits' or (in his argot) 'rompers', which he adopted during the war. As Diana Cooper wrote in October 1940, the Prime Minister dined 'in a little sort of workman's overall suit. He looks exactly like the good little pig who built his house of bricks.'[10]

Others saw a bad little pig, one possessing plenty of the animal's unamiable attributes. MPs were offended by Churchill's expressions of dissent in the House of Commons, which often took the form of grunts and snorts. Well-placed observers thought that he was not so much single-minded as pig-headed, obstinately determined, like his sometime ally Admiral Jackie Fisher, to go the 'whole hog, totus porcus'.[11] Churchill could be brutally rude to underlings, and one of his bodyguards, Detective Inspector Walter Thompson, initially described his behaviour as piggish. A pre-war chauffeur, Sam Howes, recalled an occasion when Churchill roared at him in 'rough peremptory terms', which prompted this reply: 'Excuse me Sir, I'm not a pig and I don't like to be spoken to like one.' Churchill coloured and said nothing for some time, eventually telling Howes to take no notice of his way of speaking: 'It's my military manner and it doesn't mean anything.'[12] He did not abuse Howes again, though towards others he was not always so restrained.

Brought up among aristocrats fearful of Edmund Burke's swinish multitude, Churchill had also been exposed to what he ironically termed 'correct regimental ideas' about the mob, namely that they were swine, their leaders being 'the same, with an adjective prefixed'.[13] Thus piggish insults sprang readily to his lips, as when he asserted that Boer women had little narrow-set pig eyes. Churchill freely called his critics swine and one of them, Lord Winterton, he deemed a malignant little pig. Portuguese republicans who overthrew their monarchy in 1910 were 'sanguinary swine'.[14] Soon after the rise of Italian Fascism Churchill exclaimed, 'What a swine Mussolini is.'[15] Warning the Commons about the danger of an act of unprovoked aggression in February 1939, Churchill told Daisy Fellowes, 'We are still waiting about here for our Italian and German pigs to grunt.'[16] During the Second World War he remarked that King Farouk was wallowing like a sow in the trough of luxury. And he seemed to advocate tough action against a later ruler of Egypt, Colonel Nasser, whom he deemed a malicious swine. Adopting the phrase of front-line troops in the Middle East, Churchill referred to staff officers as 'gabardene swine'.[17] The post-war Foreign Office was staffed by a lot of scuttling rabbits, he declared, and the Treasury by a lot of mean swine, though he excepted from such strictures his own private office.

As the grin accompanying this proviso indicated, his porcine characterizations were not invariably pejorative or even serious. In November 1916 he complained that his friend Archie Sinclair was a 'pig not to write more often. You will reply in the jargon of the day that in that case I am a super-pig.'[18] During the Second World War Churchill likened the government's spending departments to piglets for whom there were not enough teats. In 1953 he enjoined Britain's new ambassador in Cairo, Robert Hankey, to resist the demands of Egyptian nationalists and to oppose a dead-level scuttle by being a 'patient sulky pig'.[19] He also liked to jest about the folly of buying pigs in pokes and of burning one's house down, as Charles Lamb had alleged the Chinese did, in order to roast pig for the table.[20] Altogether earnest, though, were Churchill's dissertations on the production and consumption of pork, bacon, gammon and ham.

As late as 1930 he was still recommending that old-fashioned nostrum for social health and family happiness, the multiplication of pigs, one for every 'cottage home'.[21] This was an ideal form of individual self-help, Churchill thought, and he criticized the Bacon Marketing Board which had been set up to regulate prices and propagation. Although this body did not quite, as it claimed, bring home the bacon, it was not as costly or as cumbersome as he maintained, and between 1931 and 1937 the number of pigs in Britain increased by 50 per cent. When the wartime Ministry of Agriculture proposed drastic reductions to this population in order to save on fodder imports, Churchill complained in vain about the massacre of pigs. To his distress bacon became a luxury. In 1944 he issued a stinging rebuke to the Minister of Food, Colonel John Llewellin, for his 'very foolish prosecution' of a man who had killed his own pig and given joints of bacon to his friends: 'It shows bureaucracy in its most pettifogging and tyrannical aspect.'[22]

Churchill himself was partial to bacon which he sometimes ate for breakfast accompanied by cutlets and white wine. He also liked more elaborate pork dishes and at the Savoy Hotel he was once served a roast piglet with an apple in its mouth. This beast was the offspring of one of Churchill's own sows, her litter having been bought by the Mayor of Medicine Hat in Alberta, Canada, who flew the piglet back to London, frozen and complete with apple. However Churchill found pig's knuckles, as enjoyed by President Roosevelt, too slimy. And he evidently refused Stalin's invitation, issued in the Kremlin in the early hours of 16 August 1942, to share the head of a suckling pig. Still, the Prime Minister watched attentively as the Soviet leader 'fell upon it with zest',[23] cleaning out the cranium and putting bits into his mouth with the knife, then cutting pieces of flesh from the cheeks and eating them with his fingers. Of course, Churchill himself was not one to toy with food. But when he was presented with a magnificent local ham at Fulton, Missouri, in 1946 his response was a model of refinement: 'In this ham the pig has reached its highest form of evolution.'[24]

PLATYPUSES

O f all the zoological curiosities that fascinated Churchill, none was more peculiar than the platypus. This Antipodean prodigy has a bill like a duck, a body like a mole and a tail like a beaver. It walks like a reptile, lays eggs like a bird and suckles its young like a mammal. But the female has no teats, exuding milk through her pores, while the male has concealed testicles but two penises, neither used for urination. The animal, technically known as a monotreme, possesses sensitive electro-receptors to detect prey and large webbed feet, the back ones equipped with claws and poisonous ankle spurs which can inflict an agonizing sting. It was to this prize sport of nature that Churchill looked in 1943 for the purpose of improving Britain's relations with Australia, resulting in one of the most bizarre and least-known episodes in the Second World War.

Concentrating on the struggle against Germany, Churchill had little to offer Britain's dominions in the Pacific which were threatened by the might of Japan. After the fall of Singapore John Curtin, Australia's Labour Prime Minister, publicly expressed his compatriots' disillusionment with Britain, saying that they would have to look for protection to America. Later, in private messages to Churchill, he criticized the British government for making the defeat of Hitler the Allied priority and for underrating the Japanese as a foe. Churchill responded with sops. He sent Curtin a film entitled *Desert Victory*, celebrating the battle of Alamein in which the Australian 9th Division had 'played so fine a part'.[1] He sought to honour Australia by proposing the King's brother, the Duke of Gloucester, as the next Governor-General and he gave Australia's Minister of Foreign Affairs, Dr Herbert Evatt, a seat in the War Cabinet. Furthermore, evidently as a means of symbolizing Australia's bond with the mother country, he asked Curtin to send him six duck-billed platypuses.

This was a tall order. Not only did it contravene Australia's strict regulations protecting the platypus but it disregarded the creature's extraordinary voracity and sensitivity. Churchill might have learned about such characteristics from the 'very informative book on the life and habits of the platypus'[2] for which he thanked Evatt, who also sent him a stuffed and mounted specimen of the animal. This he placed on view in No. 10, beaming all over, pretending to be a showman at a fair and saying to visitors: 'This way to the flat-billed platypus, gentlemen.'[3] Called 'Splash', it had died after four years in captivity, during which time it had consumed three-quarters of a ton of worms, 2,400 duck eggs and thousands of tadpoles. The Australian naturalist David Fleay, superintendent of the Healesville wildlife sanctuary in Victoria where he bred platypuses in captivity for the first time, was charged with meeting Churchill's request. But appreciating the difficulties of exporting members of this 'exceptionally nervous species'[4] and declaring that no person or institution 'could feed six platypuses',[5] he got the number reduced to one. In April 1943 Fleay caught a suitable male and christened him, inevitably, Winston.

When Brendan Bracken learned that the Australian government had suspended its cherished law preventing the platypus from leaving the country, he sent Churchill this droll memorandum:

> One is now on its way to you accompanied by 50,000 specially chosen worms! The Australian Government believes that these ample rations will keep the platypus happy and well until it becomes attuned to our climate and to British worms.
>
> Now that you have achieved your ambition to possess a platypus, you must decide where you are going to house the little creature. If you decide to keep it near you, you must send your cat Nelson into exile. The pussy could (and probably would) slaughter the platypus in a few fell minutes.[6]

Rather than risk such a calamity, Churchill decided that the platypus should go to London Zoo. Clementine, who had seen captive platypuses in Australia, welcomed news of the animal's impending arrival: 'I think this is good and great fun.' But, in a caveat with which her husband would have sympathized, she pointed out that 'the duckbilled platypus sets some store by its private life and that if the gift to the Prime Minister is a single one, its sorrow over its celibate existence will not be compensated for by the prospect of 50,000 specially selected worms'. She presumed that the zoo was well acquainted with this and hoped it would bear in mind 'the foibles of the platypus'.[7]

Such speculation was premature. No platypus had survived for long outside its native land and the elaborate preparations for Winston's long voyage and reception in England took several months – the whole enterprise being kept secret to conceal its possible failure or, in the case of success, to enhance the propaganda coup. A miniature 'platypussary' was built, weighing two tons, based on the one at Healesville which simulated conditions in which the platypus lived in the wild. It consisted of a water tank, with artificial burrows and a sleeping place at either end. The portable platypussary would be home to Winston on his journey and would be placed in a corner of the Aquarium at London Zoo, previously occupied by a manatee, until more permanent quarters could be provided.

The zoo's superintendent, Geoffrey Vevers, proposed to drum up publicity for the exciting acquisition – 'one of the most primitive of all existing mammals ... separated from our age by a gulf of millions of years' – by asking the public to help supply its diet. He informed Churchill that he planned to appeal 'to those interested in this unique animal to assist them in maintaining an adequate supply of worms ... [which should be] packed in leaf mould or moist tea leaves in tins, wooden boxes or glass containers and sent to the Superintendent, Zoological Society'.[8] Also enlisting the co-operation of Kew Gardens, Vevers hoped to build up a stock of 100,000 worms for the winter, though it might have to be supplemented by steamed eggs which would be hard to obtain in wartime. Churchill said that he 'would, if necessary, spend up to £50 personally on the platypus in providing [for] extra needs'.[9]

On 21 September 1943 Winston the platypus sailed from Melbourne aboard the motor vessel *Port Phillip*, a fast refrigerator ship of almost 10,000 tons recently built by Swan Hunter. He was looked after by a specially trained cadet and his ravenous appetite was satisfied by 750 worms a day augmented by helpings of custard. He appeared lively and never missed a meal but delays occurred and by the time Winston reached the Panama Canal he was running short of food. The ship's master, W. J. Enright, recorded: 'I had fifteen niggers digging for two days to get about eight thousand worms.'[10] These did not seem to disagree with Winston but further delays, caused by Atlantic convoy requirements, rationed him to 600 a day. His resistance was thus lowered when the *Port Phillip* came under attack from a German submarine and dropped depth charges. The shock evidently killed him, perhaps by upsetting the electro-sensory organs in his bill, which were so delicate that they could detect the flight of a mosquito. Churchill, who had been 'earnestly' hoping for the creature's 'safe arrival',[11] telegraphed Herbert Evatt on 22 November 1943: 'Am grieved to have to tell you that the platypus you kindly sent me died on the last few days of its journey to England.'[12]

Winston's body was preserved in a bottle of fluid thoughtfully provided by David Fleay in case of his demise. When the taxidermists had done their work, Winston Churchill presented his stuffed namesake to the Royal College of Surgeons to replace their own specimen, which had been lost in the Blitz. It was a sad end to a strange odyssey about which he had nursed such great expectations.

POLO PONIES

Churchill called polo, which had been invented by Persian warriors and became fashionable among Victorian officers, the 'emperor of games'.[1] And he spent a king's ransom on polo ponies – horses fourteen to sixteen hands high, distinguished by their speed, strength and agility. He bought his first mount with a loan of £100 from Cox's Bank when taking up the sport seriously as a fledgling hussar. It quickly became an obsession: in order to play well, he said, he would almost be prepared to give up any other ambition. In August 1895 he was in the saddle for eight or nine hours a day and completed some eighty seven-minute chukkas a week. By spring the following year he had acquired five quite good ponies and was badgering his mother to lend him £200 (around £20,000 today) to buy in addition a really first-class animal. He tried to persuade her that the expenditure would be an investment, while admitting that it would produce pleasure rather than profit. In order to have the best chance of winning the inter-regimental polo tournament in India, the 4th Hussars purchased the Poona Light Horse's entire stud of twenty-five seasoned ponies. Churchill appraised these beasts with a discriminating eye and, according to the Aga Khan's cousin, no one in his regiment was 'a better judge of a horse'.[2]

Despite having dislocated his right shoulder and being obliged thereafter to ride with his elbow strapped to his side, Churchill became an outstanding polo player. His own performances perfectly illustrated his conviction that it was a martial exercise. A contemporary, Patrick Thompson, wrote:

> He rides in the game like heavy cavalry getting into position for the assault. He trots about, keenly watchful, biding his time, a master of tactics and strategy. Abruptly he sees his chance and

Churchill regarded polo as 'the finest game in the world' and he played aggressively well into middle age.

he gathers his pony and charges in, neither deft nor graceful, but full of tearing physical energy – and skilful with it, too. He bears down opposition by the weight of his dash and strikes the ball. Did I say 'strikes'? He *slashes* the ball.[3]

Indeed, according to his cousin Shane Leslie, he 'played hard enough to have ponies killed under him'.[4] Against the odds, the 4th Hussars were victorious at the Meerut inter-regimental tournament in 1899 and Churchill, despite the injury to his arm, scored several goals.

He was correspondingly indignant when, three years later, the Secretary of State for War, St John Brodrick, proposed to abolish such competitions because they added to the expense of serving in cavalry regiments. In a long letter to Brodrick, Churchill asserted that for mounted soldiers the game was an education as much as a recreation, developing 'very strongly qualities of nerve and judgement quite apart from horsemanship'.[5] Elsewhere he maintained that mimic combat on the polo ground took the toper out of the mess, imbued him with pluck, temper and equestrian skill, and achieved the salvation of the subaltern in India. Later, during the Second World War, he visualized

Spitfires as steeds and made every effort to ensure that 'the pilots have good polo ponies'.[6]

Elected to parliament in 1900, Churchill justified his continuing to play polo on the grounds that it would provide him with the physical exercise and mental stimulus which the 'late hours and continual sittings of the House absolutely require'.[7] He remained a keen contestant up to and after the Great War. In 1920 he bought two more ponies for £150 each. In 1921 he organized a Commons team to compete against one from the Lords, expecting to 'beat them to blazes'[8] and telling his cousin Lord Wimborne that if the peers shirked the challenge they should 'hand over the Cup to the custody of the popular Chamber and cease illegitimately, and indeed fraudulently, to keep it in your gilded hands'.[9] In 1922 he sent two grooms and four ponies across the Channel so that he could play near Biarritz. And he struggled to keep fit. Churchill informed the Prince of Wales that he was practising daily with dumb-bells to prolong his polo-playing life and expatiated on the delights of the fast Indian game, with its 'smaller ponies and lighter ball and smoother ground'.[10]

That year, however, Churchill suffered a bad accident on the polo field. As he told Lord Curzon:

> I had got into the habit, through long years of impunity, of dismounting on the offside by throwing the left leg over the horse's head and slipping to the ground. I have done it thousands of times without misadventure but it is unquestionably slovenly and careless. On this occasion, just at the very second when I was swinging my left leg over the pony's head, the brute gave a violent leap with the result that I shot through the air in a circle and alighted on my head and shoulders. A very little further to fall and you would not have been plagued by me any more.

For nearly a week he was 'like a beetle on its back'.[11] The doctors forbade him to play the game for the rest of the season and he lent two of his ponies to his friend Archie Sinclair, keeping a couple for recreational riding.

Churchill was not put off polo. As late as 1924 he was paying over £40 a month to stable his ponies in Roehampton, to say nothing of the extra cost of vets, blacksmiths, transport, equipment and so on. At the same time he was laying out large sums to renovate Chartwell. Eventually the expense, compounded by his increasing girth and age, decided him to abandon the game – 'It is dreadful giving it up for ever'[12] – and to sell his polo ponies. Churchill was slow to part with them. One of his ponies, Energy, was 'too excitable for polo', and so was sent to stud. Churchill determined to keep her at least until she foaled, saying that she 'is a beautiful hack in ordinary circumstances on the road'.[13] In August 1925 he solicited Lord Wodehouse's help in selling Bay Rum and Ostrich while wondering whether to keep them until the following spring. They were not speedy so much as serviceable, he wrote, but 'really fine ponies to play, the best I have ever ridden in my life'.[14] Early in 1927, at the age of 52, he took part in his last game, organized by his friend Admiral Sir Roger Keyes in Malta. Churchill told the Admiral, 'You must realize that I am very bad at Polo.'[15] But, he added, 'If I expire on the ground it will at any rate be a worthy end.'[16]

POODLES

Winston Churchill had his first recorded encounter with a poodle at the age of eight, when his mother took him to a pantomime at the Aquarium Theatre in Westminster. As she reported to her husband, 'there was a large poodle, who was brought on the stage and introduced as "Ld R. Churchill". Winston said "& it ran & barked & squeaked at everyone."'[1] Natural zanies, poodles by this time often performed in fairs, circuses and music halls, though they had originally been bred on the Continent as gundogs, their coats clipped so that they could retrieve game more easily in marshland, with pompoms and bracelets being left over the joints to guard against rheumatism. Their increasingly elaborate, often comical, coiffure made them attractive to the Victorian beau monde and miniature poodles (smaller than the standard size and sometimes used to hunt for truffles) became especially fashionable as lapdogs. But Churchill himself did not acquire one until late in life, when it became the most adored of all his pets. 'No one should not know the companionship of a dog,' he said with double-negative emphasis. 'There is nothing like it.'[2]

Apparently the delay was caused by his conviction that dogs never liked him very much. However the chocolate-brown miniature poodle that was his frequent companion throughout the Second World War, named Rufus (presumably after the first of that colour to be bred, in 1891), seems to have returned his affection. Admittedly there were occasional tiffs. Once, as Lord Kilmuir later recalled, Rufus was alarmed by an outburst of Churchillian bad temper and responded with a frenzy of wails and woofs. 'Take that dog away,' his master roared. 'We cannot both be barking at once.'[3] But Rufus sometimes slept on the Prime Minister's bed. He often sat on Churchill's lap, accompanying him on car journeys and being given pride of place at Chartwell, Chequers and 10 Downing Street. He even ventured into the Cabinet Room during a meeting. 'No, Rufus,' said Churchill. 'I haven't found it necessary to ask you to join the wartime Cabinet.'[4]

In October 1947 Rufus was run over and killed. Churchill was at the Tory Party Conference in Brighton and the news was kept from him until it was over. When told he was devastated, so much so that he could not forgive the maid who had let the dog off the leash and never spoke to her again. He sought a substitute, which was provided by Walter Graebner, the American journalist who arranged the serialization of Churchill's war memoirs in *Life* magazine. Graebner found a lookalike poodle of championship class at the Duke Street Kennels, which had supplied Rufus in the first place. Churchill was not immediately hooked, telling Graebner, 'I'd like to try living together before coming to a permanent arrangement.'[5]

His caution seemed justified when the new poodle developed distemper and later suffered from 'a slight case of chorea ... "twitching" in his leg'.[6] Churchill therefore decreed that 'the marriage can't take place'.[7] In January 1948 he told Bella Lobban, who ran the Duke Street Kennels, that after his sad loss he did not wish to own another dog at the moment. She persisted, saying that the poodle would surely recover and that he was so lovable and elegant that she would like to keep him herself. But Churchill was insistent: 'I do not want to have the poor little dog.'[8] However, as Graebner observed, the attachment grew and at some point Churchill took to introducing the poodle thus: 'His name is Rufus II – but the II is silent.'[9]

Churchill's vet, Leslie Pugh, knew all too well how susceptible he was to animal magic. So when Pugh's partner, J. W. Bruford, examined Rufus II in March 1948, he gave Churchill his 'firm opinion that you should not allow yourself to become attached to this dog, as it is likely that he will be an unsatisfactory companion within a year or so'. His view was based on the fact that Rufus II was highly strung and affected with chorea. 'He has also a bad set of teeth owing to a severe illness when he was puppy, and he will probably suffer from very objectionable breath for the rest of his life.'[10] Meanwhile Churchill seems to have kept Rufus on trial. In May, at any rate, he gave a local man £10 as a reward for finding the poodle, who had escaped from Chartwell and spent a night in the rain – the man's wife replied 'respectfully' and touchingly that 'We were very glad to do a small thing for one who has done so much for us all.'[11]

On 3 June the vet wrote a second and still more damning report on Rufus II. In addition to his other defects, it was 'probable that this will be an unthrifty dog, subject to attacks of gastritis and possibly rheumatism'. Furthermore, when in 'a sitting position his penis is constantly exposed, and in consequence there is a constant discharge from the sheath'.[12] Obviously disappointed, Churchill told Miss Lobban that in view of the vet's verdict he would not retain Rufus despite his 'many good qualities'.[13] Instead he now thought of acquiring a bitch. During the course of the month, however, Churchill again changed his mind. Never one to be impressed let

To mark Churchill's 80th birthday the *Illustrated London News* devoted an entire page to 'A Great Englishman With his Dog'. Churchill even contemplated being buried next to Rufus.

alone intimidated by experts, he succumbed to Rufus II's charm and allowed his heart to rule his head. 'I have at last found a miniature poodle who is both attractive and companionable,' he wrote, 'and whom I intend to keep.'[14]

In some respects the vet's assessment proved correct. Rufus's health was erratic, his jaw was troublesome and by 1956 he had lost all his teeth.[15] Although the worst of his chorea cleared up, he remained subject to muscular spasms. Despite meticulous shaving and grooming, he got fleas and other pests which made him scratch. His halitosis was appalling: Anthony Montague Browne said that he had 'breath like a flame-thrower'.[16] Rufus never became fully house-trained. Belying his ancestry as a waterdog, he disappointed Churchill by his reluctance to swim – the poodle had to be pushed into the swimming pool at Chartwell, with his master's valet, Norman McGowan, acting as lifeguard. Rufus was highly temperamental and inclined to mope, especially when Churchill was too busy to do much more than bid him 'Good morning'. In 1958 Clementine told Lord Moran, 'Rufus has been a great failure.'[17]

Yet Churchill himself would have entirely disagreed. He established a swift, enduring and passionate relationship with Rufus, who also captivated his staff. Within two months of the poodle's becoming a fixture in Churchill's household one of his secretaries wrote to Miss Lobban, 'Rufus is adorable and the greatest fun now. He was absolutely heartbroken when Mr Churchill went away, but he is being well looked after and has settled down all right until his return.'[18] Churchill's absences were frequent and he expected they would cause Rufus to have a good howl. Absence certainly made Churchill's heart grow fonder. He was quite capable of leaving a Commons debate to institute telephone enquiries about the poodle's well-being and he telegraphed from abroad to ask how Rufus was. Diana Cooper later recalled, 'I have watched him mobilize tired notables at a house party to seek a lost poodle in twilight, and he once held up a meeting of urgency to wait for a vet's verdict.'[19] Churchill loved Rufus's welcomes and he was miffed on one occasion when, at a railway station, the dog greeted his valet first. 'In future, Norman,' he instructed, 'I would prefer you to stay in the train until I've said hullo.'[20] Churchill was further hurt when Rufus showed a partiality to Grace Hamblin, telling her, 'You've stolen my dog's affection.'[21]

Rufus was equally keen to come first in Churchill's affections and did not hide his jealousy of rivals, particularly Toby the budgerigar and Tango the marmalade cat. He was prepared to be civil to visiting dogs and, as Churchill noted, he 'made tremendous friends' with Puff, Pamela Lytton's little white Peke, 'although both are boys'.[22] But Rufus seems to have resented regular intruders and he apparently once provoked a fight with Mary Soames's Labrador, earning a scolding from Churchill, who put a table napkin over his head. In general, though, Rufus reconciled himself to the competition, not least because Churchill so obviously revelled in their rapport. 'He owns me,' Churchill once said. 'He has taught me to throw sticks.'[23] He also threw balls for the dog and they played together happily in the grounds of Chartwell. Rufus's desire to please was palpable and he lived up to the French adage, 'loyal as a poodle'.[24] Like his predecessor, he often slept on Churchill's bed, though he was removed when his licking of his master's hands and face became too importunate. Rufus made himself at home in Downing Street, curling up on the knees of visitors. He was accorded special privileges in the Chartwell dining room, where he ate with the family, though his table manners were far from perfect – he once tried to maul the ornamental cat on top of Churchill's birthday cake. Churchill persistently indulged him: 'Poor darling, come and talk to me.'[25] Rufus often sat in a special chair next to his master or on his lap, notably when watching film shows at Chequers. During the scene in David Lean's *Oliver Twist* where Bill Sikes tries to throw the police off his track by killing his bull terrier, Churchill put his hand over Rufus's eyes and said, 'Don't look now, dear. I'll tell you about it afterwards.'[26]

In January 1955 Rufus received a proposal from 'Jennifer', who described herself as 'a standard poodle, first-class pedigree, very accomplished and a nice good-tempered character', asking him to consider 'giving me your kind services so that I can have some puppies by you'.[27] The reply came by telegram: 'I AM CONSIDERING YOUR

PROPOSAL AND WILL COMMUNICATE WITH YOU SHORTLY. RUFUS.'[28] Churchill consulted Miss Lobban, who said that mating pet dogs was likely to give them bad habits: 'they think every dog they see is a bitch on heat, and run after them, and sometimes go off on their own to look for bitches. Also they sometimes run after people.'[29]

Once again Churchill ignored professional advice and his secretary reported that Miss Lobban would 'very pleased to arrange Rufus' marriage' and that only two or three hours would be required to complete the 'ceremony'.[30] Rufus therefore wrote:

> My dear Jennifer,
> On the 10th of April I shall be going to stay with a great friend
> of mine, Miss Lobban, who has very nice kennels in London. I
> should be very glad to receive you there; and Miss Lobban says
> she will make every arrangement for your comfort.

This letter was marked 'VERY PRIVATE'.[31]

Churchill was not the first person or even the first Prime Minister to write in the name of his dog: the poet William Cowper sent a note as from his spaniel Beau and Lloyd George signed the visitors' book at Danny House, West Sussex, with the paw mark of his Welsh terrier Cymro. Other pets too enjoyed a vicarious epistolary existence, especially those owned by writers: Walter Pater's cat Pansie and her sister Atossa, who belonged to Edmund Gosse, went so far as to correspond in verse. Nevertheless the exchange of letters between Rufus and Jennifer was unusual, to say the least, and Churchill took care that their nuptial arrangements, made in 10 Downing Street, remained secret.

Darling Rufie, as Churchill called him, died in August 1962. He was buried near the top terrace at Chartwell beside Rufus I, whose grave had been adorned with crocuses and blue tulips, their colour chosen by their donor so as to leave Churchill in 'no doubt as to how I voted in the last Election'.[32] In animals as in humans, Churchill was not inclined to grieve over death in old age, regarding it merely as part of the inevitable tragedy of our existence here below. But he was saddened by the loss of his 'companion of many years',[33] whose intimacy had assuaged not only the cares of senescence but the loneliness of leadership. 'He was my closest confidant,' Churchill said. 'Rufus heard everything.'[34]

QUAIL

C hurchill liked eating as well as shooting quail. The only migrant game birds, they often appeared as luxurious hors d'oeuvres on Edwardian dining tables, sometimes boned, roasted and stuffed with foie gras marinated in Armagnac. In *Savrola* Churchill indicated the sumptuousness of the President of Laurania's banquet by noting that 'the champagne was dry and the quails fat'.[1] And in a speech made at Lambeth in 1910 he claimed that Tory tariff reformers believed that import duties were capable of making every Briton a millionaire – like the protectionist Germans, he added ironically, who for some reason preferred to eat horse meat when they 'could live entirely on truffles and quail'.[2]

When Molotov visited Chequers in June 1942 Churchill was determined to entertain him in style, which was made difficult because of wartime shortages and the erratic hours kept by the Russian delegation. Nevertheless an impressive dinner menu was arranged, in which quails were to be the *pièces de résistance*. Unfortunately for host, guest and the official in charge of government hospitality, Sir Eric Crankshaw, the quails had been kept in the refrigerator for too long and they turned out to be dry and tasteless. Churchill was furious. Catching the eye of his naval aide Commander 'Tommy' Thompson, he growled, 'Tell Crankshaw that these miserable mice should never have been removed from Tutankhamen's tomb!'[3]

RABBITS

On 15 June 1940 the new Prime Minister was downcast by the news that the Battle of France was almost lost but, walking among the roses in the Chequers garden after a good dinner, he cheered up while contemplating the drama about to be afforded by the Battle of Britain, occasionally murmuring: 'Bang, Bang, Bang, goes the farmer's gun, run rabbit, run rabbit, run, run, run.'[1] This song, popularized by the comedy duo Flanagan and Allen, and initially used to mock the ineffectiveness of the Luftwaffe, became a favourite of Churchill's. It perfectly summed up his view of conies as prey, which was at complete variance with his view of bunnies as pets.

Aged just sixteen and staying at Banstead Manor near Newmarket, Winston happily told his mother that he and his companions had slaughtered about eleven brace of rabbits. Some he devoured, saying, 'We exist on onions & Rabbits & other good things.' Yet in the same letter he sent her love from the tame 'rabbit I have bought'.[2] The incongruous pattern persisted. Winston quickly became a trigger-happy marksman, earning a stern rebuke from Lord Randolph for firing a double-barrelled gun out of a mansion window at a rabbit on the lawn. Yet when Winston became a father himself he wanted a country house since, as Clementine said, 'the babies must keep rabbits.'[3] When the Chartwell hutches were full, however, he was quite capable of compounding the contradictions by murdering the inmates, a perversity all the more curious since his son Randolph was nicknamed 'the Rabbit'. As Churchill's nephew Peregrine recalled, his uncle once had their Flopsies, Mopsies and Cotton-tails served up for dinner.

As late as 1947 Churchill took part in a rabbit hunt at Chartwell, not having fired a shot for nine years. Just as he arrived in his Jeep, a rabbit darted from the last remaining clump of wheat in a harvested field. 'In a flash Mr Churchill raised his gun and fired one barrel,' recorded his private detective. 'The rabbit keeled over dead. It was a wonderful shot.'[4] Although Churchill had no hesitation about killing for sport, he refused to gas the Chartwell rabbits despite his farm manager's plea that these pests, multiplying before the outbreak of myxomatosis, were doing serious damage to the estate. Furthermore in 1957 Churchill was given a final domesticated rabbit, which he cherished. He thanked its donor, Wendy Reves, the wife of his literary agent: 'The White Rabbit arrived with Miss Maturin [Churchill's secretary]. We had great fun with it. I shall take g[rea]t care of it & treat it v[er]y kindly.'[5]

Obviously he reckoned that the role of rabbits changed according to circumstances. Like foxes, they had their place in nature and even provided a model for mankind. Churchill did not favour the nationalization of land but he thought that the country would be stronger if many more citizens had a stake in the soil, on the principle that foxes had earths and rabbits had warrens. On the other hand rabbits could augment the national diet, especially in wartime when meat was in short supply. In 1941 Churchill asked the Minister of Agriculture whether he had done justice to the production of rabbits and urged that they should be bred in captivity: 'Although rabbits are not by themselves very nourishing, they are a pretty good mitigation of vegetarianism.'[6] When Clementine fed him on rabbit in the same year, she said that he wouldn't have eaten it if he had known what it was. With a grunt Churchill replied, 'Bunny was very good, but he didn't want to eat it all the time.'[7]

Occasionally he seemed to think that Brer Rabbit, a trickster full of wiles and stratagems, was typical of his kind. In October 1924 Churchill said that he and the other twenty-six anti-Socialist Liberals not facing Tory opposition at the polls must conduct a cautious election campaign: 'The twenty-seven rabbits had better lie in the Bramble patch for the present with their ears neatly folded.'[8] In 1939 the trench-digging machine that Churchill sponsored as First Lord of the Admiralty was known as 'White Rabbit No. 6', allegedly as a tribute to his conjuror's 'reputation for pulling things "out of the hat"'.[9]

Usually in Churchill's mental bestiary, though, rabbits epitomized vulnerable quarry. Merchant vessels hunted by U-boats during the First World War resembled 'hundreds of rabbits running across a ride, with only two or three one-eyed poachers to shoot them'.[10] Similarly the German battlecruisers *Scharnhorst* and *Gneisenau*, which successfully ran the Channel gauntlet in 1942, were code-named Rabbits. Churchill was ordinarily contemptuous of the species, likening enemy fighters to scared rabbits, startled rabbits, scuttling rabbits. He protested that wartime committees bred like rabbits. And he invariably disparaged political rabbits such as R. A. Butler. When asked whether Neville Chamberlain's attempt to intimidate Attlee over appeasement was not like a snake dominating a rabbit, Churchill replied, 'It's more like a rabbit dominating a lettuce.'[11]

RACEHORSES

Horse racing was in Churchill's blood. His maternal grandfather Leonard Jerome helped to found the American Jockey Club and was known as 'the father of the American Turf'.[1] Lord Randolph Churchill won the Oaks in 1889 with his handsome black filly L'Abbesse de Jouarre (known to punters as Abscess on the Jaw), whose health Winston toasted with lemon squash at Harrow and whose portrait later adorned his study at Chartwell. He himself became an amateur jockey as soon as possible, competing for the regimental Subalterns' Challenge Cup in March 1895. Having assured his disapproving mother that he would not take part, he rode a borrowed horse under an assumed name – the somewhat transparent alias of Mr Spencer. Churchill found the race, run over 2 miles and 5 furlongs, most exciting and distinctly dangerous, since he had to jump high fences for the first time. But he came third, telling his brother Jack that it was an achievement which everyone, including himself, considered 'very sporting'.[2]

Lady Randolph begged him not to race in India where, she maintained, citing the opinion of the Prince of Wales, the sport was corrupt. But once again he resisted, arguing that many officers participated in it and not to do so would 'rob my life out here of one strong interest'.[3] Moreover Lord William Beresford (husband of Winston's aunt Lily, herself widow of the eighth Duke of Marlborough) had given him a racing pony, also called Lily. He quickly put her into training, hoping that she would win him prize money. But he was disappointed. In November 1897 Winston told Lord William that he feared the mare wouldn't do well since she could not beat very ordinary ponies in India. He believed that the warm climate had spoiled her courage and concluded philosophically, 'These sort of things are all luck – and for one you get that turns out well, twenty go wrong.'[4] However he derived immense pleasure from racing his other ponies, announcing that chocolate-pink sleeves and cap (his father's racing colours and today the colours of Churchill College, Cambridge) would appear on Indian soil for the first time. And he enjoyed taking part in a number of races himself, one with 'a ripping line of forty-nine fences'.[5] He never won but came third three times and was elected to London's Turf Club.

These experiences were followed by an extraordinary hiatus: for half a century, lacking both time and money, he gave up horse racing. Indeed, as Chancellor of the Exchequer he alienated the racing fraternity by imposing a betting tax in his 1926 budget. It was designed not just to raise revenue but to regulate gambling, which he described as an evil despite his own addiction to it, claiming that 'personally I have not been able to take a particular interest in horses'. Churchill argued that the levy would not be to the detriment of racecourses and the beautiful beasts that ran on them. But it proved so unpopular that he twice reduced and finally abolished it, adding to his reputation as a political chancer – 'the man who put the Chance into Chancellor!'.[6] However, in 1928 he set up the Horserace Totalisator Board, a state-controlled

Churchill's champion was so popular that Lord Derby told him the 'Tory cry at the next election would be "the Conservatives and Colonist"'.

bookmaker (privatized in 2011) which pleased the punters and returned some of their losses to the sport. Churchill often speculated and seldom thus accumulated, but the Tote was a venture that paid off handsomely.

Through all vicissitudes he continued to think in horse-racing terms. Relishing the jumps, he described politics as a steeplechase, but he also liked competing on the flat. In his first election campaign he told the voters of Oldham that the contest reminded him of the Derby. Other mounts 'might make the running, but when they come into the straight and the judge's box is in view, the noble animal of Tory Democracy and the Union responds to the call that is given to him, and coming up with a rush at the finish has made it definitely certain that he will win'.[7]

As a rank outsider at Westminster during the 1930s, Churchill likened his hopes of getting the premiership to winning the Derby.[8] And after he won the military race in 1945 he complained that politically, thanks to the electorate, he had been warned off the turf. Whatever the odds and whatever the ground, he never lost his full-blooded capacity for thrusting and boring. Princess Daisy of Pless, who met Churchill at Cliveden in 1909, pitied him for it: 'He is like a race-horse wanting to start at once – even on the wrong race-track; he has so much impetuousness that he cannot hold himself back, and he is too clever and has too much personal magnetism.'[9]

Much to the surprise of his wife, Churchill took up horse racing again in 1949, registering his father's racing colours and acquiring some half a dozen thoroughbreds. Clementine was perhaps unaware that as Prime Minister he had strongly deprecated anything that 'threatened to terminate horse racing in time of war or ruin the bloodstock industry'.[10] Certainly she believed that he had hardly been on a racecourse in his life and she greeted this new enterprise with horror.[11] Others feared that his participation in the sport might cost the Tories votes. In an era of austerity it was a gross extravagance, and long gone were the days when ministers had habitually suspended business at Westminster in order to concentrate on more important matters at Epsom or Newmarket. The Jockey Club, of which Churchill became a member in 1950, was an elite institution in a democratic age. Yet the raffish world of racing still attracted those from both ends of the social scale, recalling Lord Randolph Churchill's celebrated remark that the aristocracy and the working class were 'united in the indissoluble bonds of a common immorality'.[12] When Churchill's most famous horse, Colonist II, romped past the post, racegoers cheered, 'Winnie wins.'[13]

Encouraged by his son-in-law Christopher Soames and flush with cash made by his volumes on the Second World War, Churchill had bought the grey, French-bred three-year-old for £1,500. Like the Conservative leader himself, Colonist II was not especially impressive in appearance but he raced from the front and, it was noted, he did best on courses veering to the right. Possessed of a strong jaw, good quarters and splendid hocks, he was, moreover, a 'wonderful battler who would never give in'.[14] He won thirteen races in three seasons and netted his owner £12,000 in prize money. Churchill also backed him heavily, being as thrilled by not having to pay tax on his racing gains as he was by seeing the animal victorious. Moreover Colonist II afforded Churchill a political advantage when, after he had delivered a philippic about how Attlee's government was ruining the country, an MP shouted, 'Why don't you sell your *horse?*' According to A. P. Herbert, Churchill replied, 'Well, that at least is a property which has increased in value since it came under my control…. As a matter of fact I was strongly tempted to sell the horse, but I am doing my best *to fight against the profit motive*.'[15] Shortly before Churchill did in fact sell Colonist II, for 7,000 guineas at the end of 1951, he was asked whether he would put him out to stud. 'To stud?' he allegedly replied. 'And have it said that the Prime Minister of Great Britain is living on the immoral earnings of a horse?'[16] But Colonist II *was* put out to stud and to one enquirer Churchill helpfully explained that 'he has given up racing. He is now rogering.'[17]

Churchill established his own stud, first at Chartwell and later at Newchapel in Surrey, where Queen Elizabeth II visited it in 1958, paying careful attention, going into detail and, as Mary Soames told Clementine, all the while 'looking very dewy & pretty'.[18] Churchill himself took a close interest in breeding as well as training. In April 1950, for example, he reported to Clementine:

> The brood mare Poetic went to Lord Derby's to have her foal, which is a colt with three white anklets and a white star, said to be very good looking. He is by King Legend and might well be a valuable animal. Poetic will be married this week to Lord Derby's Borealis, and it is thought that this progeny will also be valuable. I may buy another brood mare with a colt foal in order to keep company with the new foal by Poetic.[19]

Attending race meetings whenever he could, Churchill also kept a critical eye on his trainer Walter Nightingall. In 1954 he considered taking his horses away from Nightingall and when First Light came second at Newbury the following year, he remarked, 'I never thought five furlongs would be his specialty.'[20] Churchill was not infallible about thoroughbreds. In 1953 he bought Pigeon Vole from Baron de Rothschild for £3,500 and sold him for £440 a year later. But until Churchill gave up the sport in 1964 he was one of the most successful breeders and owners in Britain. In fifteen years he had seventy winners and among his total of thirty-six racehorses were Le Pretendant, Vienna, High Hat, Dark Issue and Pol Roger, whom Churchill called 'the dear animal'.[21] He might have said of the whole experience what he said of Colonist II – that the horse had been sent by Providence as a comfort in his old age.

Churchill commissioned two portraits of Colonist. The first, to be a companion to Lord Randolph's picture of the Abbesse, was by Sir Alfred Munnings who inspected the grey at Newmarket in 1950 and enthused, 'What a horse! What a hind leg, what hocks! I could paint him with my eyes shut.'[22] The second was a portrayal of Colonist with his owner by Raoul Millais, which hung over the fireplace in the drawing room at Chartwell. Churchill's friend Paul Maze also sent him a lively sketch of horse and man.[23] And Theodore P. Cozzika, a wealthy Greek businessman who had originally bred Colonist, gave him what Churchill called a 'charming picture by [Ernest] Meissonier of Napoleon's famous grey horse. I shall greatly value this, and feel that it also commemorates the fine performance of Colonist II.'[24]

In fact Churchill surrounded himself with all sorts of racing artefacts, among them bronze horses made by Herbert Haseltine. As Prime Minister he put his name to the foreword of an exhibition catalogue of the sculptor's work. He admired the perfection of physical detail which Haseltine achieved, having lived for some years with one of his 'Thoroughbred Horses in my dining room at Chartwell. I might say, with greater truth, that the Thoroughbred Horse has lived with me, for it has seemed to be far more than a mere representation of a horse in bronze.' In what might stand as his last word on the sport of kings, Churchill said that Haseltine's thoroughbreds were 'above all for the delectation of those who, like himself, have loved and understood horses'.[25]

RATS

When Lord Randolph Churchill could not pursue foxes or hares, he liked nothing better than to spend 'an afternoon with a terrier hunting a rat in a barn'.[1] Winston was introduced early to such rustic sport, telling his mother that, having killed rabbits on New Year's Day 1891, 'Tomorrow we slay the rats.'[2] However he felt no particular animus towards these creatures. After escaping from the Boers in 1899 he hid in a coal mine where rats ran over him and ate his candle. Luckily, as he later wrote, he had no horror of rats as such. The antithesis of Winston Smith in Orwell's *Nineteen Eighty-Four*, he actually thought them 'rather nice little beasts, quite white, with dark eyes which I was assured in the daylight were bright pink'.[3]

Gorged on corpses, of which they devoured the eyes first, rats in the trenches of Flanders during the Great War were more numerous and more menacing. From the front line Churchill depicted a nightmarish shambles raked by enemy fire:

> Filth & rubbish everywhere, graves built into the defences
> & scattered about promiscuously, feet and clothing breaking
> through the soil, water & muck on all sides; & about this scene
> in the dazzling moonlight troops of enormous rats creep &
> glide.[4]

Churchill was happy under the hammer of Thor but Clementine was more appalled by the rats than by the bullets. These voracious creatures, often as big as cats, were indeed repellent, rattling the barbed wire, infesting the dugouts, gnawing at the feet of exhausted men. However, as General Edward Spears later recalled, 'Winston pointed out that they played a very useful role by eating human bodies.'[5]

Still, Churchill understood the revulsion which rats provoked. He sympathized with the besieged Parisians who in 1870 had been forced to consume these rodents and other 'atrocious foods'. And during his first election campaign, at Oldham in 1899, he first used 'rat' as a term of political abuse. Churchill described as cowardly and treacherous a local MP who had opposed his own government in the Commons, saying that the verdict of voters would be: 'Rats are plentiful, but they are not very popular in Lancashire.'[6] The tables were well and truly turned on him in 1904 when he deserted the Conservatives and joined the Liberals over the issue of Free Trade. Accused of betraying not only his party but also his caste, Churchill was bitterly denounced as 'the Blenheim Rat'.[7] It was a stigma he bore for the rest of his life.

In 1911, for example, when Churchill was, as Home Secretary, temporarily in charge of government business in the Commons, he was ragged by a group of aristocratic Tory MPs led by Lord Hugh Cecil, who caused him to lose his temper by making a continual noise and calling out 'Rats!'. Churchill was sometimes forced to a standstill by these disruptive tactics which were, ironically, similar to those used by Lord Randolph and his so-called Fourth Party against Gladstone's ministry during the 1880s – outside parliament Lord Randolph was even rougher, once declaring that Lord Derby belonged to 'a tribe of political rodents!'[8] As Winston's friend Wilfrid Scawen Blunt remarked, it was 'strange to see him hoist with his father's petard'.[9] But even in general society Churchill could not shake off the aura of rat, as appears from the curious trinity of images coined by the writer Wilfrid Meynell. He said that the three things Churchill most resembled were 'a seraph, a rat and ... a rat-catcher'.[10]

Churchill made matters worse on 21 September 1914 when he said in a speech at Liverpool, to loud cheers, that if ships of the German fleet did not come out and fight 'they will be dug out like rats in a hole'.[11] The following day a German submarine sank three British battlecruisers in the North Sea, with the loss of some 1,450 lives. Churchill bore the brunt of the public outcry, which started at the top. The King, who deemed his remark undignified, said that the rats had come out of their own accord to British cost. In the Navy there was widespread condemnation of Churchill's vulgar boasting. The press became increasingly critical, accusing him of Napoleonic bombast. When later challenged in the House of Commons, Churchill candidly acknowledged that it was 'a very foolish phrase, and I regret that it slipped out'.[12] But he was more equivocal in *The World Crisis*, attributing the 'unhappy phrase' to his weariness and claiming that it was 'true enough in thought'.[13] Dark, murine thoughts certainly haunted his mind when he was ousted from the Admiralty in May 1915. He accused Lloyd George of failing to help him and said that he stood by 'just as if they had been killing a rat'.[14]

Lloyd George had warned Churchill that no man can rat twice. But that, of course, was precisely what Churchill did in the early 1920s, quitting the Liberals and re-joining the Conservatives. His overt motive was to resist the rise of Socialism at home and abroad. But the move was seen as yet another example of Churchill's unscrupulous opportunism and he was excoriated for lack of moral principle as well as lack of political loyalty. Debate about this will echo down the ages: with equal justice Churchill can be represented as a born Whig, an instinctive Liberal, an atavistic Tory and, perhaps most convincingly, an adherent of the party assembled under whatever eccentric hat he happened to be wearing at that moment. But the Judas charge hurt and characteristically he sought refuge in humour. 'Any fool can rat,' he memorably observed, 'but I flatter myself that it takes a certain ingenuity to re-rat.'[15]

Churchill gave lesser rats walk-on parts in the music-hall comedy of his life, he himself being author, impresario and star. Maintaining that he never had any objection to the rat as such, Churchill professed shock at the shameless manner in which William Jowitt crossed the floor in 1929 to become Attorney-General in the new Labour government: 'He has disgraced the name of rat.'[16] In 1935 Churchill expressed surprise when his son contracted a rare form of infection derived from bacilli in the urine of rats, known as sewerman's disease, saying that 'Randolph could not recall having encountered any rats – except Buchan Hepburn!'[17] (Patrick Buchan-Hepburn, who had served as Churchill's unpaid private secretary during the late 1920s, accepted a minor post in the 1931 National Government, with which his former patron was now at odds.) When the maverick Air Vice-Marshal Donald Bennett, formerly a Tory, stood as a no-hope Liberal in the North Croydon by-election of 1948, Churchill said that it was the first time 'he had heard of a rat actually swimming out to join a sinking ship'.[18]

These were private remarks and behind closed doors Churchill was happy to revile as rats those, like Samuel Hoare, whom he deemed double-dealers. Suspecting an intrigue against him in September 1944, he even promoted Attlee from mouse to rat. But Churchill had evidently learned his lesson about the pejorative use in public discourse of a creature so generally abhorred – his son Randolph, like his grandparental namesake, was less cautious, incensing 'a large number of people' during a political row in 1934 by calling Lancashire MPs 'rats'.[19] However Churchill was quick to adopt the nickname 'Desert Rats', given to the 7th Armoured Division by their first commander, Major-General Percy Hobart – their shoulder flash was initially based on a jerboa in Cairo Zoo. Turning the savage, cunning, virulent stereotype on its head, Churchill admired their aggression, cleverness and courage. In a paean of praise delivered after the Allied Victory Parade through the German capital on 21 July 1945, he said: 'Dear Desert Rats, may your glory ever shine. May your laurels never fade. May the memory of this glorious pilgrimage which you have made from Alamein to the Baltic and Berlin never die.'[20]

RHINOCEROSES

s Home Secretary in 1911, Churchill attempted to liberalize the law relating to trade unions only to discover that they eluded precise legal definition – like the rhinoceros, he said, they were difficult to define yet instantly recognizable. Having seen quite a number on his East African safari a few years earlier, he himself was entirely familiar with the pachyderm, which he described as a grim straggler from the Stone Age. Short-sighted, thick-skinned and ill-tempered, this titanic survivor had made an indelible impression on his mind, 'roaming about the plain as he & his forerunners had done since the dawn of the world'.[1] The rhinoceros represented a supreme challenge to Churchill the sportsman. And although his predatory instincts were curiously (but not unusually) alloyed with feelings of pity and guilt, he eagerly embraced the chance to engage in what he called 'battle with Behemoth'.

He described the first rhinoceros he spotted on the savannah as a jet-black silhouette grazing placidly under the snow dome of Mount Kilimanjaro. As Churchill and his companions stalked their prey, they encountered two more rhinos and he fired the opening shot. 'The thud of the bullet,' he wrote, 'which strikes with an impact of a ton and a quarter, tearing through hide and muscle and bone with the hideous energy of cordite, came back distinctly.' The wounded animal stumbled, turned and charged towards them with nearly the speed of a galloping horse. It met with a terrific fusillade but came on remorselessly like a monstrous engine, seemingly impervious to 'the frightful concussion of modern firearms'. Finally it swerved, collapsed and died. But during its onrush, Churchill said, the hunters had time to reflect that

> we were the aggressors; we it is who have forced the conflict by an unprovoked assault with murderous intent upon a peaceful

Like Teddy Roosevelt, Churchill celebrated the hunter's manliness by posing
beside the carcass of what both regarded as a monster from the past.

herbivore; that if there is such a thing as right and wrong
between man and beast – and who shall say there is not? – right
is plainly on his side.

Churchill concluded that the encounter had been as thrilling as any
military skirmish but whereas war involved the call to duty and the
hope of glory, 'here at the end is only a hide, a horn, and a carcass, over
which the vultures have already begun to wheel'.[2]

Since prehistoric times man had revered as well as hunted animals,
and big-game hunters in Churchill's day often expressed remorse
about their own sanguinary nature as well as sympathy for the brutes
that they had slain. Typical was the Duchess of York (the future
Queen Elizabeth the Queen Mother), who went on a Kenyan safari
in 1925 and told King George V, 'I shot a rhinoceros which nearly
broke my heart.'[3] But humane sentiments (whether sincere or self-

serving) seldom converted devotees of blood sports to the principles and practices of such as Bernard Shaw, who wrote: 'I have sufficient fellow-feeling with a rhinoceros to think it a frightful thing it should be killed for fun.'[4] Churchill himself would have agreed with his improvident uncle Moreton Frewen, known to the family as Mortal Ruin, who asserted that 'the sporting instinct implies a great deal more than *killing*: the love of new and wild experiences, the artistic soul, the love of untutored nature'.[5] Rhinoceroses, in Churchill's estimation, were 'picturesque and fascinating nuisances' whose proper fate was to be exterminated in settled areas, or driven away from them and confined to the ample reserves of uninhabited territory. All the same, in the wilds of Uganda he went on to shoot three rare white rhinos in the space of a few hours. The first he hit hard with both barrels of his heavy rifle and down it went, 'to rise again in hideous struggles – head, ears, horn flourished agonizingly above the grass'. This achievement by itself, he remarked, was 'an event sufficiently important in the life of any sportsman to make the day on which it happens bright and memorable in his calendar.'[6]

Theodore Roosevelt admired his feat though he disliked Churchill personally, despite the many similarities between them, regarding him as a cheap and vulgar egotist. Nevertheless the past President congratulated the future Prime Minister on having secured a 'rare and valuable trophy'.[7] Moreover he hoped to emulate the younger man's hunting prowess on his own African expedition in 1909–10, which he described as taking 'a trip back to the Pleistocene'. In fact he vastly exceeded Churchill's total bag, killing over 500 animals. His culminating achievement was to equal Churchill's tally of three white rhinos. Yet, as an ardent conservationist, Roosevelt knew that they were an endangered species and condemned, as did Churchill, the wanton carnage carried out by 'game butchers'.[8] It was a horrid contradiction that neither the American Bull Moose nor the British Bulldog could or would resolve.

SEA ANEMONES

Winston first encountered sea anemones as a small boy playing on the beach at Cromer in Norfolk. Aged ten, he wrote to his mother that after breakfast 'we go on to the rocks and hunt for Sea Anennomies [sic]. I have got a hundred of them.'[1] But although he found these quiescent creatures attractive he was evidently not much excited by them, preferring bolder, gaudier beasts.

Similarly, as an adult influenced by Victorian propriety as well as Regency licence, Churchill was apt to divide the women he admired into two categories: innocent lambs and soiled doves. The purity of the former must be treasured, but the latter were also to be admired – as mature adventuresses unafraid to grapple with the seamy side of life. One such, Churchill told Asquith's daughter Violet, was Maxine Elliott, whom he likened approvingly to 'a tigress' in the jungle. But when Violet, who twitted him on the romantic naivety of his attitude towards unsullied virgins, asked him what went on in the jungle, he refused to tell her: 'Not for you the savage claws of predatory beasts....' However Churchill did make her privy to his own anti-Puritan creed during a birthday party given to him by his cousin Venetia Montagu in the early 1930s, at which most of the ladies were women of experience. 'Yes – this is the sort of company I should like to find in heaven,' he said. 'Stained perhaps – stained but *positive*. Not those flaccid sea-anemones of virtue who can hardly wobble an antenna in the turgid waters of negativity.'[2]

SHEEP

Churchill's Spencer ancestors had made their fortune from wool and he himself always valued sheep. Having earned almost £10,000 from writing and lecturing after his escape from the Boers in 1899, he handed the whole sum to the financier Sir Ernest Cassel with the instruction, 'Feed my sheep.'[1] Cassel invested the money prudently and the sheep fattened. But as Churchill said, somewhat underestimating his prodigious appetite, he ate one or two of them each year until the flock was entirely devoured.

In East Africa, a few years later, Churchill pointed to the economic advantages of improving the breed of native sheep, hairy creatures rather resembling small goats. He extolled the practice of crossing these animals with Sussex or Australian stock, whose descendants were transformed into the 'woolled beast of familiar aspect'.[2] Later still, as a Home Secretary who had progressive ideas about penal reform and was harrowed by letters from gaol which gave 'the feeling of souls in agony',[3] Churchill intervened to remit a severe prison sentence passed on a Dartmoor shepherd, one David Davies. A frequent rifler of church poor boxes (on the plausible ground that they were labelled 'For the Poor' and he himself was poor), Davies was celebrated for 'his unusual gift of calling individual sheep by name'.[4] Churchill tried to give him a fresh start but almost at once the shepherd committed another theft and the Home Secretary, to his chagrin, was mocked for being soft-headed as well as soft-hearted.

Churchill farmed sheep himself at Chartwell, where he took a keen interest in breeding, lambing and rearing. A ram called Charmayne he bottle-fed in person, though not with the happiest results. Charmayne grew cheeky with age, Churchill said, 'swollen with pride at his fertile harem'.[5] He also became aggressive, chasing and butting those who intruded into his domain. He alarmed children, wrote Sarah Churchill, who considered him an 'absolutely horrible beast'. Clementine had Charmayne castrated in an attempt to make him less fierce and when this didn't work she wanted to get rid of him altogether. But her husband would have none of it: 'How ridiculous, you don't have to be frightened; it is very nice and knows me.' Eventually, however, the ram butted Churchill in the back of the legs, knocking him flat. As Sarah recorded, 'Charmayne was never mentioned again and was banned from Paradise!'[6]

A similar fate overtook the sheep Friendly which was purged when it became unfriendly, though not before participating in what Churchill took to be an extraordinary instance of ovine telepathy. Sitting over lunch at Chartwell in January 1937, drinking port and smoking a cigar, he found himself musing about feeding Friendly some bread. All at once he spotted the sheep marching, then trotting and finally cantering down the opposite hill towards him. It was, he told Clementine,

> an amazing case of thought transference and this most intelligent animal realized my intention to give him bread. Needless to say I gathered up whatever bread there was on the table and hastened down to the lake where I rewarded him for his occult intelligence. If you had seen what happened you would have thought it remarkable. It appears to me these things do not depend on the will power at all or in any conscious exercise of the intellect. It is only when there is a thought which forms subconsciously that sometimes it is transferred. In this case the key was simple, namely bread, which Friendly could understand as well as I.[7]

Perhaps Churchill would have been less impressed by Friendly's psychic powers if he had recalled Robert Burns's pet ewe Mailie: 'A lang half-mile she could descry him/Wi' kindly bleat, when she did spy him/She ran wi' speed.'[8]

As a small boy Winston had been so naughty that his relations regarded him as 'the black sheep of the family'.[9] The same epithet was applied to him as a man. He repudiated it while in the role of Colonial

Secretary, saying that since his economies reflected those advocated in the Geddes Report 'the blackest sheep in the flock ... has left court without a stain on his character'.[10] In 1925, though, Churchill happily denominated himself a lamb in a letter to Lord Beaverbrook, who had been harrying Baldwin's Chancellor with lupine ferocity in the *Daily Express*:

> the whole of our relations during the present year have been
> those of the Wolf and the Lamb. The Wolf has made repeated
> and extremely spiteful attacks upon the Lamb, and has avowedly
> compassed his destruction. The Lamb, on the other hand,
> conscious not only of his innocence, but of the strength of
> the fold, and sustained by the sympathy of the Shepherd and
> the other Sheep, has preserved a moody silence not, however,
> unaccompanied by some complacency.[11]

Beaverbrook admired this imagery, with its hint of irreverence. But the press baron claimed that he himself did not bite, only howled, and advised Churchill to have no faith in some of the sheep sharing his pasture.

It was advice Churchill eventually took, consigning himself to the political wilderness during the 1930s. Throughout he retained his faith in the worth of wool, painting some of his flock as they grazed on a hillside in a picture entitled *Landscape with Sheep*[12] – which sold for £1 million in 2007. When he became Prime Minister in 1940 Churchill objected to clothes rationing as recommended by his new President of the Board of Trade Oliver Lyttelton, asking why everyone couldn't wear woven boiler suits as he did. Lyttelton had to stop himself from retorting that Churchill's unconventional attire was made from the finest vicuña and that even if less exotic one-piece garments were manufactured for the masses they would consume 'most of the Australian wool clip'.[13]

Although Churchill set such store by sheep he often used them, in standard fashion, as metonyms for meekness. Military discipline, which gave scope to elan and individualism, was, he liked to insist, that of a pack of hounds, not that of a flock of sheep. Social discipline was also vital but, he declared during the Great War, it had to be freely accepted by active citizens – as opposed to 'the docile sheep who serve the ferocious ambitions of drastic kings'.[14] War itself, he told Clementine in 1916 when condemning the sloth of his successors in high office, 'is action, energy, & hazard. These sheep only want to browse among the daisies.'[15] Sir James Wolfe Murray, Chief of the Imperial General Staff, who was wholly submissive to Kitchener at the War Office, Churchill nicknamed 'Sheep' Murray.[16] In 1937 he declared that the Japanese were no more moved by Christian pacifism than wolves by the bleating of sheep. During the Second World War Churchill agreed with Stalin that the Germans were like sheep, blindly following their leader. But when talking to his senior military advisers he qualified this verdict: 'They are carnivorous sheep.'[17] Employing a similar oxymoron, he described a broadcast that Attlee made in 1950 as 'ferocious bleating'.[18] Apparently part of the large body of Churchill aprocrypha, however, is the oft-quoted story that he called the Socialist Prime Minister 'a sheep in sheep's clothing'.[19]

SKUNKS

C hurchill naturally shunned skunks. In Canada he gave these noxious creatures a wide berth and at home he kept his distance from the human variety. To attack them was to risk contamination. Churchill cited T. B. Macaulay on indecent Restoration plays: they were protected from criticism by their own foulness since, like the skunk, they were 'too noisome even to approach.'[1] Of course, Churchill was happy to surmise that Mussolini's troops would 'fight like skunks'.[2] And he did enjoy company which exuded a whiff of sulphur, such as that of the bibulous lawyer F. E. Smith and the Mephistophelean press magnate Lord Beaverbrook.

However Churchill was enough of a Victorian to set store by an aura of respectability, especially that surrounding social or political eminence. Even after his mortifying dismissal from the Admiralty in 1915, he would probably have accepted Clementine's view that Asquith was 'not a skunk tho' a wily old tortoise'.[3] On the other hand someone like Tom Driberg, a flagrantly homosexual, high-Anglican, left-wing Labour MP who flitted between the public lavatory, the cathedral and the Kremlin, stank in Churchill's nostrils. 'That's the fellow,' he was quoted as saying, 'who brought sodomy into disrepute.'[4] Churchill would have certainly endorsed the comment penned by someone in his private office on a letter concerning Driberg: 'He is a dirty skunk.'[5]

SNAKES

On a walk with his nanny Mrs Everest and his infant brother Jack near the Cascades in the grounds of Blenheim Palace, seven-year-old Winston told his father, 'we saw a snake crawling about in the grass. I wanted to kill it but Everest would not let me.'[1] The primeval human enmity towards the infernal serpent could not have been expressed more starkly and throughout his life Churchill was repelled by these reptiles, sometimes attributing their venomous character to his foes. In this respect he differed from Lord Randolph, who appreciated that the traditional image of the snake was ambiguous: it was a symbol of sagacity as well as an emblem of evil. Thus he maintained that to defeat Gladstone required 'the wisdom of the serpent',[2] yet he found in the Grand Old Man's conversion to Home

Rule 'more of the trail of the serpent than I do of the silvery wings of a dove'.[3] Winston's antipathy to snakes was unequivocal, as appeared in his account of how the legendary ninth-century Viking Ragnar Lodbrok, known as 'Hairy-breeches', was cast into a Northumbrian pit filled with a 'coiling mass of loathsome adders'.[4]

Unsurprisingly, therefore, Churchill directed his choicest ophidian invective at the Bolsheviks, whom he compared to 'a snake creeping along on its slimy stomach, and then suddenly striking at its prey'.[5] In 1920 he wanted to expel the Soviet trade delegation led by Leonid Krasin, likening it to a swarming nest of vipers – whereas, he complained, Lloyd George regarded the Russians as tame cobras. Churchill also wished to persuade Austria to send the exiled Hungarian Communist leader Béla Kun to Soviet Russia on the grounds that a few additional serpents in that nest would make 'no appreciable difference to its poisonous character. They can bite each other if they like.'[6] Seeking an antidote to the international spread of revolutionary doctrines, Churchill hopefully maintained that the Bolsheviks were so alien that it was as impossible for British working men and women to get on with them 'as it would be to make a pet of a poisonous snake'.[7]

Ironically Churchill himself was compared to a snake after his capture by the Boers in 1899. General Smuts observed him, a squat, scruffy, unshaven figure complaining bitterly (and speciously) that as a war correspondent he should be released: 'He was furious, venomous, just like a viper.'[8] Churchill too was liable to visit serpentine vilification on his own sometime friends. On 20 May 1915, as the Dardanelles disaster unfolded and he was about to be dismissed from his post at the Admiralty, he exclaimed to the newspaper proprietor George Riddell, 'I have been stung by a viper. I am the victim of a political intrigue. I am finished!'[9] Apparently Churchill thought that the fangs belonged to Jackie Fisher, the rancorous First Sea Lord, but that the sinuous manoeuvres behind the plot were those of the ambitious David Lloyd George.

In the tropics Churchill took careful precautions against fork-tongued assailants. He knew that there was no way of extirpating these enemies of humankind, however, and mocked the Indian government's attempt to reduce mortality from snake-bites by offering a reward for the skins of cobras: 'Forthwith cobra-farming becomes an extensive industry.'[10] But he was far from having a phobia about snakes. In fact he was fascinated by those he saw swaying to the rhythm of snake charmers in Marrakech. And he employed harmless reptilian imagery in the standard fashion, comparing rivers, trains and columns of men to gliding, twisting, creeping serpents. Apparently he could also joke about these creatures, though it is not clear that the dialogue recorded by his secretary Anthony Montague Browne is more credible than the story, which lacked solid foundation, that Lady Randolph Churchill had had a snake tattooed on her wrist. According to Montague Browne two Mormons accidentally gained entry to Chartwell and gave the aged Churchill an opportunity to recycle (as he afterwards grinningly admitted) some familiar music-hall lines when he offered them a glass of whisky:

'May I have water, Sir Winston?' one asked. 'Lions drink it.'
'Asses drink it too,' replied their host, sotto voce.
'Strong drink rageth and stingeth like a serpent,' said the other, austerely.
'I have long been looking for a drink like that,' WSC muttered.[11]

SQUIRRELS

Churchill was a squirrel. Or rather he was a squirrel in one crucial respect: he hoarded his papers. Although improvident in other ways, he kept every official record he could lay his hands on, collected copious press cuttings and photographs, retained copies of his own letters and memoranda as well as drafts of his speeches, articles and books, and preserved every communication he received.

With a shrewd grasp of the literary, historical and financial value of this huge documentary store he hung on to trivia and ephemera: a receipt for 10s and 6d paid to the Westerham Market Fat Stock Show Society; a letter of thanks to a man for giving him 'one of your cucumbers, in the shape of a "Victory V"';[1] the gory labels on game birds sent to him from Blenheim and Sandringham. Typical of the inconsequential material he accumulated was correspondence about two albino squirrels spotted in the grounds of Walmer Castle on the Kent coast, his official residence as Lord Warden of the Cinque Ports (a ceremonial post of medieval origin). These unusual creatures were, as the Bailiff of the Royal Parks Division of the Ministry of Works told him in July 1948, 'newcomers among the normal arboreal population of your domain'.

In his mandarin missive the Bailiff said that London Zoo were interested in acquiring these animals, one of which had been trapped and the other soon to be caught if the Ministry was capable of 'matching our cunning with the more cautious partner'. Meanwhile, he continued, 'tallies must be kept and observance paid to the demands of precedent, thus the zoo authorities require to know whom they are to record as presenting these two rare living specimens to their care'. Baffled by this bureaucratic idiom, Churchill exclaimed, 'What *do* they want?'[2] They wanted him to make a formal gift of the squirrels in his capacity as Warden, which Clementine thought would be 'very nice'.[3] He was glad to comply and the zoo was proud to display albino examples of *Sciurus vulgaris* with such illustrious provenance.

Churchill was enchanted by the sprightliness of bushy-tailed red and grey English squirrels and he was also attracted to their North American cousins, chipmunks and marmots. He met the 'chumpwick', to use his own term, in the Rocky Mountains in 1929, telling Clementine that it was 'about quarter of the size of our squirrel, but beautifully marked on its sides with black and yellow stripes, and in manner lively and confiding. These charming little animals soon become tame, and at the Tea House above Lake Louise they came in twos and threes and ate crumbs out of our hands, putting their little paws on our fingers and sitting up and eating their food in the prettiest manner.'[4] In a rugged glacial valley Churchill also encountered several marmots. Continuing with his lyrical nature study, he wrote:

> This animal looks like a Beaver and is about two to three feet long including the tail. It wears Iron Grey fur down to its waist turning to Reddish Auburn to its tail, which is Black. He lives among the rocks and has disguised himself to look exactly like them. He is possessed of a great curiosity which led him to pry upon us as we picknicked, and he, too, allowed himself to be fed, though quite wild.[5]

Agile and active, squirrels also provided Churchill with rhetorical opportunities where opponents were concerned. In January 1942, for example, he complained about the hopeless inconsistency of the 'naggers in the Press', who 'spun round with the alacrity of squirrels.'[6] Such was Churchill's post-war loathing for Herbert Morrison, at whom he once directed rude gestures as well as harsh words, that he actually scrambled his animal imagery. He derided Morrison as Attlee's 'faithful spaniel' in one breath and in the next accused him of reverting to unreconstructed Socialism 'with a rapidity which would excite the envy of the nimblest squirrel'.[7] Stafford Cripps – a rich, left-wing barrister, a Christian, a vegetarian, a teetotaller, a non-smoker (eventually) and an eccentric who knitted his own earmuffs – was another bête noire and a prime target for Churchill's wit, real or recycled. 'Sir Stifford Crapps',[8] he allegedly said, had 'all the virtues I dislike and none of the vices I admire.' Also attributed to Churchill, but probably not original to him, was the famous remark: 'There, but for the grace of God, goes God.'[9] Still, Churchill was genuinely offended by Cripps's combination of Puritan idealism and personal ambition. 'The trouble is,' the Prime Minister told Stalin, 'his chest is a cage in which two squirrels are at war, his conscience and his career.'[10]

STAGS

Churchill espoused stag-hunting, by whatever means, as a royal and ancient pursuit. Quoting a medieval chronicler in his *History of the English-Speaking Peoples*, he recorded how William the Conqueror had exercised a strict monopoly on killing game and 'loved stags as much/As if he were their father'. Edward I also delighted in slaying the fleet hart: disdaining hounds and spear, he 'galloped at breakneck speed to cut the unhappy beast to the ground'.[1] And other kings, notably Henry VIII, were obsessed by the chase. As for Churchill himself, he had his most enjoyable experiences of pursuing monarchs of the glen while staying at Balmoral as a guest of Edward VII and George V. In 1902 he found the stalking excellent but missed the stags. Subsequently, although deploring butchery, he was more successful; and on 20 September 1913 he shot four good stags in quick succession under difficult conditions. It was, he told Clementine, 'Quite the best day's sport I have had in this country.'[2]

A couple of years earlier W. S. Gilbert was quoted as saying that deer-stalking would be a very fine sport if only the deer had guns. Neither Churchill, though he loved Gilbert and Sullivan operas, nor his wife, who once urged him to 'secure a huge stag'[3] in the Highlands, would have entered into the sentiment. For them culling stags was not only a natural process but a cherished ritual of the realm, an intrinsic part of Balmorality. It reinforced the social hierarchy, adding distinction to its regal and noble leadership. It fostered the martial arts of hunting and shooting. And it celebrated the vigour of the island race on which, as Churchill often said, the security of the British Empire depended.

This was a common view among his contemporaries but as Churchill learned, to his embarrassment, for some of them slaying deer was as much a matter of passion as prestige. After visiting the Grand Fleet on the west coast of Scotland with senior officers from the Admiralty in September 1914, the First Lord stopped to investigate a searchlight seen on top of Lochrosque Lodge near Achnasheen. Spy mania was rife and they suspected that it was being used to signal the whereabouts of British ships to German Zeppelins. Pistols in pockets, the naval party bearded the owner. He explained that the purpose of the searchlight was to locate deer on the hillsides at night by the greenish glint in their eyes, so as to secure a good bag the following day. Churchill expressed frank incredulity and insisted on dismantling the searchlight. He and his colleagues departed 'bearing with us various parts of the mechanism', Churchill wrote, 'after sullen adieux'.[4] He remained suspicious and instituted further enquiries. They revealed that the owner, Sir Arthur Bignold, was an entirely innocent and eminently respectable patriot who was ardently dedicated to the sport of stalking deer.

SWANS

On the evening of 28 July 1914 Churchill sought respite from the pressures of readying the fleet for the imminent war against Germany by watching a pair of black swans on the lake in St James's Park. He was geared up and happy, he told Clementine, since these 'preparations have a hideous fascination for me'. But he was also horrified by his own bellicose nature and by the prospect of carnage on an inconceivable scale. Stately and serene, the swans afforded him moments of calm before the storm and he particularly admired their 'darling cygnet – grey, fluffy, precious & unique'.[1] This was a prologue to Churchill's long love affair with swans, especially black swans, which, he was later pleased to learn, the Roman poet Juvenal had used as a 'synonym for something excessively rare'.[2] Like other love affairs, however, Churchill's was characterized by trouble as well as joy.

In 1927 he introduced two of these rare birds to his pair of white swans, named Jupiter and Juno, on the lake at Chartwell. The newcomers were gifts from his rich friend Sir Philip Sassoon, to whom Churchill wrote:

> The black swans arrived safely and I conducted them to their pool. The next day they were driven off by an irate Jupiter. But a wire fence has now been constructed which will protect them from his aggression until the novelty of their presence has worn off. They look lovely, and their beaks have got much redder since they arrived. They sing to one another beautifully, and dance minuets with their necks.[3]

Churchill addressed his beloved birds in 'swan-talk', whimsically claiming to have an exclusive understanding of the language.

Plainly entranced by this aquatic ballet, Churchill asked about the swans' mating and their accommodation during the winter. Sassoon replied that 'these birds are much hardier than their delicate exterior would lead one to believe'.[4] As Churchill told Clementine, they not only survived the cold but established a modus vivendi with the white swans, the whole group being 'very sweet'.

In the spring of 1928 Jupiter and Juno built a nest and incubated three eggs, taking it in turns to sit on them. Churchill paid Jupiter a visit on the nest and reported:

> He was most affable and tried to explain to me exactly what he was doing. Juno has been reduced to law and order by the black swans. She is allowed to go on to the upper lake; but the moment she misbehaves or is the least bit above herself, the new female black swan swims quietly up to her, looks her full in the eye, and without even a hiss or a splash or a peck, orders her off, with which command Juno immediately complies.

Soon the black swans were seen carrying bulrushes and reeds in their beaks, from which Churchill inferred that they too were building a nest. He endeavoured to protect their privacy. In the typescript of his Chartwell bulletin to Clementine he inserted this delicate information by hand: '*Ils font l'amour chaque matin.*'[5]

Churchill's bevy expanded as a result of both acquisition and propagation, the latter process affording him ironical amusement at the expense of prudery. All the black swans were mating, he noted in March 1935, not only father with mother but brothers with sisters. 'The Ptolemys always did this and Cleopatra was the result,' he informed Clementine. 'At any rate I have not thought it my duty to interfere.'[6] Churchill was not alone in extracting comedy from the irregular liaisons of wildfowl. Evelyn Waugh once observed that his elder peacock had developed an 'unnatural passion' for a Muscovy drake, approaching it '*backwards* with tail spread. The drake is entirely normal and much disgusted.'[7] But Churchill took the breeding of his black swans very seriously, and he was concerned that although practising incest they 'have so far shown no signs of fertility'.[8] He listened to their mellifluous morning serenades and watched attentively as one pair established their nest on an island in the lake. Eventually the mother laid four or five eggs, while the father harried all the other birds, including his own offspring, at the least sign of a threat.

The tranquillity of Churchill's waters was often disturbed by such skirmishes. Despite occasional aberrations, swans are essentially monogamous, models of fidelity notwithstanding their classical reputation for lechery. Churchill wanted his couples to congregate harmoniously like a gaggle of geese and he later got London Zoo to send a keeper to assist in this undertaking. But as the zoo told him, inducing the swans to flock together would be rather difficult since 'they are by nature non-gregarious'.[9] The Wildfowl Trust, which Churchill later consulted, endorsed this opinion: 'We normally tell people that they cannot keep more than one pair of swans per pond.'[10] His own swans continued to fight, one resident cob severely injuring an alien pen introduced by Clementine in what she acknowledged to be a 'disastrous'[11] attempt at matchmaking. Eventually John Yealland, the zoo's Curator of Birds and a distinguished aviculturalist, suggested putting up another fence to segregate the 'quarrelsome birds'.[12] Since swans can fly and Churchill resisted having their wings clipped, no such remedy could keep the peace. In fact the lakes at Chartwell were the scene of recurrent alarums and excursions.

The excursions that most perturbed Churchill were long-distance flights. Black swans are semi-migratory birds and occasionally one or more of his flotilla would head for the horizon. In the summer of 1938, for example, Churchill announced that three had gone missing and offered a reward for their return. A widespread search ensued. Correspondents reported seeing the birds from Sheerness to the Isle of Wight, and one of them apparently came to rest on a millpond at Emsworth in Hampshire, where it piqued the interest of local people as well as resident waterfowl. From the swan's description, Churchill told a local newspaper that it was 'certain to be one of his lost pets'.[13]

In June 1954 the exodus of another black swan, one of eight he then possessed, prompted an international hue and cry. Once again Churchill appealed for help, advertising in the *Sevenoaks Chronicle* and offering £5 for information leading to the bird's recovery. But this time sightings occurred not only in scattered English locations but also overseas. The most positive reports came from the Netherlands, where everyone took an interest in Churchill's loss according to one of his Dutch correspondents, while another went so far as to write him a poem about the drama. Churchill sent Clementine a jubilant telegram: 'Black swan retrieved in Holland. He was flying to Australia.'[14] But the Prime Minister was misinformed. When the British ambassador in The Hague investigated the likeliest candidate, in Huissen (which perhaps not incidentally bore a swan on its municipal coat of arms), he found that it was quite different from Churchill's bird, being very young and 'not exactly black'.[15]

Considering the recent departure of one black swan and the possibility that another would fly away too, Churchill told Clementine: 'These anxieties are grievous.' Still more upsetting were regular attacks by predators. Foxes, which also preyed on his ruddy-breasted geese, were the main culprits. Thus in January 1949 Churchill told the Marquess of Bath that 'a few months ago the mother of my herd at Chartwell was murdered by a fox while she was protecting her young. The father however protected and cared for them wonderfully and they are now fine youngsters.'[16] Apparently some swans fell victim to wild mink. And in May 1954, the Kent County Constabulary, summoned to investigate the disappearance of four eggs or (if hatched) cygnets, concluded that crows were probably responsible. Only one cygnet was left, wrote Churchill mournfully, though it looked 'very attractive riding on its Mamma's back'.[17] In the words of Norman McGowan, Churchill's valet, such killings left him 'very distraught'.[18] After one murder, Walter Graebner noted, Churchill was so 'overcome with grief'[19] that he went off his food; but not drink – he was revived by champagne.

During these crises Churchill invariably solicited advice and assistance from London Zoo. In July 1946, for instance, he informed its superintendent, Dr Geoffrey Vevers, that misfortune had overtaken one of his black swans:

This was a most friendly bird, and had already been willing to eat from our hands (before bread rationing began). I should greatly like to send back to you the remaining swan – the female, I am sure – who was none too civil to her mate, and now keeps herself very much aloof from everyone … we will organize a party to catch the lonely female.[20]

The zoo was keen to oblige its distinguished patron and made no charge for its services. So when the black swans faced dangers or difficulties at Chartwell, especially when the lakes froze, they were looked after in Regent's Park. The zoo gave guidance over breeding and from its wild animal park at Whipsnade it even provided a mate for one of Churchill's widowed birds – at the height of the Battle of the Atlantic he found time to scrawl 'I will adopt it'.[21] In June 1946, at the behest of the zoo, Churchill applied to the Ministry of Food for extra rations, four ounces of grain a day for each swan, so that his pair could 'retain their present good condition during the winter months'.[22] He was also persuaded for a time to pinion the cobs' wings in order to prevent another hegira.

Successive superintendents of the zoo sent Churchill upbeat accounts of the state of his birds in their care. In April 1948, for example, Dr Vevers reported:

> The black swans are in marvellous condition and the old male bird is becoming quite maternal and looking after the cygnets very well…. They are all feeding well, and when danger approaches they all rush to father who spreads his wings and protects them.[23]

When the boarders were returned to Chartwell, the zoo's keepers tried to ensure that they settled down safely. Churchill himself took increasingly elaborate defensive measures on their behalf, encouraged by Brendan Bracken, who made various suggestions about protecting 'your swans from four-footed Gaitskells'.[24] Churchill not only built the birds a 'citadel'[25] but erected an 'Iron Curtain'.[26] He also set up a swinging searchlight and an explosive device that emitted periodic bangs to deter marauders, looking out last thing at night, when he was partial to a bowl of turtle soup, to ascertain that they were working.

When two black swans escaped from their fox-proof enclosure he induced his private secretary, Anthony Montague Browne, to swim after them and herd them back. 'They didn't like it,' Montague Browne recorded, 'and expressed their views in strong Western Australian voices.' The private secretary fled, pursued by Churchill's 'exhortations and cries of contempt'.[27] Churchill himself was not to be intimidated. One cold afternoon his hungry swans, dissatisfied by the bread he brought them, advanced on him menacingly with outstretched necks and flapping wings. As his research assistant Denis Kelly recorded, 'Churchill sprang at them, waving his hat and stick and yelling, "Don't you dare talk to me like that."'[28] They retreated.

Churchill's efforts to safeguard his black swans were never wholly successful and over the years their numbers fluctuated alarmingly, but he was seldom short of replacements. Indeed, during the Second World War the Australian Ministry of Foreign Affairs used these birds to conduct a little animal diplomacy of its own. In May 1942 Churchill promised its head, Herbert Evatt, three squadrons of Spitfires to combat Japanese air raids on Darwin and elsewhere. However the following month he diverted most of these fighters to Egypt in order to stem the German advance, during which Rommel captured Tobruk. Bitterly disappointed, the Australian Prime Minister John Curtin sent Churchill a sharp reminder of his country's 'most urgent need for the three squadrons'.[29] However, as Churchill had been privately informed, 'no one is more anxious to seek improved relations between Mr. Curtin and yourself than Dr. Evatt'.[30] Thus on 9 July the emollient Evatt telegraphed Churchill sympathizing with his anxieties and expressing confidence that he would now tell Charles Portal, Chief of Britain's Air Staff, 'to fulfil our Spitfire plan to fullest point of efficiency'. He added that Churchill's black swan had been 'allocated and will arrive after Plumage attaches itself in August'.[31] On 4 August a shipment of forty-five Spitfires left England for Australia. In October Churchill received a pair of black swans, which he put on display in Regent's Park. They had been supplied by Melbourne's Zoological Gardens, whose Board also sent him a message 'to say how you, personally, have been and still are our wonderful inspiration in the fight for freedom'.[32]

Of course the provision of the aircraft did not depend on the dispatch of the swans, but the gift helped to oil the wheels of the creaky Anglo–Australian relationship.

Churchill received more such presents after the war. In September 1949 he thanked Ross McLarty, the premier of Western Australia, for sending him four black swans which were in excellent condition and had already given him great pleasure:

> They are extremely fine-looking birds and appear to have settled down in the enclosure I have had made for them on my lake here. So far I have not let them mix with the older ones, but each family can see the other through the wire netting which keeps them apart. I am full of hope that they will soon make friends.[33]

Integration provoked the usual squabbles and predation took its accustomed toll. So three years later Churchill had to express his gratitude to McLarty, who had volunteered to make up the deficit, for a further consignment: 'The black swans have arrived safely, weary but undaunted … I look forward to welcoming them to their citadel at Chartwell. I value so much your gift of these magnificent birds.'[34] This pattern continued and one of the last letters Churchill signed, in June 1964, was to thank Robert Menzies for a new pair of swans to replace those recently killed by foxes.

On the sunny morning of 19 May 1940, as German panzers advanced swiftly through France and Churchill could only hope that the 'tortoise is thrusting his head very far beyond his carapace',[35] he found some moments of relief at Chartwell, feeding his goldfish and his remaining black swan. It was an echo of his behaviour on the eve of the Great War and an indication of the soothing effect such animals had on him. He cherished swans partly for aesthetic reasons, as embodiments of elegance reflected on still waters. Like W. B. Yeats, Churchill was uplifted by the sight of these brilliant creatures. He immortalized his own black swans on canvas in 1948 and in the same year, despite his reverence for royalty, he refused to part with a single one of them when requested to do so on behalf of the Queen Mother of the Belgians. However, Churchill mainly liked to relate to them in a personal and paternalistic fashion: to call out to them and hear their answering cry, to give them bread and feel them nibbling at his fingers, to look at them and look after them with 'tender solicitude'.[36]

TIGERS

At the age of ten Winston wrote to his father, who was off to India, 'Will you go on a tiger hunt while you are there?'[1] He did indeed venture into the jungle on a hunting expedition, during which a large variety of lesser game fell to his gun. Finally, as Winston recorded in his biography, Lord Randolph sent home an excited account of how he had also 'had the great good fortune to kill a tiger'. It emerged from the undergrowth quite unexpectedly and he and his companion fired several times in quick succession, wounding it badly. The tiger hid in a patch of grass: 'How he growled and what a rage he was in!' More shots finished it off: 'Great joy to all.' It was, wrote Lord Randolph, a 'magnificent specimen', 9 feet 7 inches long. Such creatures in the zoo gave little idea of what the wild animal was like. Tiger-hunting, he concluded, was 'the acme of sport'.[2]

Evidently Winston himself found no time to indulge in it when he went to India, being preoccupied with soldiering, collecting butterflies, playing polo and educating himself for a political career. Still, it was a strange omission, particularly as his military patron, General Sir Bindon Blood, had slain thirty tigers with his own rifle and other members of the Churchill clan followed enthusiastically in Lord Randolph's footsteps. In January 1898 Winston's cousin Sunny, the ninth Duke of Marlborough, 'got 3 tigers'. Leonie Leslie, a member of the ducal party, reported to her sister Jennie, Winston's mother:

> we watched them through the jungle as they appeared – the
> second one was wounded & came on to us - & Jack polished
> him off. It was a big sight later ... to see the natives carrying
> down the three tigers on litters made of branches like the Swan
> in Parsifal.

Leonie extolled the pleasures of the hunting trip, in which they were ably assisted by Colonel Herbert of the Bengal Lancers who 'swears hard in Hindustani'[3] at the Indians. She urged Lady Randolph to visit the subcontinent with her lover (soon husband) George Cornwallis-West to enjoy the sport.

Winston clearly felt a pang at not having done so himself. During the Second World War he told the wife of a Chinese diplomat of his ambition to shoot a Manchurian tiger, though this was hard to reconcile with his later aspiration to return to life as a tiger. However, his experience of hunting the largest, fiercest and most charismatic of the big cats was altogether vicarious. He nonetheless used it to excellent histrionic effect, stippling his prose and adding bite to his discourse with tigerish imagery. In *The River War*, for example, he wrote that Kitchener, 'terrible antagonist' of the Dervish leader Osman Digna, 'watched him as a tiger gloats on a helpless and certain prey – silent, merciless, inexorable'. Weakened and demoralized by a war of attrition, the victim was powerless to fly. 'The tiger crept forward two measured strides ... crouched for a moment, and then bounded with irresistible fury upon its prey and tore it to pieces.'[4] Insisting on implacable resistance to Hitler during a discussion with President Roosevelt's envoy Harry Hopkins in the early hours of 25 January 1941, Churchill said that a negotiated settlement would leave open the way for another and final 'spring of the tiger'.[5]

Of course the great striped beast has been seen down the ages as the incarnation of ferocity. Classically Shakespeare's Henry V urged his forces to 'imitate the action of the tiger'.[6] From the time of Tipu Sultan, furthermore, the triumph of the British Lion over the Bengal Tiger was celebrated in song and story, notably by Kipling, whose man-eater Shere Khan was finally killed by Mowgli, his intended victim. So Churchill was anything but original in drafting the tiger into his rhetorical armoury. Indeed, his anti-appeasement confederate Major Desmond Morton employed the familiar trope when writing to him in 1935: Germany's 'strength and cunning, compared with Italy, are as the attributes of a Bengal tiger compared with those of a common tom-cat (and not even a ginger one either!)'.[7] Still, Churchill savoured the tiger's cruelty with peculiar satisfaction and brought his own brand of humour to the menace it embodied.

Thus he wrote that the Pathan warrior was as 'fierce as the tiger, but less cleanly; as dangerous, not so graceful'.[8] The Dervishes were tigers who had tasted blood. Trying out a figure of speech that he later applied to Hitler and Mussolini, Churchill declared in 1908 that during electoral contests with the Tories the Liberal candidate had to fight the Protectionist tiger while all the time a Socialist Jackal was snapping at his heels. As Minister of Munitions in 1917 he stressed the need for more 'moving power' – tanks – at the Front, since 'blasting power' was not enough to 'stop the tiger'.[9] In January 1941 he compared the attitude of Prince Paul of Yugoslavia, whom he nicknamed Prince Palsy, to 'that of an unfortunate man in a cage with a tiger, hoping not to provoke him while steadily dinner-time approaches'.[10] Complaining to George VI about critics in parliament and the press after the fall of Singapore, Churchill said that he felt as if he were 'hunting the tiger with angry wasps about him'.[11]

Of course, tigers were good to have as allies. Churchill hugely admired Georges Clemenceau, asserting that the Old Tiger would have made a truer mascot for France than the Gallic cock. Having seen him speak in the Chamber of Deputies, Churchill said that he 'looked like a wild animal pacing to and fro behind bars, growling and glaring'. And when France opened the cage and let the Tiger loose as Prime Minister in 1917, he inspired terror on all sides: 'With snarls and growls, the ferocious, aged, dauntless beast of prey went into action.'[12] Something of the same galvanic force surged within the breast of Lord Beaverbrook, whom Churchill also admired, though their relationship was beset by squalls. During the abdication crisis in

1936 Churchill acted with him on the monarch's side, telling Edward VIII that the press baron was 'a tiger in a fight.... A *devoted* tiger! Very rare breed...'.[13] This was hardly the case since Beaverbrook's main aim was to exploit the King's matter to get rid of the Prime Minister. But Baldwin won the day, belying his appearance as a somnolent tabby – Beaverbrook, and maybe Churchill too, derived wry amusement from the fact that Lucy Baldwin called her husband 'Tiger'.[14]

Churchill himself was occasionally likened to a tiger. On the eve of the Great War the most intellectually distinguished member of the cabinet, Lord Haldane, exclaimed that Winston 'is perfectly splendid, like a tiger'.[15] After returning from his hopeless attempt to defend Antwerp against the German onslaught in October 1914, Churchill appealed to Asquith to be allowed to grapple with the foe in person, giving up his post at the Admiralty for a glittering military command. His savage instincts matched his Napoleonic ambitions. Asquith wrote to his epistolary inamorata Venetia Stanley about the impetuous First Lord: 'Having, as he says, "tasted blood" these last few days he is beginning like a tiger to raven for more.'[16] Churchill also bared his teeth and claws in parliament, though he sometimes failed to secure his prey. Attacking the War Minister Leslie Hore-Belisha in December 1938, he fumbled with the evidence and his speech was a flop. As Harold Nicolson observed, 'He is certainly a tiger who, if he misses his spring, is lost.'[17]

TOADS

C hurchill noticed toads not as living creatures but as poisonous ingredients in a cauldron of invective that he sometimes filled to the brim and brought to the boil. He was especially prone to vituperation as a young Conservative and in one of his earliest political speeches, all the more offensive for having been carefully prepared, he said that the Liberal Party, which consisted of 'prigs, prudes and faddists', was not dead: 'It is hiding from the public view like a toad in the hole; but when it stands forth in all its hideousness the Tories will have to hew the filthy object limb from limb.'[1]

If Churchill learned a measure of oratorical discretion in later life, the same could not be said of his son Randolph, who rashly stood as an Independent Conservative in the 1935 Liverpool Wavertree by-election, split the Tory vote and let in the Labour candidate. Although embarrassed by his aggressive campaign, Winston supported it out of paternal loyalty and pride that Randolph was defending British rule in India. And he leapt to his son's defence when Duff Cooper, a junior member of the National Government, accused Randolph of stating that its leaders, Ramsay MacDonald and Stanley Baldwin, were 'two toads on the lion's nostrils'.[2] Telegraphing Cooper, Churchill asserted that Randolph had referred to unnamed 'party bosses' not to specific ministers and that 'your natural mistake [was] due to elision'.[3] Cooper apologized and suggested that he should admit his mistake in *The Times*, an offer Churchill accepted. But his letter was not quite what Churchill had in mind. Cooper wrote that he had relied on the chief newspaper backing Randolph, the *Daily Mail*, which had quoted him as saying, 'Our present party leaders ... sit like toads on the nostrils of the British Lion.' He was not clear about the identity of the caucus bosses to whom Randolph claimed he was referring. But one of them must be the gentleman who had led the Tory party for a dozen years, so 'I will cheerfully acknowledge that Mr. Churchill compared Mr Baldwin only to a part of a toad and not to the complete batrachian.'[4]

During the war Winston Churchill admitted to being a complete batrachian himself. Ravaged by the strain, he often behaved in an ugly fashion to those around him. It was as if Churchill had, as he once accused Kitchener of having, a spitting toad in his head. On one occasion he lost his temper with his devoted secretary Elizabeth Layton. Seeing her upset, he exclaimed, 'Good heavens. You mustn't mind me. We are all toads beneath the harrow, you know.'[5]

ULREYI, MOLLIES, GUPPIES AND OTHER TROPICAL FISH

In March 1925 Churchill took his two older daughters to London Zoo, where he admired the wonderful new aquarium and was charmed by some fish that had recently arrived from Java, 'about three inches long and painted with the most brilliant yellow and white belts. No ordinary gold fish could look at them for shame.'[1] Nevertheless it was to goldfish and golden orfe that he largely confined his underwater interests for the next twenty-five years and it was not until 1950 that he developed a serious passion for tropical fish – warm-water creatures requiring heated tanks. According to Grace Hamblin, his enthusiasm was sparked when a small boy turned up at the door of his London house, 28 Hyde Park Gate, with a birthday present, 'a tin of black mollies'.[2]

Churchill at once arranged that they should be taken to Chartwell, that an expert should be consulted and an aquarium installed. Soon he acquired red mollies but their propagation was problematic. One 'died in childbirth'[3] and her babies were apparently eaten by other fish. Derrick Cawston, an authority on tropical fish, recommended segregation and something he called 'Operation Fish Elevation'.[4] Churchill asked Grace to get another tank fixed up 'at the same temperature in which to put the red mollies till they have got over their interesting condition'.[5] Before long he had three tanks and so many different inmates that he compiled a muster roll, headed 'Parade Strength as at 16.6.51'.[6] On the list were three tiger barbs, one Siamese fighter (called 'Cocky'), two harlequins, four neon tetras, two mountain minnows, one red platy, three beacons, two penguins, two serpae, three zebras, two rosaceous (rosy tetras), four ulreyi (sparkling broken-stripe characins from Paraguay), and assorted mollies. Churchill told one of his suppliers, 'The Black Mollies are breeding at so great a rate and the other children are growing up so fast that we shall soon have to move out on to the lawn.'[7]

Churchill had distinct preferences. For some reason he refused to buy corydoras even though he was told that they were 'friendly and quite comic as they will wink at you if you watch them'. Furthermore corydoras obviated the need for snails (which he did not much like) since they were 'first class scavengers'.[8] On the other hand Churchill was so intrigued by Siamese fighting fish that he quickly obtained a pair, naming them Golly and Cleopatra, and encouraged them to breed. They had three days together, he reported in August 1951, 'but she remained coy, protected in her grove, and would not come out under the nest he had made. I have therefore returned them to their separate apartments and will have another try soon.'[9] Churchill's new craze did not go unnoticed. The *Yorkshire Evening Post* published a cartoon entitled a 'A Bit Fishy' which depicted a smouldering Havana over a glass tank in which one fish says to another: 'It does get a bit sick'ning – keep getting covered all over with cigar ash!'[10]

Churchill was offered shoals of tropical fish by admirers touched that 'a great and busy man like yourself' could devote time to our 'finny friends'.[11] He refused most gifts but he did accept exotica such as two rare black guppies and a superb pair of blue-red platys. As Prime Minister once more he also accepted, after much hesitation and on the assurance that there would be no publicity, a dazzling haul from Irving L. Straus, President of the Aquarium Institute of America. It included cardinal fish, mosquito fish, American flag fish, Cuban lamp-eyes, scissor-tail rasbora, silver-tip tetras, orange medaka, Queensland rainbow fish, garnet fish, checkerboard tetras and talking catfish, which had the 'ability to produce a very human sound'.[12] Churchill told Straus:

> I am most complimented by your very kind offer to send the thirty or forty attractive and interesting fish you mentioned in your list. I am making all preparations for their welcome including a Guard of Honour. Alas I cannot manage anything over two inches owing to the small size of our Island and rising increases in population! Please let me know which ones hate each other. I shall be much obliged for any advice.[13]

Straus provided detailed information – the flag fish 'will thrive best on a diet of Algae or boiled spinach'.[14] He hoped that the consignment would give Churchill many hours of pleasure and relaxing enjoyment, and saluted him as the world's 'foremost tropical fish hobbyist'.[15]

In his letter of thanks for this 'splendid collection' Churchill said that the fish had 'arrived quite safely and seem to be settling down happily and suffering no ill-effects from their journey and change of environment'.[16] Their new quarters could hardly have been more magnificent. Churchill had installed five aquaria in his favourite place at Chequers, the Hawtrey Room, where he dictated many of his speeches. There, amid old masters, rich tapestries and antique furniture, the tropical fish constituted a scintillating piece of kinetic art. Churchill was mesmerized by them. Here and at Chartwell, where he had several tanks in his study, he would gaze at these slivers of quicksilver for twenty minutes at a time, calling them by name, extolling their beauty, lauding their colours, exclaiming on their antics, dilating on their love life and even conjuring up a comic fantasy about participating in it himself. He revelled in showing off distinctive varieties, particularly, as one of his research assistants recalled, 'a little black chap called a Molly, who was about the size of a sixpence. And he liked to point out that the Molly was a peculiar creature because, unlike other fishes, it suckled its young like a mammal.'[17]

Not content with admiring his tropical fish, Churchill endowed them with human personalities. The sculptor Oscar Nemon, who visited Chequers in November 1952, gave a vivid account in his unpublished memoir of how his host, standing in front of the aquaria, identified individuals in the water:

> A lean and haggard looking fish with a pronounced nose swam
> by. 'That's Monty,' he said. 'That's Max' (Beaverbrook) was
> how he referred to a round fish with a puckish face. A massive
> looking black fish pushed its way to the front: 'Mussolini.' A
> rather unpleasant fish with a tuft of hair sticking up on its head
> thrust itself forward. 'Ah, there's Hitler.' A neatly spotted and
> speckled fish came into view. 'There's Anthony [Eden] – and
> that one there is a widower.' 'How do you know? I asked in
> surprise. 'We buried his wife yesterday.'

At this point in the exposition Churchill was informed that Eisenhower had defeated Adlai Stevenson, the Prime Minister's preferred candidate, in the American presidential election. 'And now I shall have a fish that can talk,' remarked Churchill. Nemon said that he never knew such a fish existed. 'Believe me, it does,' replied Churchill, 'and this one speaks with an American accent.'[18]

Churchill made every effort to ensure the welfare of his tropical fish. He took instruction from British aquarists about cleaning, heating and aerating his tanks. He learned about lighting and discovered that both fish and plants needed an eight-hour day. He informed himself about diet, finding that angelfish, leopards and Siamese fighters were most in need of live fare such as tubifex worms and Daphnia (water fleas). Churchill enjoyed feeding (often overfeeding) his fish and when he forgot he sometimes climbed out of bed in the middle of the night to do so. Moreover he summoned his valet to assist, being all too apt, in the patrician manner, to treat his servants with less consideration than his animals. However, perhaps sensing an incipient domestic revolt, he once undertook this task on his own, with consequences that might have proved fatal. He dropped the lid of a tank, smashing the immersion heater that kept the temperature at 80 degrees Fahrenheit, and when he put his hand into the water to retrieve the lid he got a terrific shock.

Looking after all these tropical fish involved so much work that when Churchill left office for the last time in April 1955 he lent the bulk of his collection to London Zoo. It was 'honoured' to receive the fish, some 150 species. Among them were two moon fish (*Metynnis roosevelti* – named after Theodore not Franklin), buff-coloured natives of South America as round as they were long, which had never before been exhibited in Regent's Park. The zoo arranged for the removal of four tanks from Chequers and placed them, as Churchill suggested, on a special base 'so that it will not be possible for children to interfere with the electrical apparatus'. The Curator of the Aquarium expected a substantial increase in visitors 'when it is known that your fish are on exhibition here'.[19] Churchill particularly wanted to keep the strain of black mollies going and the Head Keeper promised that 'we shall do our best to breed them'.[20] In retirement Churchill was glad to visit his fish in their new home but sad that only a few remained at Chartwell where, a living kaleidoscope, they continued to beguile him.

VULTURES

Despite the vital cleansing role these scavengers fulfilled, Churchill took the conventional view that they were repellent corpse-eaters and birds of ill omen. Unusually, though, he saw the funny as well as the sinister side of vultures. He first encountered them en masse in India, when serving with the Malakand Field Force in 1897. As festering bodies accumulated on the battlefield, he wrote, 'great numbers of vultures quickly assembled and disputed the abundant prey with odious lizards'. Churchill was appalled by this grisly banquet, but when wounded mules had to be shot he could not suppress the wry observation that the vultures 'watched the proceedings with expectant interest'.[1] Yet their nauseating gluttony prompted a serious reflection on the bestial character of frontier warfare. Churchill wrote to his friend Reggie Barnes:

> After today we begin to burn villages, every one. And all who resist will be killed without quarter. The Mohmands need a lesson and there is no doubt we are a very cruel people. At Malakand the Sikhs put a wounded man into the cinerator & burnt him alive. This was hushed up.... I feel rather like a vulture. The only excuse is that I might myself become the carrion.[2]

In war Churchill's watchword was Resolution, but it might well have been Ruthlessness, since he seldom shrank from drastic expedients – dum-dum bullets, concentration camps (in South Africa), poison gas, area bombing and atomic weapons. Clearly he believed that the law of the jungle must prevail, that there was no escaping the evolutionary imperative: devour or be devoured.

A year later the winged scavengers entered Churchill's life again as he advanced into the Sudan with Kitchener's invading army as a supernumerary lieutenant in the 21st Lancers. Passing through a camp abandoned by the Dervishes on the dun-coloured plain of Metemma, he saw fat, bald-headed vultures wheeling lazily overhead or rooting through the filth and offal that littered the ground. Some, he noted, 'waddled composedly up to the cavalry, as if speculating on the value of their reversions'. More inauspiciously still, about a hundred of these birds, flying or hopping from bush to bush but always keeping a beady eye on the horsemen, accompanied his column as it rode towards Omdurman. In *The River War* Churchill wrote:

> Throughout the Soudan it is believed that this portends ill-fortune, and that the troops over which vultures circle will suffer heavy losses. Although the ominous nature of the event was not known to us, officers and men alike were struck by the strange and unusual occurrence; and it was freely asserted that these birds of prey knew that two armies were approaching each other, and that this meant a battle, and hence a feast. It would be difficult to assign limitations to the possibilities of instinct. The sceptic must at least admit that the vultures guessed aright, even if they did not know.[3]

Over 10,000 Dervishes were killed at Omdurman, though to Churchill's regret the 21st Lancers with whom he charged the foe did not incur a properly 'historic'[4] number of casualties – seventy dead or wounded, plus 119 horses. Still, the vultures got their feast.

Churchill's most celebrated and most comical confrontation with a vulture occurred in South Africa in 1899. After breaking out of the Boer prison in Pretoria and smuggling himself aboard a freight train which took him about 70 miles eastwards, he hid in a grove of trees overlooking the mining and farming district of Witbank. 'My sole companion was a gigantic vulture,' he reported, 'who manifested an extravagant interest in my condition, and made hideous and ominous gurglings from time to time.'[5] This image seemed too good to be true and it attracted much mockery in the shape of jokes, cartoons and squibs. For example, in the satire *Clara in Blunderland*, in which Churchill appears as a green Caterpillar, the heroine recites this verse:

> How doth a timely vulture lend
> Improvement to a tale,
> A Verne-Munchausen-Crusoe blend,
> Which makes de Rougemont pale.

The Caterpillar complains that despite his strikingly handsome appearance the silly bird wanted 'to treat me merely as a little grub'. But in the end it didn't eat him because of his verbal colour: 'You see the vulture couldn't swallow my statements.'[6] Eventually the young politician tried to face down the scoffers. In a speech at Manchester in 1905 he recounted the story of his escape and his meeting with the vulture and added: 'Nobody will believe in my vulture. I don't care whether anybody believes it or not. There was a vulture. ('Hear, hear,' and laughter.)'[7]

Otherwise Churchill invariably conjured up vultures as emblems of menace and horror. Time and again he identified them with real or impending evils. Pioneering provisions of state welfare in 1909, he aimed to guard against the hovering vultures of unemployment, accident, sickness and the death of a breadwinner. Condemning Bolshevism as the vilest tyranny that ever existed, he said that the Russian masses were 'gripped by a gang of cosmopolitan adventurers, who have settled down on the country like vultures and are tearing it to pieces'.[8] Between the wars Churchill warned against the vultures of protectionism and Socialism at home. In 1938 he compared hostile air raiders to vultures and urged the building of more British bombers to attack their nests abroad. Two vultures hung over Britain in 1941, he declared, the threat of invasion and the assault of the Luftwaffe. Other vultures of uncertainty poised above him, Churchill variously said, were his anxieties about the D-Day invasion, his concerns about the continuing war with Japan and his apprehensions about the outcome of the 1945 general election.

Soon after the Labour Party's victory at the polls he rallied Tory supporters by declaring that the 'gloomy state vultures of nationalization hover over our basic industries',[9] illustrating the prospect by slowly flapping his arms, a gesture which convulsed his audience. He harped on this theme, emphasizing the rapacity of the Socialist state with its two outstretched claws, one enforcing uniformity and the other grasping monopoly. But even on trivial occasions vultures gnawed at Churchill's intellectual vitals or loomed above him as harbingers of affliction. In April 1950, for example, he complained to Clementine of the 'Primrose League & Reading Dinner hanging like vultures overhead'.[10]

WARTHOGS AND WILD BOARS

At Harrow Winston had a hostile encounter with a younger boy, Richard Meinertzhagen, who saw in his glance a menacing intensity that he 'recognized later in the eyes of a wild boar about to charge him'.[1] In adulthood Churchill proved equally capable of ferocity, never more so than in the pursuit of feral pigs, particularly African warthogs and their bigger but less heavily tusked European cousins, sometimes known by their French name as *sangliers*. He seems to have shared the view expressed by that champion of pig-sticking and hog-hunting, Robert Baden-Powell, that both man and beast achieved a kind of savage consummation in their enjoyment of this 'brutal sport'.[2]

Killing wild boars had been a test of manhood in ancient Greece[3] and ranked among the deeds of chivalry during the Middle Ages; but Churchill's delight in the exercise was something more, amounting almost to theriomania – an insatiable passion for hunting wild animals.

Churchill, with the immensely rich Duke of Westminster to his right, was plainly thrilled by the success of this boar hunt.

'Joyous times', he exclaimed, when describing how he galloped down 'great fierce wart-hogs' on the savannahs around Mount Kenya in 1907, impaling some and shooting others with his revolver. 'One made a very ugly charge at me,' he told his brother Jack in a euphoric letter, 'but luckily I plugged him in the neck with my spear, so hard that it broke, and the brute escaped with a foot of it sticking in its body.'[4] The victims were not only worthy of their executioner, they also fulfilled a splendid destiny. 'Let no one reproach the courage of the pig,' wrote Churchill. 'These great fierce boars, driven from their last shelter, charged out in gallant style – tusks gleaming, tails perpendicular – and met a fate prepared for a king.'

Perhaps feeling that this majestic finale was a somewhat implausible justification for human bloodlust, Churchill went on to say, in *My African Journey*, that the warthog was 'regarded as dangerous vermin who does incredible damage to native plantations, and whose destruction – by any method, even the most difficult – is useful as well as exciting.'[5] The thrill never palled and afterwards Churchill took every opportunity to repeat it. As Violet Asquith recorded when cruising with him on board the Admiralty yacht *Enchantress* in May 1913 off the Albanian coast, the First Lord 'stayed behind for a wild-pig hunt at three in the morning & caught us up next day at Corfu in a destroyer'.[6] In January the following year the Prime Minister, Violet's father, reported that Winston had returned from boar-hunting 'with his own tusks well whetted and all his bristles in good order'.[7]

Set in wood, silver or ivory, the bristles of the boar were often used as elegant wipers for Victorian pens, which explains Churchill's nickname for the beasts that he often hunted on the estates of his friend, the Duke of Westminster, in Gascony and Normandy. Occasionally his host was absent and Churchill would send him a triumphant telegram announcing 'killed pig penwiper'.[8] Churchill's mother had hunted boars and his wife urged him on, hoping that he would 'get a penwiper or two – Please bring me back their gleaming tusks'.[9] He did his best, though sometimes he only managed to slay a sow. Sometimes, too, the boar proved less aggressive than he was, though even a fruitless chase made the blood surge in his veins. In March 1920 he gave Clementine a rapturous account of galloping after a fat, dark pig for over an hour,

> as fast as we could go through the sunlit woods with all the hounds chiming in frantic chorus. But, alas, instead of losing his wind and sitting down to fight, this obstinate animal continued his career, made for the river and swam as if followed by all the hounds.[10]

The hunters lost the pig and most of the hounds and despite coursing round in every direction, spending five hours in the saddle, they had to abandon the quest. But Churchill was not so much exhausted as exhilarated. Aptly enough, when he became Prime Minister, Russia's state security organization the NKVD, in its secret wireless traffic, gave him the alias BOAR.

WHALES

I n 1947 Churchill wrote to the Director of London's Natural History Museum, Sir Clive Forster Cooper: 'I was interested to learn that in my capacity as Lord Warden I may lay claim to certain whales, porpoises etc., which may be stranded around the Cinque Ports area.'[1] Elsewhere such 'royal fish' were the property of the Crown, which handed them over to the state. Churchill duly abrogated his own right to beached cetacea, acceding to the Natural History Museum's request to make what scientific use of them it wished. But although he had no call for leviathans in the flesh, he set great store by them as images. Monsters of the deep, they surfaced now and again to express his more extravagant or apocalyptic sentiments.

In a doom-laden speech delivered in 1931, for example, he warned about the fate of the nation should it lose its empire, its sea power and its share of world trade, likening Britain to an enormous whale which swam into a bay 'upon the tide and then was left to choke and rot upon the sands'.[2] Churchill later chided himself for repeating the simile but it was certainly a memorable one, never more so than when applied to the unsuccessful amphibious operation at Anzio in January 1944: 'We hoped to land a wild cat that would tear out the bowels of the Boche. Instead we have stranded a vast whale with its tail flopping about in the water!'[3]

A happier outcome, this time involving man-made 'Whales', occurred later in 1944 when Allied seaborne forces invaded Normandy. Churchill believed that, in his paraphrase of Bismarck, the British whale would show its superiority over the German elephant, and as early as 1917 he had conceived the idea of creating artificial harbours on hostile coastlines to supply the lack of a port. In 1942 he had issued his famous memorandum demanding piers for use on beaches that would float up and down with the tide. This resulted, after much toil and sweat, in two prefabricated 'Mulberry' harbours, linked to the French shore by long, flexible, steel roadways code-named 'Whales'. Protected by 'Phoenix' breakwaters and supported by pontoons, the Whales enabled the Allies to disembark 2.5 million men along with vehicles and supplies in the ten months after D-Day. This achievement was all the more remarkable since the Mulberry at Omaha Beach was wrecked by a storm and the one at Arromanches, nicknamed Port Winston, had to bear the full weight of the traffic – Churchill was fascinated to witness DUKWs (amphibious trucks) swimming through this 'synthetic lagoon' and 'waddling ashore'.[4] Members of the construction staff, in their spare time, made him 'charming silver models of "Whale" and "Phoenix"' which he was 'delighted to receive'.[5]

Churchill showed no fellow feeling for the largest animal on the planet. During the war, indeed, he regarded whale oil simply as a commodity to be kept out of the hands of the enemy. In old age he heard a lot about whales from Aristotle Onassis, who had made millions from their indiscriminate slaughter and perhaps told Churchill, as he told other guests on his yacht, that the *Christina O*'s bar stools were upholstered with the foreskin of the minke whale. In person, however, Churchill, who wallowed in the bathtub two or three times a day and spouted bubbles as he finished his ablutions, was strangely reminiscent of the great aquatic mammal. His valet Norman McGowan listened for the signal telling him that his master was about to emerge: 'a noise like a whale "blowing"'.[6]

WOLVES

Churchill believed that man is a wolf to man, that ours is 'a wolfish world'.[1] In youth he witnessed humans behaving with lupine savagery, identified Pathan warriors as wolves and feared, after the cavalry charge at Omdurman, that the Dervishes would 'devour me like wolves'.[2] After 1917 he inveighed against the Bolshevik wolves who, with wild ululations and slavering jaws, were tearing Russia to pieces. Their alien creed even seemed able to transform home-grown proletarians, changing their nature as if by lycanthropy. Assailed during the general election of 1923 by howling, foaming, spitting crowds, the most hostile he had ever seen, Churchill said that they were more like Russian wolves than British workmen. In August 1938 he condemned the imminent sacrifice of Czechoslovakia to Nazi Germany, declaring that it was a fatal delusion to think that safety could be purchased by throwing a small state to the wolves. In March 1944, anxious about growing Soviet might and about maintaining Britain's position as a great power after the war, Churchill observed: 'We live in a world of wolves – and *bears*.'[3]

When Stalin's successors turned on his most vicious henchman, Lavrenti Beria, in 1953, Churchill remarked that he 'was thrown to the wolves without a moment's hesitation. They are like wild beasts.'[4] The theme of saving oneself by tossing tasty morsels to pursuing wolves was a favourite of Churchill's and he harped on it in various ways. As early as 1901 he oddly maintained that making political mistakes did not matter since it was like 'throwing babies to the wolves: once you stop, the pack overtakes the sleigh'[5] – and the government falls. After his own fall and that of Field Marshal Sir John French in 1915, Churchill asserted that Asquith would throw anyone to the wolves to keep himself in office. When the Labour Chancellor Philip Snowden cut ministerial salaries by 20 per cent in 1931, Churchill said that cynics would compare him to a man in a sledge who threw one of his five children to chasing wolves so that he could run on a little longer with the other four. During the mid-1930s Churchill denounced as 'suicidal absurdities' proposals to hand over British colonies to 'the "Have not" Powers and thus, by throwing our children to the wolves, stave off the hungry dictators for a few more years'.[6]

Supporters of Chamberlain's appeasement policy accused Churchill of crying wolf. They had some justification since his judgement was as fallible as his ambition was palpable. Indeed, he was sometimes said to possess 'genius without judgement'.[7] But when making the most important judgement of his life, Churchill proved triumphantly right. He recognized the bestial nature of Hitler, who adopted the alias Herr Wolf and called his eastern headquarters the Wolf's Lair. And he resolutely opposed the Nazis, wolves at the door of the world.

During the Second World War, it must be acknowledged, Churchill gave vent to certain wolfish propensities of his own. Most notably, soon after Dunkirk had deprived Britain of other offensive capacities, he aimed to initiate 'an absolutely devastating, exterminating attack by very heavy bombers from this country upon the Nazi homeland'. This was not intended as a strategy of genocide but it did lead to a massive onslaught on civilian targets, especially those which were easiest to hit from the air, namely the crowded, working-class districts of enemy cities. The policy of 'area bombing' was justified as a response to Hun barbarism and disguised as an assault on 'industrial centres'.[8] But it prompted C. P. Snow, who as a government scientist witnessed the development of the bombing campaign, to say that future generations would rightly ask whether Britons had not resigned their humanity during the conflict, whether 'we were wolves with the minds of men?'.[9] Churchill, who afterwards suppressed his instructions to terrorize Axis populations, evidently had similar qualms at the time. Watching a dramatic film shot during an RAF raid on Ruhr cities in 1943, he suddenly exclaimed: 'Are we beasts? Are we taking this too far?'[10]

WORMS

During a game of golf with the newspaper magnate George Riddell in 1911, Churchill came across a worm in the fairway, which he removed tenderly and placed in nearby bracken, saying, 'Poor fellow! If I leave you here, you will be trampled by some ruthless boot!'[1] He was similarly compassionate at home. When the croquet lawn at Chartwell became pitted with worm casts, Clementine ordered the gardener to put down a chemical killer and proudly showed her husband the results. He was most upset, telling her that 'it is very wrong to kill poor worms for they all have their place in Nature's grand design'.[2]

As usual, though, Churchill was inconsistent. He ridiculed the views of two Croydon councillors, one opposed to angling because it gave pain to fish and the other lamenting 'the greater agonies of the worm, with his three deaths – first, when he is put on the hook; second, when he is drowned; and third, when he is devoured by the fish!'.[3] Furthermore Churchill derided those whom he regarded as human invertebrates. Censuring Viscount Halifax's shifts over appeasement and playing on his earlier title, Lord Irwin, Churchill called him Lord Worming and Squirming. (In the same vein, though using a different image, he denominated the French politician Paul Reynaud a *poisson gelé*.) He was equally unkind about the former French ambassador Charles Corbin. Although pro-British, Corbin would not take a firm stand against Marshal Pétain's Vichy regime and when in 1944 Violet Bonham Carter sympathized with the Prime Minister for having to deal with such spineless creatures, her old friend replied: 'My dear – there must be some worms in this world for you & me to tread on.'[4]

It was during his first meeting with Violet Asquith, as she was in 1906, that he made his best-known pronouncement on the topic of worms. After an abstracted silence the thirty-two-year-old Churchill subjected her to a long monologue about himself, concluding abruptly: 'We are all worms, but I do believe I am a glow-worm.'[5] No aphorism better illustrates his mastery of the luminous image and the glittering phrase – to which, of course, he was sometimes also the slave.

In general, though, he evinced the standard reaction to worms in their different varieties, expressing his feelings in conventional or proverbial terms. Churchill loathed and evaded Africa's parasitic worms, expatiating on the horror of guinea-worm disease (*dracunculiasis*, popularly known as the 'fiery serpent')[6] and the habits of the chigger, which 'will enter your foot and raise a numerous family'.[7] However the parasitic worm did at least suggest to Churchill a method inducing neutral Portugal to let the Allies use the Azores in 1943: 'The great thing is to worm our way in and then, without raising any question of principle, to swell ourselves out.'[8]

Earthworms were more prosaic. They turned. Or early birds caught them. In April 1912 Churchill telegraphed Admiral Fisher, perhaps to acclaim progress being made in developing airships: 'An early worm juicy.'[9] Or they were a source of humour: Churchill was much amused by the columnist Nathaniel Gubbins, who in the *Sunday Express* portrayed himself as an ageing worm prostrated by his duties in the Home Guard, rather like Private Godfrey in *Dad's Army*. Churchill scorned his own university-educated contemporaries as mere bookworms, 'quite undisciplined and irresponsible'.[10] Incorrigibly juvenile himself, he could not resist the vermicular pun repeated by generations of schoolboys – many of whom bred silkworms, as he did at Harrow. In conversation with his private secretary Jock Colville in December 1940, Churchill expressed his distaste for the complicated post-war European Confederations that would have to be formed 'with their Diets of Worms'.[11]

ZOOS

On 11 July 1891 Winston was taken by Count Kinsky, who was probably the favourite among his mother's lovers, to see an exhibition of wild animals at the Crystal Palace in Sydenham. Kinsky drove them in his phaeton and they attended an elaborate series of events, culminating in a firework display, staged in honour of the visiting Kaiser – whose eagle-topped helmet the sixteen-year-old Winston admired. However his chief enthusiasm was reserved for Carl Hagenbeck's menagerie of performing lions, tigers, cheetahs, leopards, bears and boar hounds. Hagenbeck was a prolific collector and would later establish the first so-called 'zoo without bars' at Stellingen, outside Hamburg, a wildlife park which gave animals an 'illusory freedom'.[1] But he was essentially a showman and at the Crystal Palace he put on a series of acts befitting the sawdust ring: lions and tigers standing on revolving globes; two lions on a see-saw with a bear balanced in the middle; harnessed tigers drawing a chariot containing the king of the jungle dressed in crimson and attended by two boar hounds acting as footmen.[2] Winston was thrilled. He wrote to his brother Jack: 'Wild Beasts. (wonderful never seen anything like them.)'[3]

Thereafter Churchill eagerly embraced opportunities to witness such spectacles. Moreover he tended to equate zoos and circuses, regarding both as places of entertainment, theatres of the exotic. This was a common conflation, often encouraged by London Zoo in order to attract visitors. After taking his older daughters to Regent's Park in 1925, Churchill wrote elatedly: 'The Keepers made all the beasts do their tricks. The elephant took a bunch of keys as well as a lot of buns in his trunk and gave back the bunch of keys to the keeper each time without dropping the buns.'[4]

No doubt Churchill appreciated the zoo for reasons familiar to rulers down the ages, as a symbol of personal, national or imperial power. Obviously he also valued it as a repository of expert advice and assistance in relation to his own menagerie. But this itself was not an expression of scientific curiosity or aristocratic grandeur; it was a source of constant interest and enjoyment. As he said in 1928, the Chartwell 'zoo has been full of incidents'.[5] Shortly before the Second World War his daughter Mary sent him a letter bearing this printed address: THE HAPPY ZOO, CHARTWELL, WESTERHAM, KENT.[6]

The prospect of war suggested to Churchill that London Zoo might become the scene of more apocalyptic excitement. Visiting Regent's Park to see the giant panda, he asked how the zoo would cope with an aerial onslaught. Julian Huxley replied that dangerous creatures would be shot to prevent escapees from running amok among the civilian

The Churchills visited London Zoo for this classic 'photo opportunity' just two days after Allied bombers destroyed Carl Hagenbeck's Tierpark at Stellingen.

population. This was a phantasmagoria, notes a recent scholar, that had 'haunted animal keepers for centuries'.[7] But it had long appealed to Churchill. 'What a pity,' he said on hearing of Huxley's plans:

> Imagine a great air raid over London – squadron after squadron of enemy planes flying in – Dropping their explosive on the people and the buildings of this great capital city – Houses smashed to ruins – Fires breaking out everywhere – The ruins crumbling into ashes – The corpses lying about in the smoking ashes – and the lions and tigers roaming the ruins in search of the corpses. And you're going to shoot them – What a pity![8]

There was a genuine element of relish in this vision but of course Churchill spoke in jest, conjuring a blood-and-thunder melodrama out of a potential tragedy. Its potential was soon hideously realized on the Continent. Of the Luftwaffe's attack on Belgrade, which presaged that on Russia, Churchill himself wrote:

> Out of the nightmare of smoke and fire came the maddened animals released from their shattered cages in the zoological gardens. A stricken stork hobbled past the main hotel, which was a mass of flames. A bear, dazed and uncomprehending, shuffled through the inferno with slow and awkward gait down towards the Danube. He was not the only bear who did not understand.[9]

What Churchill didn't record was the holocaust that consumed German zoos, including those in Berlin, Dresden and Frankfurt, as a result of Allied air raids. In July 1943, during the cataclysmic fire-bombing of Hamburg, code-named Operation Gomorrah and personally approved by the Prime Minister, Carl Hagenbeck's Tierpark at Stellingen was devastated. Nine of his men lost their lives, as did 450 animals.

Churchill's fondness for zoos was evidently little affected by his life-long aversion to durance vile, whether human or animal. Confined by the Boers in youth, he felt like a wild beast in a cage. When faced as Prime Minister with competing inter-service demands on scarce resources, he compared himself to 'a keeper in the zoo distributing half-rations among magnificent animals'.[10] Releasing butterflies at Chartwell in old age, he said that he could not bear their captivity. Yet he must always have been aware that zoos were penitentiaries in which the animals were serving life sentences that often resulted in their premature death. They were designed for the amusement of visitors and the convenience of keepers rather than the welfare of inmates, and their architects, intent on erecting monuments to themselves, were plausibly said to be 'the most dangerous animals in the zoo'.[11]

At any rate, in 1943 Churchill was presented with the case against these iron and concrete jungles, set out in an impassioned letter appealing against Rota's incarceration in Regent's Park. It was sent by Mildred Ransford, the sister-in-law of Sir Arthur Conan Doyle, who implored him not

> to carry out your intention to add to the number of poor
> unhappy wild animals at the Zoo, which are kept in small
> (compared to the size of many) cages and obliged to tramp
> up and down on concrete floors and be stared at through iron
> bars – this last must be very galling to proud, intelligent and
> grand animals such as lions, tigers, etc. One only has to look
> at … the sad appealing expression of the monkeys to realize
> the cruelty which our idea regarding the education of children
> entails on these helpless creatures. Surely children can learn
> from photographs and books all that is *really* necessary for them
> to know without imbuing them with a kind of *Hun* indifference
> to suffering…. It seems so unlike you to encourage all this, you
> the best of good men, especially when you have seen all these
> animals in their natural surroundings.

The letter concluded by begging Churchill to send Rota and any cubs to Whipsnade 'to lessen some of their misery', since even when animals were born in captivity they were bound to develop 'instincts for the forests and freedom'.[12] One of the Prime Minister's secretaries, who sympathized with these views (though not with the way they were put), responded that they would be brought to his notice at a convenient opportunity. Perhaps they were, but there is no evidence that he sent a reply.

In 1952, however, Churchill did append his name to a message of support for the 600-acre wildlife park at Whipsnade on its coming of age, solicited by its Scientific Director L. Harrison Matthews on account of the Prime Minister's 'much appreciated interest in its affairs'.[13] Churchill wrote:

> It is difficult to believe that twenty-one years ago there was only derelict downland where the Park now stands, and the change that has been wrought is evidence of the increasing knowledge of and interest in animals that is becoming so much a part of our daily life.[14]

In the issue of *Zoo Life* containing Churchill's good wishes, a copy of which was sent to him, Matthews paid tribute to Carl Hagenbeck, whose pioneering work had influenced the creation and development of Whipsnade. The old idea of a zoo, which packed the largest number of animals into the smallest possible space, was now, wrote Matthews, as dead as the dodo or the quagga. The new principles were superior both ethically and practically: 'The animals are no longer conscious prisoners, but lead full and happy lives in conditions as near as possible to their natural habitats.'[15] He protested too much and his principal interest was actually still presentation rather than conservation. Churchill would doubtless have endorsed this priority. Yet he had been offered a glimpse of a future in which zoos might be transformed from crowded jailhouses into ample panopticons, arks in parks capable of saving endangered species from extinction.

NOTES

The place of publication is London unless otherwise stated.

INTRODUCTION

1   R. Rhodes James (ed.), *Winston S. Churchill: His Complete Speeches* [henceforth *Speeches*] VII (8 vols., 1974), 6824.

2   H. Vickers, *Gladys: Duchess of Marlborough* (1979), 196.

3   C[hurchill]A[Archives]C[entre], CHAR 2/124B/159, Archie Sinclair to Churchill, 13 September 1922.

4   CAC, CHAR 28/14/7, Winston to his mother, 23 March 1887.

5   CAC, CHAR 1/4/14, Mrs Everest to Winston, 2 October 1891.

6   CAC, SCHL 1/1/8, Sarah to her father, 27 July 1948.

7   W. Manchester, *The Last Lion: Winston Spencer Churchill* (1983), 776–7.

8   R. Boothby, *Boothby: Recollections of a Rebel* (1978), 55.

9   *Letters Written by the … Earl of Chesterfield …* III (1775), 220.

10 Mr Jorrocks actually said that fox-hunting was 'the prince of sports. The image of war without its guilt, and only half its danger.' (R. Surtees, *Jorrocks's Jaunts and Jollities* [1965 edn.], 67).

11 J. Serpell, *In the Company of Animals: A Study of Human–Animal Relationships* (Cambridge, 1996), 235.

12 K. Halle, *The Irrepressible Churchill* (2010), 285.

13 A. Montague Browne, *Long Sunset: Memoirs of Winston Churchill's Last Private Secretary* (1995), 145.

14 S. Churchill, *A Thread in the Tapestry* (1967), 27.

15 Manchester, *Last Lion*, 778.

16 CAC, EADE 2/2, 11 September 1942.

17 CAC, CHUR 1/58A-B/227.

18 D. Gilmour, *The Long Recessional: The Imperial Life of Rudyard Kipling* (2002), 196. Gilmour is wrong, however, in suggesting that Churchill was unaware of Kipling's hostility towards him. (See *Speeches* VI, 5905.)

19 H. Nicolson, *Harold Nicolson: Diaries and Letters 1930–1964*, edited by S. Olson (1980), 317.

20 Commenting on her inability to live a normal married life, Sarah told her father in 1947: 'I suppose every now and then, something goes wrong and a mule is born.' (CAC, CHUR 1/45/12.) She signed many of her family letters with drawings of a mule in various comic poses.

21 Such preferences were at least as old as classical antiquity. According to Plutarch, Julius Caesar once rebuked visitors to Rome for lavishing on puppy-dogs and monkeys embraces that would have been better given to their own children.

22 J. S. Churchill, *Crowded Canvas: The Memoirs of John Spencer Churchill* (1961), 31.

23 CAC, SCHL 1/1/7, Sarah to her mother, 1 July 1944.

24 W. S. Churchill, *The Second World War* III (6 vols., 1948–54), 757.

25 J. Kennedy, *The Business of War: The War Narrative of Major-General Sir John Kennedy* (1957), 79–80.

[26] R.S. Churchill (first 2 vols.) and M. Gilbert, *Winston S. Churchill* [henceforth *Churchill*] V (8 vols., 1966–88 plus companions, hereafter designated C.), 245.

[27] *Speeches* VII, 6741.

[28] M. Holroyd, *Bernard Shaw* III *1918–1950: The Lure of Fantasy* (1991), 227.

[29] W. S. Churchill, *The World Crisis* [henceforth *World Crisis*] IV (6 vols., 1923–31), 40.

[30] *Speeches* III, 3023. Churchill may have had in mind the hybrid leopard-man in H. G. Wells's science-fiction novel about vivisection, *The Island of Doctor Moreau* (1896).

[31] CAC, CHAR 2/235/90, Churchill to Lord Rothermere, 12 May 1935.

[32] *World Crisis* IV, 38.

[33] P. Brendon, *Winston Churchill: A Brief Life* (1984), 92.

[34] Job XII, 7.

[35] *Churchill* VIII, 1075.

[36] *Finest Hour* 166 (Winter 2015), 33.

[37] Montague Browne, *Long Sunset*, 280.

ALBATROSS

[1] J. A. Cross, *Sir Samuel Hoare* (1972), 172. Churchill also called him, along with stronger epithets, 'a snake'. (A. Eden, *The Eden Memoirs: The Reckoning* [1965], 96.) Talking off the record to the journalist Frank Owen in 1937, Churchill was especially contemptuous of Hoare for quitting the Admiralty to go to the Home Office: 'The only man who chose to leave Jack Tar for Jack Ketch.' (Parliamentary Archives, BBK/C/86.) In 1911, of course, Churchill himself had exchanged the Home Office for the Admiralty.

[2] *Speeches* VI, 5638.

[3] A. Lascelles, *King's Counsellor: Abdication and War: The Diaries of 'Tommy' Lascelles*, edited by D. Hart-Davis (2006), 60.

[4] D. Dilks (ed.), *The Diaries of Sir Alexander Cadogan 1938–1945* (1971), 287.

ALLIGATORS

[1] CAC, CHUR 2/351/f408, 30 March 1955.

[2] H. Nicolson, *Harold Nicolson: Diaries and Letters 1930–1939*, edited by N. Nicolson (1966), 328.

ANTELOPE

[1] R. S. Churchill, *Men, Mines and Animals in South Africa* (1892), 215.

[2] *Churchill* I, C. 1, 237, 248 and 260.

[3] W. S. Churchill, *Ian Hamilton's March* (1900), 166.

[4] W. S. Churchill, *My African Journey* (Toronto, 1909 edn.), 202–3.

[5] CAC, CHAR 1/72/34, 8 March 1908.

ANTS

[1] *Churchill* I, C. 1, 103.

[2] R. Baden-Powell, *Scouting for Boys* (1908), 117.

[3] *Churchill* V, C. 1, 1313. Churchill, who was writing to George Bernard Shaw, did not blame humanity for its plight since the real fault lay with the Creator: 'and there is no apparent way of bringing it home to him. "He just keeps rolling along."'

[4] J. F. M. Clark, *Bugs and the Victorians* (2009), 101.

[5] W. S. Churchill, *Thoughts and Adventures*, edited by J. W. Muller (Wilmington, Del., 2009), 272–3. Churchill may have been influenced by Maurice Maeterlinck's *The Life of Termites* (1926), as was General de Gaulle.

APES

[1] B. Roberts, *Churchills in Africa* (1970), 30.

[2] T. H. Huxley, *Evolution and Ethics*, edited by J. G. Paradis and G. C. Williams (Princeton, 1989), 109–110.

[3] *Speeches* VI, 6185.

[4] W. Shakespeare, *Measure for Measure*, Act II, Scene 2.

[5] F. Glueckstein, 'Churchill and the Barbary Macaques' in *Finest Hour* 161 (Winter 2013–14), 53 and 55.

6   CAC, CHUR 2/188/63, Churchill to General Gordon MacMillan, 8 November 1952.

BABOONS
1   Churchill, *Ian Hamilton's March*, 342.
2   *Oxford English Dictionary*.
3   *Churchill* IV, 275.
4   *Speeches* III, 2671.
5   D. Rayfield, *Stalin and His Hangmen* (2004), xxi.

BADGERS
1   W. S. Churchill, *A Roving Commission: My Early Life* (New York, 1930), 91.
2   E. Thomas, 'The Combe'.
3   See CAC, CHUR 1/21/22, Roland Ward Ltd to Churchill, 23 December 1949, for details of the preserving, dressing and mounting of the badger skin, which was lined with black linen and edged and pinked with red felt, and originally intended for the floor rather than the wall. The work cost £11 15s.
4   Lord Moran, *Winston Churchill: The Struggle for Survival 1940–1965* (1966), 417.

BATS
1   CHAR 28/25/13, Winston to his mother, 22 May 1898. Cf. *Churchill* I, C. 2, 938, where the holograph letter is not transcribed with complete accuracy; it looks as though Churchill wrote 'fatten' rather than 'batten'.
2   *Speeches* III, 2725.
3   CAC, CHAR, 20/147B/174, Churchill to Brigadier Whitby, 15 October 1944.
4   *Churchill* VII, 938.
5   W. H. Thompson, *I Was Churchill's Shadow* (1951), 55.

BEARS
1   W. S. Churchill, *The River War: An Historical Account of the Reconquest of the Soudan* II, edited by J. W. Muller (South Bend, IN, forthcoming), 143. I am grateful to Jim Muller for letting me see the text of his definitive

edition of this book well in advance of publication.
2   M. Soames (ed.), *Speaking for Themselves: The Personal Letters of Winston and Clementine Churchill* (1998), 182. Churchill called his friend Archie Sinclair's sleeping bag the 'Bosom of the Amorous Pole Cats'.
3   S. Ball, *The Guardsmen* (2004), 114.
4   W. S. Churchill, *A History of the English-Speaking Peoples* II (1956), 311.
5   D. Dilks, *Churchill and Company: Allies and Rivals in War and Peace* (2012), 74. Another version of this remark, which shows signs of having been 'improved' by its second-hand source, went thus: 'In his native forests, the gorilla is an object of awe and terror: in our Zoological Gardens he inspires vulgar curiosity: in our wife's bed, he is a cause of *potential* embarrassment and anxiety.' (E. Marsh, *Ambrosia and Small Beer* [1964], 178.)
6   Churchill, *Second World War* IV, 279. What the powder was, or was for, Churchill did not specify.
7   *The Churchill Documents*, edited by L. Arnn *et al.*, (Hillsdale, MI, 2006 onwards) [henceforth *Churchill Documents*], XVI, 750.

BEAVER
1   Churchill, *Early Life*, 160.
2   CAC, CHAR 8/286/1, Thomas W. Gibson to Churchill, 27 January 1931. I am grateful to Jim Muller for drawing my attention to this letter.
3   Quoted by R. Toye, *The Roar of the Lion: The Untold Story of Churchill's World War II Speeches* (Oxford, 2013), 22.

BEES
1   T. Paterson, *A Seat for Life* (Dundee, 1980), 270.
2   A. G. Gardiner, *Prophets, Priests and Kings* (1908), 110.
3   M. Maeterlinck, *The Life of the Bee*

(1901), 5. Maeterlinck cites Virgil, who suggested that bees had a share in the divine mind, but he does not mention Shakespeare, who provided the classic account of how honeybees 'by a rule in nature teach/The act of order to a peopled kingdom.' (*Henry V*, Act I, Scene 2.)

4   V. Bonham Carter, *Winston Churchill As I Knew Him* (1965), 219. Churchill was not put off by his wife's response, as late as 1941 urging Lord Halifax to read Maeterlinck.

5   H. Pelling, *Winston Churchill* (1974), 757.

BIRDS

1   H. Salt, *Killing for Sport* (1915), xi. For good measure Bernard Shaw added that 'people who are sickened by the figures of a battue do not turn a hair over the infantile death rate in … the slums of Dundee' – which happened to be Winston Churchill's constituency. Shaw's argument was not original: in a famous polemic against fox-hunting written five years before Churchill was born, the historian E. A. Freeman had inveighed against the 'contemptible hypocrisy' of those who subjected animals to suffering in the name of sport yet acted as 'patrons of societies for the prevention of cruelty to costermongers' donkeys'. (Quoted by A. Taylor, '"Pig-Sticking Princes": Royal Hunting, Moral Outrage and the Republican Opposition to the Animal Abuse in Nineteenth- and Early Twentieth-Century Britain' in *History* 89, No. 293 [January 2003], 37–8.)

2   *Times*, 18 August 1883.

3   *Hansard* (7 March 1883), columns 1684–5.

4   *Speeches* VIII, 7945. To Captain Arthur Soames, who had invited him to shoot pheasants, Churchill wrote on 4 November 1949: 'I am afraid my shooting days are over.' (CAC, CHUR 2/165/88.)

5   E. and J. de Goncourt, *Journal* II, edited by J. Laffont (1989), 773.

6   *Churchill* V, 10.

7   *Speeches* I, 345.

8   A. Fort, *Prof: The Life of Frederick Lindemann* (2003), 144–5.

9   S. Bradford, *George VI* (1989), 303.

10   Churchill, *African Journey*, 178.

11   Soames (ed.), *Speaking for Themselves*, 399–400.

12   *Churchill* VIII, 744. In the same vein Clementine once called Winston 'a sweet Darling Lamb Bird!!'. (S. Purnell, *First Lady: The Life and Work of Clementine Churchill* [2015], 56.)

13   Quoted by H. Vickers, *Cocktails and Laughter* (1983), 68.

14   J. Meacham, *Franklin and Winston* (2005 edn.), 213.

15   G. Pawle, *The War and Colonel Warden* (1962), 338.

16   CAC, CHUR 2/165/71.

17   B. Pimlott (ed.), *The Political Diary of Hugh Dalton 1918–40, 1945–60* (1986), 587.

18   *Speeches* VII, 7155.

BIRDS OF PARADISE

1   Churchill, *River War* II, 211. He also likened distinguished personages who gathered to witness battle to vultures.

2   Bonham Carter, *Winston Churchill*, 143.

3   Dilks, *Churchill and Company*, 23.

4   A. Chisholm and M. Davie, *Lord Beaverbrook: A Life* (New York, 1993), 399.

BOA CONSTRICTORS

1   Churchill, *Lord Randolph Churchill* (1907 edn.), 376.

2   Churchill, *River War* II, 368.

3   W. S. Churchill, *Step by Step 1936–1939* (1939), 259.

4   Comte de Buffon, *Natural History of Birds, Fish, Insects and Reptiles* V (London, 1808), 74.

5   *Speeches* VI, 6373.

BUDGERIGARS

1   G. Gorodetsky (ed.), *The Maisky Diaries* (2015), 124.
2   CAC, CHUR 1/59/138, Fogg Elliot to Churchill, 6 April 1956.
3   Montague Browne, *Long Sunset*, 114.
4   CAC, HAMB 1/3.
5   J. Colville, *The Churchillians* (1981), 187.
6   R. A. Butler, *The Art of Memory* (1982), 159.
7   Montague Browne, *Long Sunset*, 114.
8   P. Catterall (ed.), *The Macmillan Diaries: The Cabinet Years, 1950–1957* (2003), 385.
9   CAC, CHUR 1/59/137, Churchill to Fogg Elliot, 2 May 1955.
10 E. Murray, *Churchill's Bodyguard* (1987), 124.
11 Montague Browne, *Long Sunset*, 205.
12 *Daily Telegraph*, 9 November 2006.
13 CAC, MCHL, 5/7/52, Clementine Churchill to her daughter Mary, 3 August 1959.
14 Moran, *Struggle for Survival*, 623.
15 R. Howells, *Simply Churchill* (1965), 82. Howells recorded that Onassis supplied a substitute for Toby named Byron, 'a vicious little thing which would bite and draw blood'. Churchill commented, 'He's all right, but it's not Toby.' Churchill's secretary, Anthony Montague Browne, told Lady Dunn on 21 February 1961 that Churchill was now 'philosophical' about the loss of Toby, 'though naturally sad'. (CAC, CHUR 2/522A-B/118.)

BUGS

1   L. Strachey, *Portraits in Miniature* (1931), 193.
2   *Churchill Documents* XVIII, 1254.
3   Dilks (ed.), *Diaries of Cadogan*, 471.
4   N. Davies, *Europe at War 1939–1945: No Simple Victory* (2006), 190.
5   *Churchill* VII, 442.
6   M. Soames, *A Daughter's Tale* (2011), 288.
7   Moran, *Struggle for Survival*, 313.
8   M. Wolff (ed.), *The Collected Essays of Sir Winston Churchill* IV (1976), 419.
9   *Speeches* VIII, 7987.

BULLDOGS

1   R. G. Martin, *Lady Randolph Churchill* I (1969), 214.
2   H. Ritvo, *The Animal Estate: The English and Other Creatures in the Victorian Age* (1990 edn.), 110.
3   Quoted by S. Baker, *Picturing the Beast: Animals, Identity and Representation* (Manchester, 1993), 52. Kingsley used the phrase in his novel *Two Years Ago* (1857).
4   See Miles Taylor's entry on John Bull as the epitome of Englishness in the *ODNB*. He might have cited Lord Killearn's view, expressed in Cairo in 1945, that Churchill himself was 'the epitome of the perfect "John Bull"'. (T. E. Evans [ed.], *The Killearn Diaries 1934–1946* [1972], 328.)
5   *Speeches* I, 41. Churchill was addressing the voters of Oldham on 27 June 1899.
6   *Speeches* III, 2331.
7   Gorodetsky (ed.), *Maisky Diaries*, 239.
8   Dilks (ed.), *Diaries of Cadogan*, 292. A year later Cadogan changed the image: anticipating Sir Humphrey Appleby, he remarked severely that ministers were given to 'thinking' at weekends and he compared Churchill to 'a spider in the middle of his web' who tickled them all up. (*Diaries*, 413.)
9   C. Perry, *Boy in the Blitz* (1972), 121.
10 Gorodetsky (ed.), *Maisky Diaries*, 378.
11 For some wonderful images of the bulldog Churchill see D. Hall, *The Book of Churchilliana* (2002), 26–7. And for a round-up of further effigies and cartoons see D. J. Hall, 'Bulldog Churchill: The Evolution of a Famous Image' in *Finest Hour* 106 (Spring 2000), 18ff.
12 CAC, CHUR 2/406/165–6, Mrs Doris Whitehorn to Churchill, 11 November 1952. Churchill's reply was dated 14 December 1952.

[13] CAC, CHAR 2/253/34, Sir Hughe Knatchbull-Hugessen to Anthony Bevir, Churchill's private secretary.

[14] CAC, NEMO 3/1/66–8.

[15] M. Soames, *Churchill: His Life as a Painter* (1990), 192.

[16] R. Berthoud, *Graham Sutherland* (1982), 186.

[17] CAC, DEKE 2, 'Churchill Memories', Chapter VI, 17.

BUTTERFLIES

[1] Churchill, *Early Life*, 41–2.

[2] CAC, CHAR 28/152A/68, Winston to Jack, 2 December 1896.

[3] Churchill, *River War* II, 10. The butterfly was a common churchyard motif but Jim Muller notes that Churchill was referring to a poem by Felicia Dorothea Browne Hemans (1793–1835), 'Written after visiting a Tomb, near Woodstock, in the County of Kilkenny' (1831). It contains the lines: 'Then didst thou pass me in radiance by,/Child of the sunbeam, bright butterfly!'

[4] W. S. Churchill, *London to Ladysmith via Pretoria* (1900), 340.

[5] Churchill, *African Journey*, 79 and 154.

[6] Churchill, *Early Life*, 28.

[7] CAC, DEKE 2, Chapter IV, 15.

[8] Moran, *Struggle for Survival*, 713 and 416.

[9] CAC, CHUR 1/130/9, Churchill to Newman, 13 June 1946.

[10] L. Hugh Newman, *Butterfly Farmer* (1953), 164.

[11] CAC, CHWL 8, Newman to Churchill, 20 June 1947.

[12] CAC, CHUR 1/20/214, Newman to Churchill, 30 April 1949. Newman's article was published in *The Entomologist* LXXXII (June 1949), 140.

[13] P. Barkham, *The Butterfly Isles: A Summer in Search of our Emperors and Admirals* (2010), 219. However, Barkham wrote in the *Guardian* on 7 April 2018 that changing climatic conditions could now permit the reintroduction of the black-veined white into southern England and that Churchill might 'simply have been seven decades ahead of his time'.

[14] *Churchill* I, 385. Churchill may have exaggerated the figures for effect but he must have known that butterfly wings have scales, not feathers.

CAMELS

[1] W. S. Churchill, *The Story of the Malakand Field Force* (1916 edn.), 184.

[2] Churchill, *River War* I, 358.

[3] Churchill, *River War* II, 38, 275 and 37.

[4] C. Knox, *It Might Have Been You* (1938), 223.

[5] J. H. Lehmann, *All Sir Garnet* (1964), 357.

[6] T. Fishlock, *Conquerors of Time: Exploration and Invention in the Age of Daring* (2004), 294.

[7] Churchill, *River War* II, 267.

[8] W. Thompson, *Beside the Bulldog* (2003), 50.

[9] C. Eade (ed.), *Churchill by his Contemporaries* (1954), 245.

[10] R. Toye, *Churchill's Empire: The World That Made Him and the World He Made* (2010), 148.

CATERPILLARS

[1] S. Leslie, *Long Shadows* (1966), 25.

[2] C. Lewis [i.e. Harold Begbie, M. H. Temple and illustrator J. Stafford Ransome], *Clara in Blunderland* (1902), 15 and 20.

[3] W. S. Churchill, *Marlborough: His Life and Times* I (1947 edn.), 749.

[4] Moran, *Struggle for Survival*, 84. Moran quoted him as saying 'enamel caterpillar' but in the Commons Churchill said 'enamelled'. (*Speeches* VII, 6749).

[5] Churchill, *Crowded Canvas*, 37.

[6] Soames (ed.), *Speaking for Themselves*, 170.

[7] *Churchill* III, 534. But see Robin Prior's justification for Haig's use of tanks in *Finest Hour* 172 (Spring 2016), 34.

8   *News of the World*, 24 April 1938. Churchill also thought tanks might be made 'which can turn themselves into moles by sinking into the ground'.

9   Soames (ed.), *Speaking for Themselves*, 387.

CATS

1   CAC, CHUR 2/464/306.

2   Eden, *The Reckoning*, 399. According to John Martin, the Munich Mouser had earlier received postal orders and gifts of fish but latterly he suffered under 'the stigma of appeasement'. (CAC, MART 1/3.)

3   J. Colville, *The Fringes of Power: Downing Street Diaries 1939–1955* (1985), 172.

4   I am grateful to Ronald Hyam for this anecdote, which he heard from Professor L. P. Pugh himself.

5   R. E. Sherwood, *The White House Papers of Harry L. Hopkins* I (1948), 320.

6   Montague Browne, *Long Sunset*, 318. Montague Browne is not always a reliable source and he may have been misremembering the story that Jock Colville told in his diary of 8 October 1940. Then Churchill amused Colville and Eden by his conversation with Nelson, 'whom he chided for being afraid of the guns and unworthy of the name he bore. "Try and remember," he said to Nelson reprovingly, "what those boys in the R.A.F. are doing."' (Colville, *Fringes of Power*, 259.) In another version of this story Churchill urges Nelson to summon up the spirit of the tiger.

7   CAC, CHUR 1/64/142, Mrs Hill to Churchill, 27 November 1948. I am grateful to Natalie Adams for this reference.

8   E. Nel, *Mr Churchill's Secretary* (1958), 74. This story, too, appears in other forms.

9   Kennedy, *Business of War*, 312. In another version of this story the cat is Nelson and his treachery takes place at Chequers. Churchill tells Menzies that Nelson is in touch with the pelicans on the lake 'and they're communicating our information to the German secret service!'. (R. J. Aldrich and R. Cormac, *The Black Door: Spies, Secret Intelligence and British Prime Ministers* [2016], 116.)

10 Soames, *Daughter's Tale*, 24.

11 CAC, CHUR 2/160/6 and /3, Churchill to Lady Aberconway, 3 and 9 March 1949.

12 Churchill, *Crowded Canvas*, 105.

13 CAC, CHAR 2/397/61.

14 Colville, *Fringes of Power*, 394.

15 Halle, *Irrepressible Churchill*, 8.

16 CAC, DEKE 2, Chapter III, 10.

17 F. Glueckstein, '"Cats Look Down on You …" Churchill's Feline Menagerie' in *Finest Hour* 139 (Summer 2008), 50ff.

18 W. Graebner, *My Dear Mr Churchill* (1965), 102. Mickey died in 1953 and for some reason his death was not revealed to the press. (CAC, CHUR 1/59/106, Elizabeth Gilliatt to Grace Hamblin, 1 January 1955.)

19 *Churchill* III, 707.

20 CHAR 1/118A/48–9, Clementine to Winston, 31 January 1916.

21 W. Churchill, *Great Contemporaries*, edited by J. W. Muller (Wilmington, Del., 2012), 240.

22 CAC, EADE 2/2, 11 September 1942.

23 Halle, *Irrepressible Churchill*, 201.

24 Moran, *Struggle for Survival*, 312.

25 Montague Browne, *Long Sunset*, 140.

26 According to *The Independent* (21 September 2001), this was a staple joke in the financial press.

27 Manchester, *Last Lion*, 644.

28 *Churchill* V, C. 1, 145.

39 *Churchill* VIII, 1059.

30 I owe this story, with thanks, to Edward Beaumont.

31 *Churchill* V, C. 1, 571.

32 Soames (ed.), *Speaking for Themselves*, 574.

33 *Churchill* VIII, 898.

34 H. White-Smith, *My Years with the Churchills* (Ascot, 2010), 29.
35 *Churchill* VII, 849.
36 CAC, DEKE 2, Chapter VI, 15–16.
37 CAC, CHAR 2/472A-B, Kathleen Hill to Grace Hamblin, 8 August 1943.
38 Glueckstein, *Finest Hour* 139 (Summer 2008), 50ff.
39 CAC, CHAR 2/466/146, Jacqueline Lampson to Churchill, 3 February 1943.
40 Moran, *Struggle for Survival*, 766. Churchill was not unique: Rorschach ink blots are commonly seen as animals.
41 CAC, MART 1/3.
42 CAC, MCHL 5/1/192, Clementine Churchill to her daughter Mary, 17 February 1964.
43 I owe this story, with thanks, to Minnie Churchill.

CATTLE
1 CAC, CHAR 1/125/20–22, Clementine to Winston, 18 August 1918.
2 Lord Alanbrooke, *War Diaries 1939–1945*, edited by A. Danchev and D. Todman, (2002), 631.
3 Wolff (ed.), *Collected Essays* IV, 18.
4 CAC, CHUR 1/30/160, Churchill to Major Marnham, 23 August 1946.
5 Soames (ed.), *Speaking for Themselves*, 393.
6 CAC, CHAR 1/286/40, Churchill to Hamilton, 30 October 1936.
7 CAC, CHAR 2/466, Churchill to Hamilton, 11 October 1943.
8 CAC, MCHL 5/7/41, Mary to her mother, 2 August 1949.
9 CAC, CHUR 1/46/111, 6 March 1948.
10 Leslie, *Long Shadows*, 30.
11 *Speeches* IV, 3459.
12 *Ibid.*, V, 5385.
13 A. Bryant, *Triumph in the West 1943–1946* (1959), 214.
14 *Churchill* VIII, 527.
15 D. Gillies, *Radical Diplomat: The Life of Archibald Clark Kerr, Lord Inverchapel 1882–1951* (1999), 130.
16 *Churchill Documents* XVIII, 1310.
17 R. Rhodes James (ed.), *Chips: The Diaries of Sir Henry Channon* (1967), 312 and 269. Another diarist, Harold Nicolson, found a different animal image to convey Churchill's antipathy to those he disliked, based on a mime the Prime Minister performed for him to show how he had greeted Count Sforza in 1944: 'Winston drew himself up with an expression of extreme disgust and gave me a hand like the fin of a dead penguin.' Churchill was delighted that Nicolson himself had referred to Sforza in the Commons as 'an elderly peacock'. (Nicolson, *Diaries and Letters 1939–1945*, edited by N. Nicolson, 417.)

CHICKENS
1 CAC, NEMO 3/1/70.
2 *Churchill Documents* XVII, 962.
3 *Churchill* V, C. 3, 108. Commenting on the inadequacies of Russian poultry farming, the author wrote: 'Literally everything I had seen was wrong.' (Arne Strom, *Uncle Give Us Bread* [1936], 77.)
4 Churchill, *Thoughts and Adventures*, 291.
5 CAC, CHAR 8/340/60, 'Land of Corn', 1933.
6 *Churchill* I, 293.
7 Churchill, *London to Ladysmith*, 265. What Churchill called 'cock's feather cockades' were actually tail feathers from the sakabula bird.
8 CAC, CHAR 20/10/13, unsigned copy addressed to Sir John Anderson, 4 September 1940.
9 CAC, MART 1/24, September 1940. Churchill raised the matter in the Commons on 5 September but reluctantly concluded soon afterwards that the intensification of air raids made it 'inexpedient to abolish the sirens at the moment'. (Churchill, *Second World War* II, 313.)
10 Lord Hankey recorded the canard

that 'Winston is like a chicken in front of a cobra before Beaverbrook'. (S. Roskill, *Hankey: Man of Secrets* III [1974], 498.)

11 Bonham Carter, *Winston Churchill*, 239. At the Admiralty once again early in the Second World War, Churchill code-named the aerial mine, which he championed on Lindemann's advice, 'the Egg-layer'. He instructed that these explosive contraptions (which were spectacularly useless) should be released when the aircraft carrying them were 'ordered by wireless to "lay"'. (CAC, CHAR 19/6, First Lord of the Admiralty Printed Minutes No. 262, 11 March 1940.)

12 M. and E. Brock (eds.), *H. H. Asquith Letters to Venetia Stanley* (Oxford, 1985 edn.), 285 and 287. By contrast, to protect ships against attack from the air in 1939, he wanted some 'made into tortoises'. (*Churchill Documents* XIV, 275.)

13 *Churchill* V, C. 3, 943.

14 *Speeches* VI, 6545.

CRANES

1 CAC, CHAR 1/282/64, James P. Clanchy (Bailey's secretary) to Churchill, 23 August 1935.

2 *Churchill* V, C. 3, 673.

3 CAC, CHAR 2/236/177, Churchill to Bailey, 17 May 1937.

4 CAC, CHAR 1/324/48, Churchill to Bailey, 25 September 1938.

5 CAC, CHAR 1/344/4, Mary to her father, 22 January 1939.

6 CAC, CHAR 2/236/177, Bailey to Churchill, 27 August 1935.

CROCODILES

1 Churchill, *African Journey*, 164–5.

2 *World Crisis* IV, 43.

3 *Speeches* IV, 3820.

4 M. Gilbert, *Churchill: A Life* (1991), 632.

5 CAC, CHAR 20/180/64, Churchill to Geoffrey Lloyd, 24 August 1944.

6 Alanbrooke, *War Diaries*, 516.

CRUSTACEANS

1 Churchill, *Lord Randolph Churchill*, 372.

2 J. Pearson, *Citadel of the Heart: Winston and the Churchill Dynasty* (1993 edn.), 134.

3 CAC, CHAR 8/344/59, 'Land of Corn', 1933.

4 C. Stelzer, *Dinner with Churchill: Policy-Making at the Dinner Table* (2011), 69.

5 *World Crisis* V, 201.

6 CAC, MCHL 5/7/51, Clementine Churchill to her daughter Mary, 29 August 1958.

7 Colville, *Fringes of Power*, 678.

CUTTLEFISH

1 M. Pottle (ed.), *Champion Redoubtable: The Diaries and Letters of Violet Bonham Carter 1914–1945* (1998), 247.

2 N. Rankin, *Churchill's Wizards: The British Genius for Deception 1914–1945* (2008), 282 and 305.

3 *Churchill* VIII, 801. It is not known whether Churchill read Orwell's famous essay 'Politics and the English Language' in which dishonest writers are accused of resorting to vagueness and euphemism 'like a cuttlefish squirting out ink'. (S. Orwell and I. Angus [eds.], *The Collected Essays, Journalism and Letters of George Orwell* IV [Harmondsworth, 1979], 166–7.)

4 CAC, MCHL 5/8/4.

5 *Speeches* VII, 7776–7.

DOGS

1 A. Leslie, *The Gilt and the Gingerbread* (1981), 134.

2 CAC, CHAR 28/1/32–33, Leonard Jerome to Lady Randolph, 13 August 1873.

3 CAC, CHAR 28/25/49, Winston to his mother, 14 November 1898. Actually the black pug had become a fashionable breed since its import in 1886.

4 *World Crisis* IV, 108.

5 CAC, CHAR 12/3/3, Lord Knollys to Churchill, 5 October 1910.

6 Quoted by K. Thomas, *Man and the Natural World: Changing Attitudes in England 1500–1800* (1983), 121.

7 CAC, CHAR 1/273/37–41, Winston to Clementine, 10 March 1935.

8 Manchester, *Last Lion*, 777.

9 N. McGowan, *My Years with Churchill* (New York, 1958), 67.

10 T. Reardon, *Winston Churchill and Mackenzie King: So Similar, So Different* (Toronto, 2012), 84.

11 Soames (ed.), *Speaking for Themselves*, 370.

12 Churchill, *River War* I, 152 and II, 227. Churchill also said that the men of Colonel Thorneycroft's regiment, cut to pieces at Spion Kop, 'fought for him like lions and followed him like dogs'. (*London to Ladysmith*, 312.)

13 CAC, CHAR 13/5/22, Churchill to H. H. Asquith, 14 April 1912.

14 *Lord Riddell's War Diary 1914–1918* (1933), 14.

15 M. Gilbert and R. Gott, *The Appeasers* (1967), 19.

16 *Speeches* II, 1429.

17 *Ibid.*, 2188.

18 Churchill, *Great Contemporaries*, 283.

19 CAC, CHAR 2/207/2–1, Churchill to Cyril Asquith, 8 August 1934.

20 A. J. P. Taylor (ed.), *Lloyd George: A Diary by Frances Stevenson* (1971), 197.

21 G. S. Harvie-Watt, *Most of My Life* (1980), 63.

22 G. Farmelo, *Churchill's Bomb: A Hidden History of Science, War and Politics* (2013), 18.

23 Dilks (ed.), *Diaries of Cadogan*, 529.

24 B. Bond (ed.), *Chief of Staff: The Diaries of Lieutenant-General Sir Henry Pownall* II (1974), 135.

25 NA, FO 800/300, Clark Kerr's Report on Bracelet Conference, August 1942. The phrase is an impolite version of 'a dog with two tails'.

26 M. Gilbert, *In Search of Churchill* (1994), 210.

27 P. Foley, '"Black dog" as a metaphor for depression: a brief history', https://blackdoginstitute.org.au/.

28 *Churchill* III, 693.

DONKEYS

1 CAC, CHAR 28/13/72, Winston to his mother, 16 August 1885.

2 CAC, CHAR 28/152A/52, Winston to Jack, 4 March 1895.

3 A. Leslie, *Edwardians in Love* (1974), 210.

4 C. Millard, *Hero of Empire: The Making of Winston Churchill* (2016), 84.

5 *Speeches* I, 138.

6 Churchill, *Thoughts and Adventures*, 26.

7 *Ibid.*, III, 2906.

8 *Ibid.*, VII, 6784. Cf CAC CHAR 20/211/20, for Harold Macmillan's slavishly Churchillian telegram sent from Athens to the Prime Minister and dated 19 January 1945: 'We are trying to tame the Trotzkyite [sic] donkey by traditional use of the stick and carrot.'

9 Montague Browne, *Long Sunset*, 206.

DRAGONS

1 Churchill, *Early Life*, 26.

2 Churchill, *Malakand Field Force*, 148.

3 Paterson, *Seat for Life*, 217.

4 *Speeches* V, 5267.

5 Soames (ed.), *Speaking for Themselves*, 394 and 399.

6 Churchill, *Step by Step*, 164.

7 M. Beloff, 'Churchill and Europe' in R. Blake and W. R. Louis (eds.), *Churchill* (Oxford, 1994), 453.

8 Wolff (ed.), *Collected Essays* II, 460.

9 Montague Browne, *Long Sunset*, 151.

DUCKS

1 Churchill, *Early Life*, 163 (a bowdlerized version) and Gilbert, *Churchill*, 465.

2 *Speeches* IV, 4339.

3 CAC, CHAR 1/256/129, Sassoon to Churchill, 24 December 1934. Churchill occasionally joked about Sassoon's willingness to oblige

influential Gentiles. Sassoon served as Haig's private secretary during the Great War and Churchill described him as sitting 'like a wakeful spaniel' outside the General's door. (Soames [ed.], *Speaking for Themselves*, 143.) Churchill himself regarded Sassoon as the 'restaurant car' on his train. (K. Rose, *Kings, Queens and Courtiers* [1985], 258.)

4   CAC, CHAR 1/256/127, Churchill to Sassoon, 28 December 1934. I have punctuated this telegram.
5   *Speeches* V, 5141 and VI, 5639.
6   CAC, CHAR 1/284/86, Sassoon to Churchill, March 1936.
7   CAC, BRGS 1/2, Burgis to General Sir Leslie Hollis, 3 May 1955. I am grateful to Natalie Adams for this reference.
8   *Churchill* VIII, 1326, 1235 and 825.
9   D. Cooper, *Darling Monster: The Letters of Lady Diana Cooper to Her Son John Julius Norwich 1939–1952*, edited by J. J. Norwich (2013), 192.
10 CAC, DIAC 1/1/25/73–79.
11 CAC, EADE 2/2, 20 December 1945.
12 CAC, DIAC 1/1/26, 16 July 1946.
13 *Punch*, 10 August 1895, 63.

EAGLES
1   Churchill, *Early Life*, 34.
2   *Review of Reviews* V (April 1892), 354.
3   Lascelles, *King's Counsellor*, 437. Lloyd George said that Gladstone 'had the eye of a demon when he was angry'. (*Lord Riddell's War Diary 1914–1918*, 67.)
4   Quoted by D. Cannadine, *In Churchill's Shadow* (2002), 91.
5   Bonham Carter, *Winston Churchill*, 22.
6   *Churchill* II, C. 1, 451. Lady Randolph was more often likened to a panther; whereas in youth Clementine resembled, according to one admirer, a 'sweet, almond-eyed gazelle'. (*Daily Mail*, 23 November 2012.)
7   Alanbrooke, *War Diaries*, 691.

8   *Speeches* VII, 7349.
9   R. Lawson, 'The Genius and Wit of Winston Churchill' in *Finest Hour* 73 (1991), 19. Shortly afterwards, in March 1946, when attending a dinner at the Union Club in New York on a hot night, Churchill noticed water dripping from the wings of an eagle carved in ice holding a bowl of caviar and said, 'The American eagle seems to have a cold.' (*Churchill* VIII, 213.)

EELS
1   Wolff (ed.), *Collected Essays* II, 416.
2   *Churchill* V, C. 3, 797. Because the Red Flag associated Socialists with Communists, Ramsay MacDonald himself privately described it as 'the funeral dirge of our movement'. (W. McElwee, *Britain's Locust Years 1918–1940* [1962], 115.)
3   *Churchill* VI, 578.
4   Alanbrooke, *War Diaries*, 459.

ELEPHANTS
1   CAC, CHAR 28/96/6, Lady Randolph to Lord Randolph Churchill, 1877.
2   Churchill, *Lord Randolph Churchill*, 853, 228 and 854.
3   Churchill, *Early Life*, 120.
4   Churchill, *River War* I, 13.
5   Churchill, *African Journey*, 181–2.
6   V. Cowles, *Winston Churchill: The Era and the Man* (New York, 1953), 223.
7   D. Cooper, *Old Men Forget* (1953), 103.
8   Wolff (ed.), *Collected Essays* II, 226.
9   R. Rhodes James, *Victor Cazalet: A Portrait* (1976), 71.
10 J. Lukacs, *Five Days in London, May 1940* (1999), 23.
11 Montague Browne, *Long Sunset*, 175. Montague Browne says that this event took place on VJ Day, the celebration marking Victory over Japan on 15 August 1945, but this is incorrect since by then Churchill was no longer Prime Minister. Incidentally, Churchill also sired a rogue elephant in the person of his son. When the

Jesuit Father D'Arcy suggested him as a suitable target for conversion to Roman Catholicism, Evelyn Waugh disagreed, saying that Randolph would not be an ornament to Mother Church so much as a 'rogue elephant trumpeting in the Sanctuary'. (K. Halle, *Randolph Churchill: The Young Unpretender* [1971], 60.)

FABULOUS BEASTS

1   Gorodetsky (ed.), *Maisky Diaries*, 354.
2   *Speeches* VII, 7262.
3   W. S. Robinson, *The Last Victorians* (2014), 120.
4   D. Reynolds, *The Long Shadow: The Great War and the Twentieth Century* (2013), 219.
5   *Speeches* V, 4521. Although Churchill's conceit is reminiscent of Giovanni Battista Casti's *Gli Animali Parlanti* (Paris, 1802), loosely translated by S. W. Rose as *The Court and Parliament of Beasts* (1819), there is no reason to suppose that he knew of this work.

FERRETS, STOATS AND WEASELS

1   H. G. Wells, *Ann Veronica*: Jeanne MacKenzie's unpaginated introduction to Virago's 1979 edition.
2   CAC, CHAR 2/207/20–21, Churchill to Cyril Asquith, 8 August 1934.
3   CAC, CHAR 20/93B/144, Churchill to A. P. Herbert, 17 April 1943.
4   *Punch*, 14 April 1943, 311.
5   P. Caddick-Adams, *Monty and Rommel: Parallel Lives* (2011), 304. The phrase was coined by Brigadier 'Bill' Williams.
6   Marsh, *Ambrosia and Small Beer*, 259.

FISH

1   CAC, CHAR 28/6/49, Lord Randolph Churchill to Lady Randolph, 8 June 1877.
2   Churchill, *Early Life*, 7.
3   *Churchill* V, C. 1, 1059.
4   CAC, CHAR 2/209/30, John McDonald to Churchill, 27 October 1934.
5   W. F. Kimball (ed.), *Churchill &*

   Roosevelt: The Complete Correspondence II (1984), 297.
6   Churchill, *Second World War* IV, 712.
7   Brendon, *Churchill*, 180.
8   CAC, CHAR 20/145B/130–1, Sir George Paynter to Churchill, 19 June 1943.
9   CAC, CHAR 2/466/115, Charles Hunter to Churchill, 26 April 1943.
10 Lord Byron, *Don Juan*, Canto XIII:106. Byron maintained that no angler could be a good man; ironically, he himself had engaged in the sport.
11 CAC, CHAR 1/94/57, Duke of Westminster to Churchill, 29 June 1927.
12 http://www.anglingheritage.org/p-21645.
13 Lord Riddell, *More Pages from My Diary 1908–1914* (1934), 78.
14 Quoted by G. Best, *Churchill: A Study in Greatness* (2001), 72. Perhaps unconsciously plagiarizing Churchill, Hugh Dalton, in his diary of 8 June 1955, used the same piscine analogy to account for the ex-Prime Minister's having 'suddenly gone very old'. (Pimlott [ed.], *Political Diary of Hugh Dalton*, 672.)
15 *Speeches* V, 4913.
16 Churchill, *Second World War* IV, 702–3.
17 Soames, *Daughter's Tale*, 345.
18 Thompson, *Churchill's Shadow*, 84.
19 W. S. Churchill, *Never Give In!: Winston Churchill's Speeches* (2013 edn.), 212.
20 Churchill, *River War* I, 362 and 422.
21 Eden, *The Reckoning*, 144.
22 *Churchill* VI, 165.
23 Eade (ed.), *Churchill by his Contemporaries*, 363–4.
24 Churchill, *London to Ladysmith*, 6.
25 Moran, *Struggle for Survival*, 768.

FLIES AND OTHER FLYING INSECTS

1   Churchill, *River War* II, 13th Sudan despatch, 12 September 1898.
2   W. Shakespeare, *Titus Andronicus*, Act

III, Scene 2.

3 Moran, *Struggle for Survival*, 302–3

4 Eden, *The Reckoning*, 333. Eden replied that this was just what he did mean.

5 CAC, CHAR 10/27/66–69, Churchill to Edward VII, 27 November 1907.

6 Churchill, *African Journey*, 139–40 and 99.

7 D. Griffiths, *Blum and Taff: A Tale of Two Editors* (2013), 75.

8 Churchill, *River War* I, 33. As Warren Dockter writes, Churchill long feared that pan-Islamic fanaticism, 'the horn of a Rhinoceros or the sting of a wasp', was a major threat to the British Empire, the largest Mohammedan power in the world. (*Churchill and the Islamic World* [2015], 191.) Churchill even said that the kicking, squealing, fighting Arab horses seemed to have been infected by the fanaticism of the human inhabitants of the land of their birth.

9 Rhodes James, *Cazalet*, 96.

10 CAC, CHUR 20/75/12, Churchill to Captain and ship's company of *Wasp*, 11 May 1942. When the first batch of Spitfires was largely destroyed on the ground in Malta, Churchill had asked Roosevelt if the *Wasp* could give another sting. Its second mission was more successful. In fact, of course, it is honeybees, not wasps, that can only sting once.

FOXES

1 A. E. Freeman, 'The Morality of Field Sports' in *Fortnightly Review* XXXIV (October 1869), 369.

2 K. T. Hoppen, *The Mid-Victorian Generation* (Oxford, 1998), 358–9.

3 CAC, CHAR 28/20/39–40, Winston to his mother, 19 September 1894.

4 CAC, CHAR 20/201/31, C. C. West to Churchill, 27 May 1945, recalling a hunt which they had both been among the few to finish, in County Meath in the winter of 1902–3. The

fox was 'rolled over on the lawn of old Tom Leonard's residence', after which the hunters partook of a champagne luncheon.

5 Churchill, *London to Ladysmith*, 97.

6 Cowles, *Churchill*, 66.

7 *Speeches* II, 1152.

8 Gardiner, *Prophets, Priests and Kings*, 110.

9 *World Crisis* IV, 18. In *A Woman of No Importance* (1893) Wilde wrote: 'The English country gentleman galloping after a fox – the unspeakable in full pursuit of the uneatable.' Lloyd George went further than Curzon, of course, wanting to hang the Kaiser.

10 A. Roberts, 'The Holy Fox': A Biography of Lord Halifax* (1991), 3.

11 The reasons for the bill's defeat are discussed by A. N. May in *The Fox-Hunting Controversy, 1781–2004* (Farnham, 2013), 133–4.

12 Montague Browne, *Long Sunset*, 58. Here the Foreign Office mandarin Sir Orme Sargent is given credit for this canard, which has also been attributed to Aneurin Bevan. Churchill himself may have repeated it given his penchant for playing, sometimes rudely, on people's names.

13 CAC, CHUR 2/187/338, Duke of Marlborough to Churchill (n.d.), with Churchill's comment on the bottom of the letter.

14 CAC, CHUR 2/187/333, 27 October 1952.

15 R. Carr, *English Fox Hunting* (1976), 199.

16 McGowan, *Years with Churchill*, 70.

17 *Churchill* VIII, 1043.

FROGS

1 NA, FO 800/300, Clark Kerr report.

2 Churchill, *African Journey*, 199.

3 Gilbert, *Churchill* VIII, 175.

4 CAC, CHAR 28/11/42–43, Lord Randolph Churchill to Lady Randolph, 7 November 1891.

5 I. Hunter (ed.), *Winston and Archie: The Letters of Sir Archibald Sinclair*

and Winston S. Churchill 1915–1960 (2005), 52. A *maison tolérée* was a brothel.

6 Channel 4's documentary *Churchill's Secret Mistress* appeared in March 2018, as did the article by W. Dockter and R. Toye in the *Journal of Contemporary History*, 'Who Commanded History? Sir John Colville, Churchillian Networks and the "Castlerosse Affair"'. My refutation of the case made in the television programme is to be found online at https://www.chu.cam.ac.uk/news/2018/mar/26/churchills-secret-mistress/.

7 CAC, CHAR 1/57/62.

GEESE
1 W. P. Crozier, *Off the Record: Political Interviews 1933–1943*, edited by A. J. P. Taylor (1973), 349.
2 CAC, DIAC 1/1/3, Diana Cooper to Conrad Russell, 14 September 1934. Diana Cooper wrote that the swans were called 'Mr Juno and Mrs Jupiter … because they got the sexes wrong to start with'. But Churchill seems to have re-christened them appropriately.
3 Churchill, *Crowded Canvas*, 151.
4 CAC, CHAR 1/200/115–116, Flora Guest to Churchill, 1928.
5 Pawle, *War and Colonel Warden*, 118–119.
6 *Churchill* VII, 1189.
7 *Hansard* 58, c 1565.
8 A. Macqueen, *The Prime Minister's Ironing Board and Other State Secrets: True Stories from the Government Archives* (2013), 86–7.
9 R. Lewin, *Ultra Goes to War: The Secret Story* (1978), 64.

GIRAFFES
1 Churchill, *African Journey*, 10.
2 *Lord Macaulay's Essays and Lays of Ancient Rome* (1886 edn.), 542.
3 For a discussion of Churchill's debt to Macaulay and, still more, to Gibbon, see P. Brendon, *The Decline and Fall of*

the British Empire (2007), 205–6.
4 *Finest Hour* 142 (Spring 2009), 29.
5 Moran, *Struggle for Survival*, 80 and 763. In an illustrated album by Edmond-François Calvo, *La Bête est Morte!* (Paris, 1945), de Gaulle is portrayed as a stork while Churchill inevitably appears as a bulldog. Churchill otherwise describes de Gaulle as the 'Monster of Hampstead'.

GOATS
1 R. Rees, *George Orwell: Fugitive from the Camp of Victory* (1961), 150.
2 *Churchill* III, 589.
3 McGowan, *Years with Churchill*, 67.
4 CAC, DUFC 6/24. I have altered the punctuation and layout of this quotation, which I owe, with thanks, to Katharine Thomson.
5 *Churchill* VIII, 857.
6 M. Glover and J. Riley, *The Astonishing Infantry: The History of the Royal Welch Fusiliers 1689–2006* (2007), 225.
7 Soames (ed.), *Speaking for Themselves*, 576.
8 Eisenhower Library, White House Office of Staff Secretary, Cabinet Series, 23 October 1953.
9 CAC, CHUR 2/80/199.

GOLDFISH AND GOLDEN ORFE
1 CAC, CHAR 1/289/6, Violet Pearman, 18 August 1936.
2 Soames (ed.), *Speaking for Themselves*, 422.
3 Soames, *Daughter's Tale*, 118.
4 CAC, CHAR 1/394/273, memorandum date 26 May 1948.
5 Soames (ed.), *Speaking for Themselves*, 32.
6 Graebner, *Dear Mr Churchill*, 103. According to A. C. Benson, man of letters and Master of Magdalene College, Cambridge, Churchill himself resembled 'some sort of maggot'. (D. Newsome, *On the Edge of Paradise: A. C. Benson: The Diarist* [1980], 326.)
7 Pawle, *War and Colonel Warden*,

196. At Yalta Stalin was quick to cater for the Prime Minister's strange partiality. Churchill noted that within two days of Air Chief Marshal Portal's remarking that the large glass tank in the conservatory at the Vorontsov Palace was empty, 'a consignment of goldfish arrived'. (Churchill, *Second World War* VI, 302.) Portal fed the goldfish, Sarah Churchill observed, on bluebottles caught in the library.

8 Quoted by F. Hervey and J. Hems, *The Goldfish* (1981), 244. Churchill may have known this poem since it was anthologized by his private secretary Edward Marsh in *Georgian Poetry 1918–19* (1919).

9 CAC, CHAR 20/95A/5–6, Churchill to Sir Richard Acland, 24 March 1943. The letter Churchill did send, two days later, excused himself from discussing the current political situation.

10 CAC, CHAR 1/383/16.

11 CAC, CHUR 1/130/93, Churchill memorandum, 10 November 1945.

12 CAC, CHUR 1/130/90, Churchill memorandum, 11 November 1945. Churchill did not want the herons killed, just scared off.

13 CAC, MCHL 5/7/41, Mary to her father, 14 August 1949.

14 CAC, CHWL 4/4, Churchill to Plater, 28 April 1948.

15 CAC, CHUR 1/21/90, Parbury to Churchill, 26 May 1950.

16 Soames (ed.), *Speaking for Themselves*, 581.

17 McGowan, *Years with Churchill*, 70.

18 CAC, DEKE 2, Chapter II, 5.

19 Murray, *Churchill's Bodyguard*, 129.

20 Graebner, *Dear Mr Churchill*, 103.

21 R. Ollard (ed.), *The Diaries of A. L. Rowse* (2003), 248.

22 J. Bright-Holmes (ed.), *Like It Was: The Diaries of Malcolm Muggeridge* (1981), 411.

23 CAC, DEKE 2, Chapter II, 6.

24 Berthoud, *Sutherland*, 185.

25 CAC, CHUR 1/59/72, F. and E. G. M. Hamlyn to Churchill, 23 May 1955.

26 CAC, CHUR 2/446/39, Churchill to Lady Juliet Duff, 2 December 1961.

27 W. S. Churchill, *Savrola* (1900), 77.

28 Churchill, *Early Life*, 212.

29 *Speeches* II, 1315.

HARES

1 Churchill, *River War* II, 271 and 41.

2 Kennedy, *Business of War*, 236.

3 *World Crisis* I, 94.

4 D. Reynolds, *In Command of History: Churchill Fighting and Writing the Second World War* (2004), 335.

5 Soames, *Daughter's Tale*, 94.

HEDGEHOGS AND PORCUPINES

1 *Speeches* IV, 5330.

2 Pelling, *Churchill*, 509.

3 Halle, *Irrepressible Churchill*, 287.

4 Manchester, *Last Lion*, 401.

5 Alanbrooke, *War Diaries*, 625.

HIPPOPOTAMUSES

1 Churchill, *African Journey*, 170–1.

2 Churchill, *River War* I, 148.

3 *Speeches* VII, 7156.

4 Moran, *Struggle for Survival*, 21.

5 Colville, *Fringes of Power*, 610.

HORSES

1 A. Leslie, *The Fabulous Leonard Jerome* (1954), 57.

2 *Churchill* I, 171.

3 CAC, CHAR 28/21/16, Winston to his mother, 12 March 1895.

4 CAC, CHAR 28/21/14–15, Winston to his mother, 4 March 1895.

5 *Churchill* I, 225.

6 Churchill, *Early Life*, 62.

7 *Churchill* I, C. 1, 585.

8 W. S. Churchill, 'British Cavalry' in *Anglo-Saxon Review* VIII (March 1901), 244.

9 CAC, CHAR 28/20/39–40, Winston to his mother, 19 September 1894.

10 Churchill, *River War* II, 329.

11 T. Pakenham, *The Boer War* (1979),

366.

12 Churchill, *Ian Hamilton's March*, 65.

13 Learning to drive in July 1901, rather a dangerous period as Churchill acknowledged, he had to apologize to Lord Rosebery for disturbing his horses. Churchill's first chauffeur, Emile Violon, was also something of a scorcher, perhaps at his master's behest. Later in 1901 Violon knocked down and injured a boy in Rochdale. Churchill denied that he had been speeding but did not contest the summons, agreeing to pay compensation to the boy's father and whatever fine the magistrates might impose. He told the local police, 'I need not say how much obliged I should be if this matter could be settled without my name being publicly brought into the case.' (CAC, CHAR 1/29/44, 21 October 1901.)

14 Soames (ed.), *Speaking for Themselves*, 222.

15 D. Harwood, *Love for Animals and How it Developed in Great Britain* (New York, 1928), 74.

16 *Mail on Sunday*, 31 December 2011.

17 Nel, *Churchill's Secretary*, 37.

18 *Speeches* VII, 7547.

19 *Churchill* IV, 500.

20 Churchill continued the equine theme at the unveiling of T. E. Lawrence's memorial at Oxford High School in October 1936, quoting from Adam Lindsay Gordon's poem 'The Last Leap' – the same verse he had used after F. E. Smith's death (*Speeches* VI, 5792):

All is over! Fleet career.
Dash of greyhound slipping thongs.
Flight of falcon, bound of deer.
Mad hoof-thunder in our rear.
Cold air rushing up our lungs.
Din of many tongues.

Like Churchill, Lawrence thought it 'shameful' to exploit animals such as horses. (T. E. Lawrence, *The Seven Pillars of Wisdom* [1976 edn.], 128.)

21 *Speeches* V, 4674. Churchill used the same term to describe the industrious Neville Chamberlain, calling him in 1936 'the pack-horse in our great affairs'. (CAC, CHAR 2/252/51.) Churchill thought the quotation came from Shakespeare's *Henry VI*, disputing (without verifying) Chamberlain's correct contention that it derived from *Richard III* (Act I, Scene 3). Chamberlain told his sister that 'it was thoroughly characteristic of Winston first that he should have remembered this phrase which is not a familiar quotation then that he should have given it the wrong attribution, and finally that having had his attention called to his error he should not have bothered to look it up'. (R. Self [ed.], *The Neville Chamberlain Diary Letters* IV [Aldershot, 2005], 183.)

22 Churchill, *Second World War* II, 591.

23 Kimball (ed.), *Churchill & Roosevelt Correspondence* II, 551.

24 CAC, CHUR 1/45/130. Joseph Alsop, Stewart's brother, gives a slightly different version in his memoirs. He suggests that Churchill's remarks were fuelled by copious draughts of champagne and brandy, and says that he was in such a foul mood, having quarrelled with Randolph (who was at the lunch), that he looked 'like an ancient angry baby'. (J. W. Alsop with A. Platt, *'I've Seen the Best of It'* [1992], 285–6.)

25 Thompson, *Beside the* Bulldog, 21.

26 Kennedy, *Business of War*, 62, quoting Job XXXIX, 21. Kennedy cited several further verses and said that 'the description of the horse in Job is a much better description of Churchill than it is of any horse'.

27 Cited in an illuminating chapter entitled 'The Old Warhorse' by M. Weidhorn, *A Harmony of Interests: Explorations in the Mind of Winston Churchill* (1992), 59.

28 CAC, DEKE 2/17.

HYENAS

1 Churchill, *London to Ladysmith*, 241.
2 *Churchill* IV, 414.
3 *Churchill* VII, 447.
4 Halle, *Irrepressible Churchill*, 220. In Aesop's fable the animal in question was a bear, though Shakespeare represented it as a lion in *Henry V*.
5 *Speeches* VI, 5909. Churchill acknowledged that he had not verified the quotation. What Carlyle actually said was that hallelujahs to atheism were 'like the shout of the hyena should he find the whole world carrion'. (A. S. Arnold, *The Story of Thomas Carlyle* [1888], 356.)

INSECTS OF THE CREEPING KIND

1 Churchill, *River War* II, 59. Churchill even saved a fellow officer, F. W. Wormald, from being stung by a scorpion.
2 Churchill, *African Journey*, 140 and 94.
3 CAC, CHAR 10/27/66, Churchill to Edward VII, 27 November 1907.
4 Captain X [A. D. Gibb], *With Winston Churchill at the Front* (Glasgow, 1924), 22.
5 Moran, *Struggle for Survival*, 513.
6 J. M. McEwen (ed.), *The Riddell Diaries 1908–1923* (1986), 185.
7 Churchill, *River War* II, 41 and I, 139.
8 Wolff (ed.), *Collected Essays* IV, 431.
9 *Speeches* VI, 5806.
10 *Ibid.*, 6429.
11 C. Thornton-Kemsley, *Through Winds and Tides* (Montrose, 1974), 97. I have cited Burke's original passage (*Reflections on the French Revolution* [Everyman edn., 1953], 82), which is slightly different from Thornton-Kemsley's quotation.
12 K. Young (ed.), *The Diaries of Sir Robert Bruce Lockhart II 1939–1965* (1980), 626.
13 J. A. Lockwood, *Six-Legged Soldiers: Using Insects as Weapons of War* (Oxford, 2009), 135.

14 Colville, *Fringes of Power*, 192.

JACKALS

1 *Hansard* (24 October 1884) 293, column 165.
2 Churchill, *River War* I, 368.
3 *Speeches* VI, 6381. Churchill's bête noire Trotsky, among others, attached the jackal label to Mussolini.
4 Thompson, *Churchill's Shadow*, 155.

JAGUARS

1 Soames, *Clementine Churchill*, 336.
2 *Speeches* VIII, 8393.
3 Pimlott (ed.), *Political Diary of Hugh Dalton*, 465.

KANGAROOS

1 *Churchill* V, C. 3, 1511. In the event Churchill did not follow his own advice about the Antipodean animals.
2 Soames (ed.), *Speaking for Themselves*, 382.
3 CAC, CHUR 1/58A-B/217, 30 November 1946.
4 CAC, CHUR 1/58A-B/245.
5 CAC, CHUR 1/58A-B/208, Vevers to Churchill, 1 February 1947.
6 CAC, CHUR 1/58A-B/188, Churchill to Vevers, 26 April 1948.
7 CAC, CHUR 1/58A-B/184, memorandum of 28 February 1949.
8 CAC, CHUR 1/58A-B/179, Churchill to McCann, 31 March 1949.

LADYBIRDS

1 Alanbrooke, *War Diaries*, 395. According to Brooke, Churchill did repeat 'at home'; the wording is usually 'are gone' or, sometimes, 'alone'.
2 Manchester, *Last Lion*, 37.
3 Young (ed.), *Lockhart* II, 709.

LEOPARDS

1 *World Crisis* I, 252.
2 *Churchill* III, 637.
3 Churchill, *Second World War* II, 251. Churchill said that at the end of the war Hitler had created a spider's web of communications around himself but had fatally neglected to retain a defensive reserve to exploit

them – '*he forgot the spider*'. (*Ibid.*, 255.) Incidentally, the plan to station fifteen British observer groups on Mesopotamia's border with Turkey, which Churchill instituted at this time, was also code-named 'Leopard'.

4   Churchill, *River War* I, 29.
5   Churchill, *African Journey*, 31.
6   CAC, CHAR 2/469A-B/131, Spellman to Churchill, 26 June 1943. Churchill thanked Spellman for the 'very fine specimen', which his staff thought he could not refuse even though he had to pay 45 shillings customs duty on the gift.
7   *Churchill* II, 196.
8   Churchill, *African Journey*, 97.
9   Montague Browne, *Long Sunset* 167.

LIONS
1   CAC, CHAR 28/23/555–56, Churchill to Reggie Barnes, 14 September 1897.
2   Churchill, *London to Ladysmith*, 388–9. In the same passage Churchill showed remarkable forethought in stressing the need for public tolerance of 'men who try daring *coups* and fail!'.
3   G. Shakespeare, *Let Candles Be Brought In* (1949), 229.
4   CAC, CHAR 2/468A-B/20, Violet Melchett to Churchill, 11 May 1943.
5   Alanbrooke, *War Diaries*, 416.
6   *Churchill* VIII, 903.
7   Berthoud, *Sutherland*, 190.
8   Halle, *Randolph Churchill*, 154. The journalist Henry Fairlie witnessed this bizarre scene.
9   Halle, *Irrepressible Churchill*, 120.
10 *Speeches* VI, 6427; VII, 6775; VIII, 8418; VIII, 8691.
11 CAC, CHUR 1/58A-B/430–432, Duke of Devonshire to G. Harvie Watt, 23 January 1943. Also CAC, CHAR 20/93A/61.
12 Churchill, *Second World War* IV, 652. The private secretary apparently thought that Churchill was in a delirium. Cadogan, head of the

Foreign Office, was equally diminutive and complained in his diary that 'some damn fool has given Winston a lion – which I suppose will travel in future in my "Liberator"'. (Dilks [ed.], *Diary of Cadogan*, 514.)

13 *Churchill Documents* XVIII, 2126.
14 CAC, CHUR 1/58A-B/365, 14 October 1950.
15 CAC, CHUR 1/58A-B/359, 27 June 1953
16 CAC, CHUR 1/58A-B/352, 30 June 1953.
17 CAC, CHUR 1/58A-B/395, Vevers to Mrs Hill, 29 June 1944.
18 CAC, CHUR 1/58A-B/386, Thomson to Churchill, 18 May 1945.
19 *Daily Express*, 11 June 1945.
20 CAC, CHUR 1/58A-B/388, Vevers to Mrs Hill, 27 July 1944.
21 CAC, CHUR 1/58A-B/368, G. S. Cansdale to Churchill, 11 May 1950.
22 CAC, CHUR 1/58A-B/348, Thomson to Churchill, 18 June 1955.
23 CAC, CHUR 1/58A-B/345, Churchill to Harrison Matthews, 30 June 1955.
24 CAC, CHUR 1/58A-B/330.
25 CAC, CHUR 1/58A-B/331.
26 CAC, CHUR 1/58A-B/327.
27 CAC, CHUR 1/58A-B/344.
28 Churchill, *African Journey*, 10.
29 This couplet is often attributed to Voltaire but seems to have originated in a French song, 'La Ménagerie' (1828). Churchill knew it and on at least one occasion applied it to himself. (*Churchill* V, C. 1, 1219.)
30 Churchill, *African Journey*, 27.
31 José Ortega y Gasset advanced a comparable argument in his famous apologia, saying that the hunter, by achieving a mysterious communion with the animal in his own primordial nature, satisfied 'a deep and permanent yearning of the human condition'. (J. Ortega y Gasset, *Meditations on Hunting* [New York, 1986], 40.)

LIZARDS
1   Churchill, *Malakand Field Force*, 22.

2 Bonham Carter, *Winston Churchill*, 264.

3 Churchill, *Great Contemporaries*, 281.

4 *Churchill* VIII, 161. Actually the 6,000 species of lizards (Squamata) do not belong to the same group of reptiles as crocodiles.

5 *Ibid.*, 1299.

6 Howells, *Simply Churchill*, 29.

MICE

1 Churchill, *River War* I, 139.

2 Soames (ed.), *Speaking for Themselves*, 106.

3 *Churchill* VI, 587. Churchill had used a similar expression in *Savrola* (188).

4 *Speeches* VI, 6541.

5 *Speeches* VII, 7691.

6 Stelzer, *Dinner with Churchill*, 170.

7 D. Kynaston, *Austerity Britain 1945–51* (2009), 385.

8 N. Major, *Chequers* (1996), 200. The painting is now ascribed to Rubens and Frans Snyders, who may well have been responsible for the mouse.

9 CAC, SCHL 1/1/9, 15 September 1945.

10 Soames (ed.), *Speaking for Themselves*, 196.

11 *Speeches* VI, 6017.

MONKEYS

1 V. Sheean, *Between the Thunder and the Sun* (1943), 27.

2 *Churchill* V, 1036.

3 Pawle, *War and Colonel Warden*, 153.

4 CAC, CHAR 20/6028, Leslie Rowan (Churchill's Private Secretary) to Clifford Jarrett (Principal Private Secretary to First Lord of the Admiralty), 15 March 1942.

5 CAC, EADE 2/2, 11 September 1942.

6 Colville, *Fringes of Power*, 178.

NEWTS

1 *Guardian*, 15 December 2000.

2 *Churchill* V, 400. Churchill had used this title for an article for the *Sunday Pictorial* in the summer of 1916.

3 Nicolson, *Diaries and Letters 1939–* 1945, 258.

OCTOPUSES

1 Churchill, *Savrola*, 242.

2 Orwell and Angus (eds.), *Collected … Orwell* IV, 164.

OSTRICHES

1 Churchill, *African Journey*, 30.

2 See S. A. Stein, *Plumes: Ostrich Feathers, Jews, and a Lost World of Global Commerce* (2008), 2. The boom collapsed in 1914 and at the Treasury in 1925 Churchill decided against imposing a tax on ostrich feathers as luxury goods since it would not raise enough revenue.

3 Soames, *Clementine Churchill*, 92.

OWLS

1 CAC, CHUR 2/446/39, Lady Lytton to Churchill, 30 November 1961. The book was entitled *Le Hibou et la Poussiquette* (1961) and it contained Lear's English text as well as Francis Steegmuller's free translation.

2 M. Shelden, *Young Titan: The Making of Winston Churchill* (2013), 183.

3 CAC, CHAR 2/180B/113, Churchill to Sir Mark Hunter, Secretary of the Indian Empire Society, 17 March 1931.

OYSTERS

1 CAC, CHAR 8/340/61.

PANDAS

1 *Times*, 23 December 1938.

2 *Times*, 8 April 1939.

3 R. W. Clark, *The Huxleys* (1968), 258.

4 J. Huxley, *Memories* I (1970), 248.

5 I am grateful to Richard Langworth for sending me an advance copy of, 'Churchill and Animals II: All Creatures Great and Small', in *The Churchillian* 6:1 (Summer 2015), 6–13, at 11.

6 Nicolson, *Diaries and Letters 1930–1964*, edited by S. Olson, 151–2. In the course of his tirade Churchill maintained that Britain would benefit from having the Turks, rather

than the Italians, as allies: Italy was 'a prey, Turkey a falcon'. (R. Steel, *Walter Lippmann and the American Century* [1980], 376.) The war itself changed his view, since Turkey remained neutral almost to the end. In November 1943 Churchill wanted Eden 'to remind the Turkey that Christmas was coming'. (Bryant, *Triumph in the West*, 62.)

7   P. Clarke, *Mr Churchill's Profession* (2012), 227.
8   *Churchill* VIII, 254.

PARROTS
1   *Speeches* I, 673; IV, 3427 and 3495.
2   Soames (ed.), *Speaking for Themselves*, 435.
3   CAC, CHAR 1/344/4, Mary to her father, 22 January 1939.
4   *Churchill* V, C. 3, 892.
5   *Churchill* VI, 210.
6   *Churchill* VIII, 137.
7   C. Roberts, *Sunshine and Shadow* (1972), 390.

PEACOCKS
1   Churchill, *River War* II, 342.
2   General Patton, America's most aggressive commander, would have agreed. He accused the Army of equipping itself with pianos and ping-pong sets.
3   Kennedy, *Business of War*, 274.
4   *Speeches* VII, 7658.

PIGS
1   *Churchill* VIII, 304.
2   Soames (ed.), *Speaking for Themselves*, 196.
3   CAC, HAMB 1/1.
4   Soames (ed.), *Speaking for Themselves*, 316.
5   CAC, CHAR 1/399A/8, Churchill to Violet Pearman, 17 January 1932.
6   McGowan, *Years with Churchill*, 39.
7   *Churchill* V, C. 1, 335.
8   *Churchill* V, 201.
9   Leslie, *Cousin Randolph*, 1.
10 Cooper, *Darling Monster*, 88.
11 *World Crisis*, II, 119.

12 *Churchill* V, C. 3, 504.
13 Churchill, *Savrola*, 55.
14 *Churchill* II, 350 and 357.
15 Soames (ed.), *Speaking for Themselves*, 275.
16 CAC, CHAR 1/343/59, 24 February 1939.
17 Dilks (ed.), *Diaries of Cadogan*, 468.
18 Hunter (ed.), *Winston and Archie*, 41.
19 W. R. Louis, *Ends of British Imperialism* (2006), 615.
20 Charles Lamb's "A Dissertation upon Roast Pig" appeared in his *Essays of Elia* (1823).
21 *Speeches* V, 4929.
22 CAC, CHAR 20/152/2, Prime Minister's Personal Minutes, 26 February 1944.
23 Dilks (ed.), *Diaries of Cadogan*, 473.
24 *Churchill* VIII, 213.

PLATYPUSES
1   CAC, CHAR 20/109.110, Churchill to Curtin, 11 March 1943.
2   CAC, CHAR 20/94A/10, Churchill to Evatt, 5 July 1943.
3   CAC, BRGS 1/3. I owe this reference, with thanks, to Natalie Adams.
4   D. Fleay, *Breeding the Platypus* (Melbourne, 1944), 36.
5   N. Lawrence, 'The Prime Minister and the platypus: A paradox goes to war' in *Studies in History and Philosophy of Science* 43 (March 2011), 292.
6   CAC, CHUR 1/58A-B/313, 29 April 1943.
7   CAC, CHUR 1/58A-B/311.
8   CAC, CHUR 1/58A-B/285.
9   CAC, CHUR 1/58A-B/291.
10 CAC, CHUR 1/58A-B/275.
11 CAC, CHUR 1/58A-B/294.
12 CAC, CHAR 20/124/114.

POLO PONIES
1   *Churchill* I, 306.
2   *The Memoirs of the Aga Khan* (1954), 85.
3   Manchester, *Last Lion*, 241–2.
4   Leslie, *Long Shadows*, 23.
5   CAC, CHAR 1/33/16–19, Churchill

to Brodrick, 7 June 1902.

6 *Churchill Documents* XV, 602. Churchill also maintained that a good pilot should be able to fly various types of aircraft, just as a good horseman could ride a hunter, a polo pony or a hack.

7 CAC, CHAR 28/26/98–100, Winston to his mother, 23 March 1901.

8 CAC, CHAR 1/135/67, Churchill to Freddie Guest, 25 June 1921.

9 CAC, CHAR 1/138/66, Churchill to Lord Wimborne, 25 June 1921.

10 CAC, CHAR 2/120/7, Churchill to the Prince of Wales, 2 January 1922.

11 CAC, CHAR 1/157/22, Churchill to Lord Curzon, 24 April 1922.

12 CAC, CHAR 1/172/48, Churchill to Lord Wodehouse, 15 December 1924.

13 CAC, CHAR 2/138/35, Churchill to General Beauvoir de Lisle, 5 November 1924.

14 CAC, CHAR 1/178/38, Churchill to Lord Wodehouse, 10 August 1925.

15 CAC, CHAR 1/188/78, Churchill to Admiral Keyes, 18 December 1926.

16 *Churchill* V, 222.

POODLES

1 CAC, CHAR 29/98/32–34, Lady Randolph to Lord Randolph Churchill, 10 January 1883.

2 Graebner, *Dear Mr Churchill*, 100.

3 *Political Adventure: The Memories of the Earl of Kilmuir* (1964), 166.

4 https://www.nationalchurchillmuseum.org/winston-churchill-biography.html/.

5 Graebner, *Dear Mr Churchill*, 100.

6 CAC, CHUR 1/45/148, Miss B. Lobban to Churchill, 1 February 1948.

7 Graebner, *Dear Mr Churchill*, 101.

8 CAC, CHUR 1/45/155, 9 March 1948.

9 *Daily Mail*, 18 November 2014.

10 CAC, CHUR 1/45/158, J. W. Bruford to Churchill, 23 March 1948.

11 CAC, CHUR 1/45/159, Mrs Lilley

Bennett to Churchill, 27 May 1948.

12 CAC, CHUR 1/45/161, Bruford to Churchill, 7 June 1948.

13 CAC, CHUR 1/45/162, Churchill to Miss Lobban, 7 June 1948.

14 CAC, CHUR 1/45/165, Churchill to Mrs Nichols, 8 July 1948.

15 Rufus I's teeth had also been rotten and Grace Hamblin authorized the vet to remove them when Churchill was abroad. This did in fact improve Rufus's general health, but Churchill was furious: 'How dare you take out my dog's teeth while I was away.' (CAC, HAMB 1/3.)

16 Montague Browne, *Long Sunset*, 114.

17 Moran, *Struggle for Survival*, 735.

18 CAC, CHUR 1/45/142, 30 August 1948.

19 D. Cooper, 'The Lion's Heart' in *Atlantic Monthly* 215, No. 3 (March 1965), 59.

20 McGowan, *Years with Churchill*, 69.

21 CAC, HAMB 1/2.

22 *Churchill* VIII, 525.

23 CAC, CHUR 2/52A-B/130.

24 T. H. Tracy, *The Book of the Poodle* (1951), 5. The frontispiece of this book consists of a photograph of Rufus jumping up at Churchill, which he gave the author permission to use provided that no mention was made of his agreement. (CAC, CHUR 1/49/81.)

25 Graebner, *Dear Mr Churchill*, 102.

26 Manchester, *Last Lion*, 38.

27 CAC, CHUR 1/59/145.

28 CAC, CHUR 1/59/144.

29 CAC, CHUR 1/59/141.

30 CAC, CHUR 1/59/142.

31 CAC, CHUR 1/59/143.

32 CAC, CHUR 2/375/34, H. F. Parmiter to Churchill, 10 October 1947. I owe this reference, with thanks, to Cita Stelzer.

33 CAC, CHUR 1/59/150, Montague Browne to Graebner, 21 August 1962.

34 CAC, CHUR 2/52A-B/130.

QUAIL

1. Churchill, *Savrola*, 105.
2. *Speeches* II, 1631.
3. Pawle, *War and Colonel Warden*, 172.

RABBITS

1. Colville, *Fringes of Power*, 158.
2. CAC, CHAR 28/16/17.
3. Rhodes James, *Cazalet*, 20.
4. *Churchill* VIII, 346.
5. *Churchill* VIII, 1238.
6. Churchill, *Second World War* III, 689.
7. CAC, EADE 2/2, 24 July 1941.
8. *Churchill* V, C. 1, 223.
9. Pawle, *War and Colonel Warden*, 42. It seems more probable that the name was taken from the White Rabbit who disappears down the hole in the first chapter of *Alice's Adventures in Wonderland*. The name was soon changed to 'Cultivator No. 6', which did not save this Churchill 'funny' from being a fiasco.
10. Churchill, *Thoughts and Adventures*, 132.
11. Halle, *Irrepressible Churchill*, 129.

RACEHORSES

1. Martin, *Lady Randolph Churchill* I, 3.
2. *Churchill* I, 247. The National Hunt Committee subsequently declared the race void and disqualified all the horses from further racing under its rules because certain irregularities had taken place – perhaps the running of a 'ringer', the clandestine substitution of one horse for another.
3. *Churchill* I, 308.
4. CAC, CHAR 28/23/69–70, Churchill to Lord William Beresford, 2 November 1897.
5. K. Thomson, 'Racing to Victory: Winston Churchill and the Lure of the Turf' in *Finest Hour* 102 (Spring 1999), 27. I'm grateful to Katharine Thomson for much help over Churchill's racehorses.
6. P. Addison, *Churchill on the Home Front 1900–1955* (1992), 257.
7. *Speeches* I, 51. In 1955 Churchill said that he could not visit the Curragh to watch his filly Dark Issue, who won the Irish 1,000 Guineas, because 'the General Election was my owner and I was already entered among the runners'. (Thomson, *Finest Hour* [Spring 1999], 30.)
8. P. Addison, 'The Political Beliefs of Winston Churchill', *Transactions of the Royal Historical Society* 30 (1980), 35.
9. A. Leslie, *Cousin Randolph* (1985), 315.
10. J. Saville, *Insane and Unseemly* (Leicester, 2009), 211 and 98.
11. D. Lough, *No More Champagne: Churchill and His Money* (2015), 357.
12. R. Skidelsky, *Britain Since 1900 – A Success Story?* (2014), 59–60.
13. F. Glueckstein, 'Winston Churchill and Colonist II' in *Finest Hour* 125 (Winter 2004–5), 29.
14. J. F. Nestle, 'Sir Winston Churchill as a Race Horse Owner' in *Riding* 14, No. 8 (August 1954), 287.
15. Eade (ed.), *Churchill by his Contemporaries*, 436. Herbert seems to have embroidered this story.
16. Thomson, *Finest Hour* (Spring 1999), 30.
17. Montagu Browne, *Long Sunset*, 151.
18. CAC, MCHL 5/7/51, Mary to her mother, 16 March 1958.
19. *Churchill* VIII, 524.
20. CAC, CHUR 1/94/24, Churchill to R. N. Macdonald-Buchanan, 15 July 1955.
21. CAC, CHUR 1/94/164, Churchill to Odette Pol Roger, 26 June 1953.
22. CAC, CHUR 2/173/194, Munnings to Churchill, 30 October 1950. Munnings observed Colonist racing, 'leading the other two – ears pricked, his wall eye intent on the ultimate end, galloping [sic] on with perfect action'. The artist said that he would not paint Colonist in the autumn because he had a coat like a bear but 'he will be a picture in the Spring'.
23. CAC, CHUR 2/173/45.
24. CAC, MCHL 5/8/43, Churchill to

Cozzika, 11 May 1953.
25 CAC, CHUR 2/219. Churchill seems to have approved this foreword but not written it. Haseltine also made a Percheron mare and foal for Churchill, as well as carving Rufus in bronze – though Clementine wanted to keep the poodle out of the importunate sculptor's reach.

RATS
1 Churchill, *Lord Randolph Churchill*, 23.
2 CAC, CHAR 28/16/17.
3 Churchill, *Early Life*, 287–8.
4 Soames (ed.), *Speaking for Themselves*, 116.
5 *Churchill* III, 635.
6 *Speeches* I, 66 and 49.
7 Manchester, *Last Lion*, 361.
8 R. Rhodes James, *Lord Randolph Churchill* (1994 edn.), 140.
9 W. S. Blunt, *My Diaries* II *1900–1914* (1920), 357.
10 E. Longford, *A Pilgrimage of Passion: The Life of Wilfrid Scawen Blunt* (1979), 387.
11 *Speeches* III, 2337.
12 *Hansard* 80 (7 March 1916), 1442 and 1425.
13 *World Crisis* I, 314.
14 McEwen (ed.), *Riddell Diaries*, 119.
15 D. Dilks, 'The Twilight War and the Fall of France: Chamberlain and Churchill in 1940' in *Transactions of the Royal Historical Society* XX (1978), 62.
16 *Churchill* VIII, 1150
17 CAC, CHAR 1/273/136.
18 Bright-Holmes (ed.), *Diaries of Malcolm Muggeridge*, 244.
19 CAC, CHAR 2/206/21, Violet Pearman to Winston Churchill, 13 July 1934. The political row which Randolph made more rancorous is fully described by Carl Bridge, 'Churchill, Hoare, Derby, and the Committee of Privileges, April to June 1934' in *Historical Journal* 22, 1 (1979), 215–227.
20 M. Gilbert (ed.), *Churchill: The Power*

of Words (2012), 367.

RHINOCEROSES
1 *Churchill* II, 230.
2 Churchill, *African Journey*, 18.
3 W. Shawcross, *Queen Elizabeth the Queen Mother* (2009), 227.
4 Salt, *Killing for Sport*, xxvii.
5 P. Pagnamenta, *Prairie Fever* (New York, 2012), 255.
6 Churchill, *African Journey*, 60 and 186. Churchill stuck to the term commonly used in Uganda, Burchell's white rhinoceros, to identify these northern pachyderms. But he acknowledged that their correct name was *Rhinoceros Simus Cottoni*, and that, as his correspondent Richard Lydekker of the Natural History Museum had pointed out, 'Burchell's white rhinoceros is the designation of the southern race'. (CAC, CHAR 1/95/74.)
7 R. H. Pilpel, *Churchill in America 1895–1961* (1977), 63.
8 M. R. Canfield, *Theodore Roosevelt in the Field* (2015), 285 and 320.

SEA ANEMONES
1 CAC, CHAR 28/13/75, Winston to his mother, 25 August 1885.
2 Bonham Carter, *Winston Churchill*, 148–9.

SHEEP
1 Churchill, *Early Life*, 361.
2 Churchill, *African Journey*, 63.
3 Wolff (ed.), *Collected Essays* II, 444.
4 *Churchill* II, 391.
5 Soames (ed.), *Speaking for Themselves*, 319.
6 Churchill, *Thread in the Tapestry*, 27.
7 CAC, CHAR 1/298/23.
8 *The Complete Works of Robert Burns* (Boston, Mass., 1858), 62.
9 Leslie, *Long Shadows*, 16.
10 *Speeches* III, 3262.
11 *Churchill* V, C. 1, 573.
12 At a Royal Academy banquet in 1953 Churchill said, 'Without tradition art is a flock of sheep without a shepherd.

Without innovation it is a corpse.'
(*Speeches* VIII, 8475.)
13 Ball, *Guardsmen*, 225.
14 *Speeches* III, 2333.
15 Soames (ed.), *Speaking for Themselves*, 179.
16 S. Roskill, *Hankey: Man of Secrets* I (1970), 219.
17 Earl Mountbatten 'Churchill the Warrior', Fourth Winston Churchill Memorial Lecture (1970), 8. Like many of Churchill's animal images, this one was long in gestation. Arguing with a Boer in 1899 over the rights and wrongs of the South African war, he acknowledged that the British Empire was the wolf to the Afrikaner lamb but maintained that 'never before was a lamb with such teeth and claws'. (Churchill, *London to Ladysmith*, 165.)
18 Bright-Holmes (ed.), *Diaries of Malcolm Muggeridge*, 413.
19 McGowan, *Years with Churchill*, 155.

SKUNKS
1 Churchill, *Malakand Field Force*, 11.
2 Colville, *Fringes of Power*, 248.
3 *Churchill* III, 699.
4 Montague Browne, *Long Sunset*, 220. Churchill also commented, when Driberg married his rather plain housekeeper, 'buggers can't be choosers'. But both quips were probably unoriginal. It was widely said of the historian A. L. Rowse, for example, that he gave buggery a bad name.
5 CAC, CHAR 20/96A/19.

SNAKES
1 CAC, CHAR 28/13/8, Winston to his father, 10 April 1882. It is interesting to compare the experience of W. H. Hudson, who as a boy of about the same age saw a snake being rescued, which taught him 'to consider whether it might not be better to spare than to kill; better not only for the animal spared, but for the soul'. (*Far Away and*

Long Ago [1918], 211.)
2 Churchill, *Lord Randolph Churchill*, 492.
3 L. J. Jennings (ed.), *The Speeches of ... Lord Randolph Churchill* II (1889), 295.
4 Churchill, *English-Speaking Peoples* I, 73.
5 *Lord Riddell's Intimate Diary of the Peace Conference and After 1918–1923* (1933), 225.
6 *Churchill* IV, 392.
7 *Speeches* IV, 3328.
8 Kennedy, *Business of War*, 316.
9 McEwen (ed.), *Riddell Diaries*, 115.
10 Churchill, *River War* II, 373.
11 Montague Browne, *Long Sunset*, 305.

SQUIRRELS
1 CAC, CHAR 2/477/49, 2 July 1943.
2 CAC, CHUR 2/355/387, Major E. C. E. Hobkirk to Churchill, 14 July 1948.
3 CAC, CHUR 2/355/388.
4 CAC, CHAR 1/207/47, Winston to Clementine, 1 September 1929.
5 *Churchill* V, C. 2, 67.
6 Churchill, *Second World War* IV, 62.
7 *Speeches* VIII, 8116–8117. Churchill was touched, though, when Morrison commiserated with him over the death of one of his black swans.
8 Montague Browne, *Long Sunset*, 76.
9 P. Clarke, *The Cripps Version: The Life of Sir Stafford Cripps* (2002), xiv and 355.
10 Moran, *Struggle for Survival*, 74.

STAGS
1 Churchill, *English-Speaking Peoples* I, 126 and 209.
2 Soames (ed.), *Speaking for Themselves*, 76
3 Manchester, *Last Lion*, 430.
4 Churchill, *Thoughts and Adventures*, 98. Bignold was a magistrate, a former MP and a godson of the Duke of Wellington. Rumours of his activities

as a spy were ridiculed in the local press, where he was described as 'one of the best men who has ever taken up his abode in the north'. (*Ross-shire Journal*, 6 November 1914.) Bignold was said to have planted millions of trees to enhance the sport on his shooting estates and critics maintained that deer had driven out crofters.

SWANS

1 *Churchill* II, 710.
2 CAC, CHUR 1/58A-B/69. Churchill's informant gave him the reference – Juvenal's Satire VI, line 165 – and the Latin quotation: *rara avis in terris negroque similliana cycno*. But he did not explain the misogynistic context: Juvenal was saying that a worthy wife, like a black swan, is a rare bird. Although rare, as Churchill liked to emphasize, black swans were not unknown in England. William Cobbett encountered some in Wiltshire in 1826, never having seen any before, and wrote dismissively: 'They are not nearly so large as the white, nor are they so stately in their movements. They are a meaner bird.' (W. Cobbett, *Rural Rides*, edited by J. H. Lobban (1922), 211.)
3 CAC, CHAR 1/194/45, Churchill to Sassoon, 9 June 1927.
4 CAC, CHAR 1/194/51, Sassoon to Churchill, 13 June 1927.
5 *Churchill* V, C. 1, 1246.
6 Soames (ed.), *Speaking for Themselves*, 376.
7 M. Amory (ed.), *The Letters of Ann Fleming* (1988), 231.
8 Soames (ed.), *Speaking for Themselves*, 388.
9 CAC, CHUR 1/58A-B/121, memorandum, 7 September 1949.
10 CAC, CHWL 8, Tony Johnstone to Grace Hamblin, 27 June 1963.
11 CAC, CHUR 1/58A-B/135, Clementine Churchill to Nellie Soames.
12 CAC, CHUR 1/58A-B/53, 29 March 1953.
13 CAC, CHAR 1/332/17, *Hants & Sussex County Press*, 8 July 1938.
14 CAC, CHUR 1/58A-B/46.
15 CAC, CHUR 1/58A-B/11, Alan Davidson to Elizabeth Gilliatt, Churchill's secretary.
16 CAC, CHUR 2/160/131, Churchill to the Marquess of Bath, 30 January 1949.
17 *Churchill* VIII, 988 and 979.
18 McGowan, *Years with Churchill*, 46.
19 Graebner, *Dear Mr Churchill*, 98.
20 CAC, CHUR 1/58A-B/143, Churchill to Vevers, 23 July 1946.
21 CAC, CHUR 1/58A-B/166.
22 CAC, CHUR 1/58A-B/151.
23 CAC, CHUR 1/58A-B/141.
24 CAC, CHUR 1/58A-B/87, Bracken to Churchill, 11 August 1952, passing on advice from W. S. Robinson about putting up electric fencing and building a shelter for the swans on a light raft moored well away from the edge of the lake.
25 CAC, CHUR 1/58A-B/83.
26 *Churchill* VIII, 523.
27 Montague Browne, *Long Sunset*, 318.
28 CAC, DEKE 2, Chapter III, 7.
29 CAC, CHAR 20/77/46, Curtin to Churchill, 30 June 1942.
30 CAC, CHAR 20/72/80, Richard Casey (formerly Australia's ambassador to Washington, newly appointed to be Britain's Resident Minister in the Middle East) to Churchill, 22 March 1942.
31 CAC, CHAR 20/77/111.
32 CAC, CHUR 1/58A-B/165, H. H. Olney to Churchill, 17 August 1942.
33 CAC, CHUR 1/58A-B/108, Churchill to McLarty, 22 September 1949.
34 CAC, CHUR 1/58A-B/77, Churchill to McLarty, 6 September 1952.
35 Colville, *Fringes of Power*, 135.
36 Cowles, *Churchill*, 361. Churchill remained quite paternalistic to

the end. In a letter to Eisenhower, written in August 1954, he expressed scepticism about 'universal suffrage for the Hottentots' and said that he would not speak about democracy but choose as the theme 'for my swan song … "The Unity of the English-Speaking Peoples"'. (*Churchill* VIII, 1041.)

TIGERS

1   *Churchill* I, 64.
2   Churchill, *Lord Randolph Churchill*, 855.
3   CAC, CHAR 28/62/8–10,
4   Churchill, *River War* I, 355.
5   Colville, *Fringes of Power*, 342.
6   *Henry V*, Act III, Scene 1.
7   CAC, CHAR 2/237/163–5, Morton to Churchill, 26 October 1935. Morton, who lived close to Chartwell, was evidently referring to Tango, the marmalade cat.
8   Churchill, *Malakand Field Force*, 27.
9   Cowles, *Churchill*, 222. Tanks were transmogrified into tiger-cubs in 1941, when five shiploads were sent to Egypt during Operation TIGER; when the convoy was attacked Churchill said, 'The Poor Tiger has already lost one claw and another is damaged; but still I would close on what is left.' (Colville, *Fringes of Power*, 385.)
10 Churchill, *Second World War* III, 140. In 1940 Churchill had used the same image to describe the peril and distress of the Dutch, though he sympathized with them 'dwelling as they do in the cage with the tiger'. (*Speeches* VI, 6200.)
11 J. W. Wheeler-Bennett, *King George VI* (1956), 537.
12 Churchill, *Great Contemporaries*, 290, 298–9.
13 *Churchill* V, 817.
14 Chisholm and Davie, *Beaverbrook*, 298.
15 A. Thwaite, *Edmund Gosse: A Literary Landscape* (Oxford, 1985 edn.), 456.

16 Brendon, *Churchill*, 70.
17 Nicolson, *Diaries and Letters 1930–1939*, 382. Nicolson probably owed this image to Lord Byron, whose biography he wrote: 'I am like the tyger (in poesy) if I miss my first Spring – I go growling back to my Jungle.' (F. McCarthy, *Byron Life and Legend* [2003 edn.], 383.)

TOADS

1   Cowles, *Churchill*, 103.
2   CAC, CHAR 2/246/5–6, Duff Cooper to Churchill, 24 January 1935.
3   CAC, CHAR 2/246/4, Churchill to Duff Cooper, 24 January 1935.
4   *Times*, 26 January 1935.
5   Nel, *Churchill's Secretary*, 58. Churchill may well have had in mind Kipling's quatrain from 'Pagett M.P.':
    The toad beneath the harrow knows
    Where every separate tooth-point goes;
    The butterfly upon the road
    Preaches contentment to that toad.

ULREYI, MOLLIES, GUPPIES AND OTHER TROPICAL FISH

1   *Churchill* V, C. 1, 423.
2   Grace Hamblin, 'Frabjous Days: Chartwell Memories 1932–1965' in *Finest Hour* 117, (Winter 2002).
3   CAC, CHUR 1/59/47.
4   CAC, CHWL 8, Derrick Cawston to Grace Hamblin, 12 March 1951.
5   CAC, CHUR 1/59/46, Churchill to Grace Hamblin, 11 April 1951.
6   CAC, CHUR 1/59/45.
7   CAC, CHUR 1/59/52, Churchill to Mr Whitwell, 8 August 1951.
8   CAC, CHUR 2/392, Stanley Wagner to Churchill, 13 August 1951.
9   CAC, CHUR 1/59/52, Churchill to Mr Whitwell, 8 August 1951.
10 CAC, CHUR 1/59/46.
11 CAC, CHUR 1/59/60, Larry Verbit to Churchill, 29 February 1953.
12 CAC, CHUR 2/406/137. According to Straus's list, he sent a total of sixty-

one fish.

13 CAC, CHUR 2/406/140, Churchill to Irving L. Straus, 8 June 1952.

14 CAC, CHUR 2/406/136.

15 CAC, CHUR 2/406/134, Straus to Churchill, 7 August 1952.

16 CAC, CHUR 2/406/134, Churchill to Straus, 9 August 1952.

17 CAC, Commodore George Gordon Allen tape-recording. In fact mollies, like a few other fish such as guppies and platys, do give birth to live young but they do not suckle them. Churchill was no ichthyologist (though, arguing that the slightest detail might be of use to German intelligence during the war, he observed that an entire ichthyosaurus could be reconstructed from a single tail bone) but he might not have got this wrong; it is quite possible that Allen misunderstood or misremembered what he had said.

18 CAC, NEMO 3/1, 71–2. I have modified the punctuation.

19 CAC, CHUR 1/59/66, H. F. Vinall to Churchill, 26 May 1955.

20 CAC, CHUR 1/59/65, H. L. Ward to Churchill, 20 May 1955.

VULTURES

1 Churchill, *Malakand Field Force*, 134 and 233.

2 CAC, CHAR 28/23/55–56, Churchill to Barnes, 14 September 1897.

3 Churchill, *River War*, II, 43 and 77.

4 Brendon, *Churchill*, 27.

5 Churchill, *London to Ladysmith*, 196.

6 Lewis, *Clara in Blunderland*, 26–7.

7 *Speeches* I, 405.

8 *Speeches* IV, 3493.

9 *Speeches* VII, 7257.

10 *Churchill* VIII, 522.

WARTHOGS AND WILD BOARS

1 R. Lewin, *Churchill as Warlord* (1973), 3.

2 R. Baden-Powell, *Lessons from the 'Varsity of Life* (1932), 86.

3 See P. Cartledge, *The Spartans: An Epic History* (2013), 255–263, for

an illuminating account of Spartan hunting.

4 CAC, CHAR 28/111/4–7/5, Winston to Jack, 17 November 1907.

5 Churchill, *African Journey*, 44 and 72.

6 Shelden, *Young Titan*, 289.

7 *Churchill* II, C. 3, 1844.

8 CAC, CHAR 1/256/74, 9 November 1934.

9 Soames (ed.), *Speaking for Themselves*, 224.

10 *Churchill* IV, 387.

WHALES

1 CAC, CHUR 2/355/364, 22 January 1947.

2 *Speeches* V, 4989.

3 Bryant, *Triumph in the West*, 160.

4 Churchill, *Second World War* VI, 23. Churchill decorated one wall of his library at Chartwell with the original large diagram of the Arromanches 'Mulberry' harbour, marked with all the ships, tracks, quays and so on.

5 CAC, CHAR 20/138A/46, Churchill to Brigadier B. G. White, 10 August 1944.

6 McGowan, *Years with Churchill*, 78.

WOLVES

1 *Speeches* VI, 5674.

2 Churchill, *Early Life*, 192.

3 Colville, *Fringes of Power*, 476.

4 Moran, *Struggle for Survival*, 457.

5 *Churchill* II, 34.

6 *Speeches* VI, 5677.

7 K. Jefferys, *The Churchill Coalition and Wartime Politics, 1940–1945* (Manchester, 1995), 107.

8 R. Overy, *The Bombing War: Europe 1939–1945* (2013), 254.

9 C. P. Snow, *Science and Government* (Oxford, 1961), 49.

10 Lord Casey, *Personal Experience 1939–1946* (1962), 166.

WORMS

1 Riddell, *More Pages*, 24.

2 Murray, *Churchill's Bodyguard*, 127.

3 Wolff (ed.), *Collected Essays* IV, 454.

4 Pottle (ed.), *Diaries and Letters of*

Violet Bonham Carter, 318.

5   *Churchill* II, 249.

6   Churchill, *River War* I, 420. An editorial footnote gives an excellent account of this disease, noting that it was conveyed by drinking water infected with the worm's larvae and not, as Churchill believed, by contact with the skin. The method of extracting the worm from the body remains today exactly as it was when Churchill described it.

7   Churchill, *African Journey*, 140.

8   *Churchill Documents* XVIII, 1873.

9   CAC, CHAR 13/7/14–15, 25 April 1912.

10 Churchill, *Early Life*, 57.

11 Colville, *Fringes of Power*, 310.

ZOOS

1   E. Baratay and E. Hardouin-Fugier, *Zoo: A History of Zoological Gardens in the West* (2002), 237.

2   According to *The Times* (16 May 1891), Hagenbeck trained his animals by kindness, avoiding old-fashioned methods such as clubbing them or burning them with 'red-hot irons'. However, he was unable to procure enough freshly slaughtered meat for those appearing at the Crystal Palace and they soon died. This illustrates the fatal impact of captivity on wild beasts but not the cost of their capture and transport. It was estimated that ten animals were killed for every one that Hagenbeck exhibited. (Baratay and Hardouin-Fugier, *Zoo*, 118.)

3   *Churchill* I, 148.

4   *Churchill* V, C. 1, 423.

5   *Churchill* V, C. 1, 1321.

6   CAC, CHAR 1/344/4.

7   J. M. Kinder, 'Zoo Animals and Modern Zoos: Captive Casualties, Patriotic Citizens, and Good Soldiers' in R. Hediger (ed.), *Animals and War: Studies of Europe and North America* (Leiden, 2013), 58. Wild animals also escaped when their cages were wrecked by the Japanese earthquake in 1923; soldiers shot them down in the streets of Yokohama.

8   Clark, *Huxleys*, 264–5. Although poisonous snakes and spiders were killed, most of the big beasts were, in the event, moved to Whipsnade. What might have happened if Regent's Park had been seriously damaged in war is described in Angus Wilson's novel *The Old Men at the Zoo* (1961), 276.

9   Churchill, *Second World War* III, 155.

10 Churchill, *Second World War* III, 455.

11 R. Malamud (ed.), *A Cultural History of Animals: In the Modern Age* (2007), 109.

12 CAC, CHAR 2/477/6–9, S. Mildred Ransford to Churchill, 28 July 1943. The holograph letter, a scrawl in which Rota is referred to as a lioness, does not exactly correspond with the version typed by Churchill's secretary for him to read. For the sake of clarity I have slightly edited it.

13 CAC, CHUR 2/351/283.

14 CAC, CHUR 2/351/282.

15 *Zoo Life* (Summer 1952), 40 and 43.

ILLUSTRATION CREDITS

Page 34 Bert Hardy / Picture Post / Getty Images.

Page 40 Churchill Archives Centre: Papers accumulated by Henry Winston (Peregrine) Churchill, PCHL 8/7. Reproduced by kind permission of the Master and Fellows of Churchill College, Cambridge.

Page 47 Hulton Archive / Getty Images.

Page 54 Globe-Photos / ImageCollect.

Page 68 Churchill Archives Centre, The Broadwater Collection, BRDW 1 Photo 2/83. Reproduced with permission of Curtis Brown, London on behalf of the Broadwater Collection © The Broadwater Collection.

Page 71 Illustration from *Clara in Blunderland* by Caroline Lewis, William Heinemann, London 1902.

Page 76 Churchill Archives Centre, The Broadwater Collection, BRDW 1 Photo 1/158. Reproduced with permission of Curtis Brown, London on behalf of the Broadwater Collection © The Broadwater Collection.

Page 87 Churchill Archives Centre, The Broadwater Collection, BRDW 1 Photo 3/24, published in the Manchester Daily Dispatch, March 1904.

Page 98 Bournemouth News & Picture Services.

Page 105 Churchill Archives Centre, The Broadwater Collection, BRDW 1 Photo 3 5/45. Reproduced with permission of Curtis Brown, London on behalf of the Broadwater Collection © The Broadwater Collection.

Page 116 © Punch Limited.

Page 124 Churchill Archives Centre, The Broadwater Collection, BRDW 1 Photo 1/115. Reproduced with permission of Curtis Brown, London on behalf of the Broadwater Collection © The Broadwater Collection.

Page 131 Churchill Archives Centre: The Papers of Clementine Spencer-Churchill, CSCT 5/145. Reproduced by kind permission of the Master and Fellows of Churchill College, Cambridge.

Page 142 Leonard McCombe / The LIFE Images Collection / Getty Images.

Page 147 Churchill Archives Centre, Deposited collections relating to Sir Winston Churchill, WCHL 4/58

Page 158 Mark Kaufmann / Time & Life Pictures / Getty Images.

Page 170 Churchill Archives Centre, The Broadwater Collection, BRDW 1 Photo 1/260. Reproduced with permission of Curtis Brown, London on behalf of the Broadwater Collection © The Broadwater Collection.

Page 175 William Vanderson / Fox Photos / Hulton Archive / Getty Images.

Page 178 Churchill Archives Centre, Churchill Press Photographs, CHPH 5 F1/A/21, published in The Sphere, 19 March 1955.

Page 191 *Churchill as an octopus / Seppla*, LC-DIG-ppmsca-05363, Prints and Photographs Division, Library of Congress.

Page 198 Churchill Archives Centre, The Broadwater Collection, BRDW 1 Photo 1/254. Reproduced with permission of Curtis Brown, London on behalf of the Broadwater Collection © The Broadwater Collection.

Page 202 Winston Churchill, *Small Drawing of a Pig*, Self-portrait sketch on reverse, n.d., 4 ½ x 6 ½ x ¼ in. (11.43 x 16.51 x 0.64 cm), Dallas Museum of Art, The Wendy and Emery Reves Collection 1985.R.536.A.

Page 211 Hulton Archive / Getty Images.

Page 216 Churchill Archives Centre, The Broadwater Collection, BRDW V 3/10/22c. Reproduced with permission of Curtis Brown, London on behalf of the Broadwater Collection © The Broadwater Collection.

Page 225 Churchill Archives Centre, The Broadwater Collection, BRDW 1 Photo 1/296. Reproduced with permission of Curtis Brown, London on behalf of the Broadwater Collection © The Broadwater Collection.

Page 234 From *My African Journey*, W.S. Churchill, Hodder and Stoughton, 1908. Reproduced with permission of Curtis Brown, London on behalf of the Broadwater Collection © The Broadwater Collection.

Page 248 Churchill Archives Centre, The Papers of Sir Winston Churchill, CHUR 1/103. Reproduced with permission of Curtis Brown, London on behalf of the Broadwater Collection © The Broadwater Collection.

Page 269 © Illustrated London News Ltd. / Mary Evans.

Page 278 Topical Press Agency / Getty Images.

Front and back endpapers: photo © Professor Stefan Buczacki, taken by kind permission from his book *From Blenheim to Chartwell: The Untold Story of Churchill's Houses and Gardens*, published by Unicorn, May 2018.

INDEX